(OO)

Philosophy In and Out of Europe

Current Continental Research is co-published by The Center for Advanced Research in Phenomenology and University Press of America, Inc.

CURRENT CONTINENTAL RESEARCH 804

Marjorie Grene

PHILOSOPHY IN AND OUT OF EUROPE

1987

Center for Advanced Research in Phenomenology
& University Press of America, Washington, D.C.

British Cataloging in Publication Information Available

Co-published by arrangement with the
Center for Advanced Research in Phenomenology

Library of Congress Cataloging-in-Publication Data

Grene, Marjorie Glicksman, 1910–
    Philosophy in and out of Europe.

    (Current continental research ; 804)
    Reprint. Originally published: Berkeley :
University of California Press, 1976.
        Bibliography; p.
        Includes index.
        1. Philosophy, Modern—20th century. I. Title.
II. Series.
[B804.G65   1987]   190   87–15966
ISBN 0–8191–6324–4 (pbk. : alk. paper)

All University Press of America books are produced on acid-free
paper which exceeds the minimum standards set by the National
Historical Publication and Records Commission.

For Martin and Lore Ostwald

Contents

Preface

These essays are concerned, one way or another, with themes in twentieth century European philosophy. (Even the Appendix, which takes Hobbism as model for the catastrophe of modern thought, is written, I suppose, from something like a "continental" point of view.) That fact, and the accident that they were all written by one writer—who was not quite the same person in 1974 as she was in 1938, when the earliest essay included here was published—are perhaps the only unifying features of the collection. For their author has swung, rather like the philosophical century itself, from rebellion against what appeared to be (and partly was) European "obscurantism" to a more steadfast rebellion against that rebellion, to a sympathy for philosophers who seek to escape the dead end of scientism, not by abandoning philosophy, but by finding, somehow, a way to start afresh. Those who, in my present view, can help most in that effort, like Merleau-Ponty and Plessner, for example, I discovered—to my shame be it said—only fifteen years ago. I had been working with Polanyi since the early fifties, but we were both, I believe, more isolated than we need have been from others who were proceeding, from other starting points, in the same direction. Participation in Carnap's research seminar in Chicago in 1937-38 had sufficed to show me the impotence of logical positivism (or logical empiricism) as a foundation for philosophy; the decades wasted by so many in "logical reconstruction" I am happy not to have shared. Nor do I regret my exile from the "ordinary language" years. But a better philosophical alternative than either of these was not so easy to hit upon. I remember that when I had been asked (as a former student of Heidegger and Jaspers) to write about existentialism, holding in my hand a copy of *La Phénoménologie de la Perception,* I said to myself, "Another of Sartre's Marxists—No!" How my own thinking, or for that matter Polanyi's *Personal Knowledge,* might have developed differently had I had, in 1946, time, patience, or understanding to study Merleau-Ponty's basic work, I cannot say. The fifteen years still to intervene between the writing of my first book on existentialism and my first reading of Merleau-Ponty were not—thanks, first, to Polanyi, and then to my return to teaching—wholly a philosophic wasteland; still, they were closer to it than they might have been, had I been more perspicacious or less preoccupied. So be it; these are bits and pieces, mostly invited for one occasion or another, some for philosophical readers or hearers, some for a wider audience. In the latter case, I have not tried to provide an elaborate scholarly apparatus, except, of course, to cite the source of direct quotations. The aggregate here collected belongs, I should think, to something one might want to call "philosophical journalism" rather than "philosophy," and I see no reason to deck it out inappropriately in more academic dress.

It would be impossible as well as tedious to list all those to whom, over so long a period, I have been indebted. But I would like to acknowledge the occasions for which, or persons for whom, some of the essays were written, as well as the occasions and persons that evoked the writing of some of them. Chapter I was written for the Festschrift in honor of Helmuth Plessner's eightieth birthday, and I am grateful to Professor Günter Dux of the University of Freiburg for inviting my contribution. Chapters II and III grew out of an invitation to read a paper at a conference at Stanford University in the fall of 1974 on "International Relations in the Humanities." Chapter III was the paper in fact read; Chapter II is the expansion of part of a first draft. My thanks are due to Professor David Halliburton of Stanford for his invitation to participate on that occasion. For Chapter IV I have only myself to blame. Chapter V was an invited address to the Western Division of the American Philosophical Association in 1950. Chapter VI, published in *The Twentieth Century,* had been written for *Encounter* as a "Men and Ideas" piece, but rejected by them for my failure to touch on that untouchable subject, Heidegger's politics. Chapter VII was commissioned by the *Chicago Review* for a special issue on existentialism, and Chapter VIII was one of several reviews that I wrote for the *Times Literary Supplement,* with gratitude, always, for relief from the stifling syllabus of a British provincial philosophy curriculum, as well as for a few extra guineas in those straitened times. Chapter IX was written for the Fine Arts Festival of the University of Wisconsin at Milwaukee in 1965. Chapter X was written for the Sartre volume of the Library of Living Philosophers, from which I have regretfully withdrawn it in order to include it here. Chapter XI was the Arthur Skemp Memorial Lecture, delivered at the University of Bristol in May 1973; I am grateful to the Department of English of the University of Bristol for the honor of that invitation, to Professors Stefan Körner and Christopher Ricks for their warm welcome, and to Richard and Freya Gregory for their unfailing hospitality. Chapters XII and XIII grew out of meetings of the Study Group on the Unity of Knowledge, funded by the Ford Foundation through the University of California, Davis, from 1967 to 1972. I am happy to acknowledge the Foundation's support of the study group, and, in particular, with respect to Chapter XII, to express my gratitude to Jacques Derrida for meeting with us in Paris in the summer of 1972 and to Charles Rosen for his insistence, on that occasion, on the parallel between Derrida and Wittgenstein, as well as for a remark of his about Wittgenstein and empiricism, on which part of my argument in Chapter II depends.

Permission to reprint is gratefully acknowledged to the following: Westdeutscher Verlag, Opladen, for Chapter I, published in *Sachlichkeit* (1973) under the title "Immer noch Philosophie?" (English translations of the German passages quoted in the text have been added); *The Journal of Philosophy* (vol. 35, 1938) for Chapter IV (the subtitle being added for the present collection); *Ethics* (vol. 62, 1952) and the University of Chicago Press for Chapter V; *The Chicago Review* (vol. 13, 1959) for Chapter VII (here abbreviated); *The Times Literary Supplement* (12 April 1963) for Chapter VIII; the *Journal of the British Phenomenological Society* (vol. 1, 1970) for Chapter IX; Routledge & Kegan Paul and the University of Massachusetts Press for the Appendix (printed from my Introduction to *The Anatomy of Knowledge,* ed. Marjorie Grene, 1969). Permission to quote four lines from "Sailing to Byzantium" from *The Collected Poems of W. B. Yeats* has been given by M. B. Yeats, Miss Anne Yeats, Macmillan London and Basingstoke; and by Macmillan Publishing Co., Inc. (copyright 1928 by Macmillan Publishing Co., Inc., renewed 1956 by Georgie Yeats). Permission to quote two lines of "Little Gidding," from "Four Quartets," T. S. Eliot, *Collected Poems,* has been given by Faber and Faber Ltd. and by Harcourt Brace Jovanovich, Inc.

M. G.

University of California, Davis
August 1975

I

Still Philosophy?

1973

PHILOSOPHY, NONPHILOSOPHERS COMPLAIN, SETTLES NO PROBLEMS. Thus social anthropology, for instance, might produce an adequate theory, say, of totemism or of magic, a theory that would both suggest directions for and explain the results of empirical research; but philosophical anthropology has no such concrete outcome. Similarly, brain research produces again and again definitive results which suggest further investigation, while discussion of the mind-body problem seems to go on forever in the same vein, only with different vocabularies: instead of the reduction of mind to sensations or to corpuscles in motion we have its reduction to behavior or to neurophysiology or to machinery, reductions which some philosophers embrace with enthusiasm and others resist. We circle, as Wittgenstein said, "round and round the same landscape." And the question, what philosophy is, is one of the philosophical questions that itself keeps recurring, however many philosophers have thought it settled. Looking back at Plessner's philosophical writing, in the context as well of the history of philosophy, past and contemporary, one may ask once again: What is philosophy doing, and why does it do it in this unsettling, because unsettled, way?

My present rather desultory reflections on this metareflective question—which is at bottom the question, What is reflection and why do we indulge in it?—were occasioned by a fragment of Friedrich Schlegel in which he likens musical to philosophical themes. In volume four of the *Athenaeum* he wrote:

> Es pflegt manchem seltsam und lächerlich aufzufallen, wenn die Musiker von den Gedanken in ihren Kompositionen reden; und oft mag es auch so geschehen, dass man wahrnimmt, sie haben mehr Gedanken in ihrer Musik als über dieselbe. Wer aber Sinn für die wunderbaren Affinitäten aller Künste und Wissenschaften hat, wird die Sache wenigstens nicht aus dem platten Gesichtspunkt der sogenannten Natürlichkeit betrachten, nach welcher die

Musik nur die Sprache der Empfindung sein soll, und eine gewisse Tendenz aller reinen Instrumentalmusik zur Philosophie an sich nicht unmöglich finden. Muss die reine Instrumentalmusik sich nicht selbst einen Text erschaffen? und wird das Thema in ihr nicht so entwickelt, bestätigt, variiert und kontrastiert, wie der Gegenstand der Meditation in einer philosophischen Ideenreihe?

It habitually strikes some people as strange and silly when musicians speak of the ideas in their compositions, and also it may often happen that we see they have more ideas in their music than about it. But those who have a sense for the wonderful affinities of all arts and sciences will not at least regard the matter from the flat point of view of so-called naturalism, according to which music is supposed to be only the language of feeling, and will find a certain tending of all pure instrumental music toward philosophy not in itself impossible. Must not pure instrumental music create for itself a text? And is the theme in it not developed, confirmed, varied and contrasted, like the object of meditation in a philosophical sequence of ideas?[1]

On the appropriateness of his remarks about music I would not venture to comment; but resemblance is a symmetrical relation. Let us turn this one around, and ask what it tells us about philosophy. For my purpose it is the last sentence that matters. "Muss die reine Instrumentalmusik sich nicht selbst einen Text erschaffen?" In the soberest tone of contemporary German philosophy, far, indeed, from the Romantic strain, Günther Patzig maintains for the writing of philosophy essentially the claim that Schlegel makes for musical composition. Celebrating Frege's genius, he writes:

Die Vorzüge der Argumentationsweise eines Denkers sind nicht etwa blosse literarische Vorzüge seiner Schriften. Es handelt sich nicht um stilistische Ansprüche eines literarischen Genres, auch nicht um die Frage, ob ein Autor neben der Fähigkeit zu wissenschaftlicher Einsicht auch noch die Gabe besitzt, seine Forschungsergebnisse verständlich und ansprechend zu formulieren. Die Forderungen an die Darstellung philosophischer Einsicht sind nichts, was der Philosophie selbst äusserlich bleiben könnte. Denn die Philosophie ist nicht ein Bestand von wahren Sätzen, sondern ein Prozess der Verdeutlichung. Und wenn dies gilt, so ist ein philosophischer Text nicht mehr ein schnell zu durcheilender Weg zu gewissen wertvollen Einsichten, der nur aus pädagogischer Rücksicht der Formulierung dieser Einsichten beigegeben wird, sondern der philosophische Text ist die Epiphanie der Philosophie selbst.

The excellences of the style of argumentation of a thinker are not mere literary excellences of his writings. It is not a question of stylistic demands of a literary genre, nor of the question whether, alongside the capacity for scholarly insight, an author also possesses the gift of formulating intelligibly and pleasingly the results of his research. The demands on the presentation of philosophical insight are not something that could remain external to philosophy itself. For philosophy is not a supply of true propositions, but a process of clarification. And if this is so, then a philosophical text is no longer a road to certain valuable insights, to be hurriedly rushed through, and which is devoted to the formulation of these insights for purely pedagogical reasons; rather, the philosophical text is the epiphany of philosophy itself.[2]

Philosophy, too, in other words, must create its own text, and appears as philosophy only in that self-creation, which is also the creation of something other than itself, the text that expresses it, in which alone it can present itself.

Why is this so? Because a philosophical concept is at the same time a philosophical problem, a problem that contains potentially, not only a "solution," but the movement toward a solution, which again opens up the original problem in another direction. In a colloquium delivered in 1935 to the philosophical faculty at Göttingen, and to which Patzig refers in the context of the statement just quoted, Joseph König contrasts the factual statement "Mount Everest is the highest mountain on this planet" with Aristotle's statement "Happiness is the highest good." In contrast with the former, he points out:

Mit dem philosophischen Satz des Aristoteles steht es wesentlich anders. Denn die Eudaimonie ist ihm nicht ein Gut neben anderen Gütern, d. h. sie ist nicht ein Gut wie diese anderen, von ihnen bloss dadurch unterschieden, dass sie das höchste Gut wäre; vielmehr ist sie in einem strengen und unemphatischen Sinn das Gut schlechthin oder das unbedingte Gut. Sagt man nun gleichwohl, sie sei das höchste Gut oder das Gut schlechthin oder das unbedingte Gut, so spricht das zwar den philosophischen Gedanken aus; allein diese Ausdrücke sind wesentlich nicht so unmittelbar verständlich und durchsichtig wie der sonst analoge Ausdruck in dem Satze über den Mount Everest. Ihre Meinung, ihr Sinn ist vielmehr selber wieder ein philosophisches Problem, das mit den wenigen Bemerkungen, die ich soeben darüber machte, nur eben bezeichnet, nicht aber aufgelöst ist. Und dieses Problem ist keineswegs nur eben ein weiteres Problem, d. h. ein Problem, das man noch hinzunehmen, ebensogut aber auch beiseite lassen könnte. Denn diese Eudaimonie selber, die Sache also, wird zugänglich nur in diesem Prädikat.

The case of the philosophical proposition of Aristotle is essentially different. For happiness is not for him a good alongside other goods, that is, it is not a good like those others, distinguished from them only by the fact that it is the highest good; it is rather in a strict and unemphatic sense the good absolutely or the unconditional good. But even if we say it is the highest good or the good absolutely or the unconditional good, this does indeed express the philosophic thought, yet, in an essential fashion, these expressions are not as immediately intelligible and transparent as the otherwise analogous expression in the statement about Mount Everest. Rather, their meaning, their sense is itself again a philosophical problem, which is merely indicated but not solved by the few remarks I have just made about it. Nor is this problem by any means just a further problem, that is, a problem that one could take up but could just as well leave aside. For this happiness itself, that is, the very matter itself, becomes accessible only in this predicate.[3]

We could "know about" Mount Everest without the additional information that it is the highest mountain, and we could understand the concept "highest mountain" without knowing what mountain it is. But we only know happiness by knowing that it "means" the *summum bonum* and we only know the *summum bonum* by knowing that it is happiness. Is philosophical truth then analytic? That was the view of some positivists, but it is plainly mistaken. For the kind of meaning König is talking about is not the meaning established by stipulative definitions and manipulable so as to produce analytic statements, as we might conceive the meaning and truth of 2 + 2 = 4. Not that mathematical propositions *are* analytic either; my point is simply that philosophical propositions, even philosophical definitions, clearly are not so. It takes the whole of the *Nicomachean Ethics* to elicit the sense of the statement "Happiness is the highest good."

The conclusion of our Schlegel fragment is apposite here: "und wird das Thema in ihr nicht so entwickelt, bestätigt, variiert und kontrastiert, wie der Gegenstand der Meditation in einer philosophischen Ideenreihe?" Although the series of verbs does not correspond to any musical or philosophical vocabulary—nor even, exactly, to the rhetorical usage from which it may well be borrowed (*exponere, confirmare, refutare*)[4]—it does fit the example before us. For in the *Ethics* the concepts of happiness and of good, and of happiness as good, are developed, and so confirmed, through the investigation of moral virtues, and of the particular virtues, of voluntary action, of the intellectual virtues, of moral weakness, of pleasure in relation to happiness, and so on. The distinction between the morally good life and the contemplative life, moreover, introduces into the ethical theme a variant—or a contrast?—not only in the sense of good but even of "highest." In book ten, finally, the argument is recapitulated with the celebration of the contemplative life now seen as its triumphant issue, and the whole argument is placed once more in the context of politics from which it took its start.

Further, as Schlegel and König agree, it is typical of philosophical subject matter, and therefore of philosophical method, that the development of the thought is also the development of the *object* of the thought. True, in a sense the text produced by the problem—in this case the *Nicomachean Ethics*—is not what the text is *about*. People have lived good lives without reading Aristotle, and people have even read, and understood, Aristotle without leading good lives. Yet the organization of the *Ethics* is not just the expression of Aristotle's tidiness and skill in argument; it is the development of his theme, which is "happiness as the highest good." Short of idealism, or beyond it, we must admit that in a philosophical text the relation between fact and significance, object and meaning, is more intimate than in a geographical account of mountains, high or low. It is the "object of meditation" that is developed in a philosophical argument, not only the meditation itself: "God, the world," König remarks,

> die Seele, das Leben, das Sein, das Werden, die Vernunft, das Bewusst-sein, das Schicksal, das Glück, der Zufall, die Notwendigkeit, das Subjekt, das Objekt, die Natur, die Geschichte: alle solche spezifisch philosophischen Titel oder Gegenstände sind gewiss zwar eben Gegenstände.

> the soul, life, being, becoming, reason, consciousness, fate, fortune, chance, necessity, the subject, the object, nature, history: all such specific-ally philosophical titles or objects are doubtless indeed precisely objects.[5]

But they are objects of such a kind that the expression, the *Logos der Sache*, belongs to the problem itself. That is why philosophy is a process of elucidation, not a road, short or long, to the establishment of mere facts.

Helmuth Plessner's concept of eccentric positionality is an object in this sense. If he is correct, as I believe he is, in his basic account of the human condition, then the words "eccentric positionality" do indeed describe the characteristic way in which a human being relates himself, and is related, to his bodily existence; but eccentric positionality is not a thing to be pointed to, like a mountain. We discover what it means precisely through its development, for example, in the concrete content of *Lachen und Weinen,* where laughing and crying are seen to be what they are—really are—as varying expressions, not so much of the concept, as of the object which, in our reflection, the concept illumi-nates for us. Laughing and crying, moreover, which philosophers generally neglect, are here brought into the range of critical reflection, and as the theme of eccentric positionality is thus varied and contrasted, so also the mind-body problem itself is thereby subtly transformed. The fundamental concept itself both demands such developments and is established by them. The uniqueness of a given philosopher's treat-ment, in this case Plessner's approach to the mind-body problem through eccentric positionality, serves, as Professor Benjamin Nelson has suggested, to set the theme as it were in a given key.[6]

An analogy, however, must be imperfect. Granted that philosophy, as a process of clarification, creates its own text, and that the philo-sophical text is inseparable from the theme developed in it, the text once established can, it seems, itself speak to its reader, while the musical text can address its hearer only through the mediation of a performer. Nor does any given performance, or indeed, the interpretation of any given performer, present the work as such. It presents it under one aspect, as one monad mirrors the universe, while the universe itself is the infinite sum total of all monadic perspectives. At first sight the relation of the philosophical reader to his text seems more direct than this. But what about philosophical interpretation? Philosophical texts are not after all so perspicuous as to need no interpretation. The reader himself is an interpreter; he has his interpretation, which may change from reading to reading, as that of a musician may develop from one performance to another of the same work. Indeed, the greatest philosophical texts do in fact resemble great works of art in permitting, and even demanding, an indefinite, and themselves developing, series of interpretations which can never exhaust the work. The central books of the *Metaphysics* are an excellent example of such a text. As Richard Rorty puts it, one can only take a given passage or set of passages which one finds seminal and build one's interpretation around them.[7] Some other aspects of the argument will then be understressed, from the point of view of another reader's interpretation, or of the same reader's interpretation at another time. In Rorty's exegesis just referred to, for example, he has taken certain passages which appear to equate genus and matter as fundamental to Aristotle's central theme, while to me these appear relatively peripheral, and I would like to take the equation of genus and matter as much more qualified, if not indeed metaphorical. Besides, the culmination of the argument of Z-H seems to me to come, as it has been traditionally believed to do, in Z 17, which Rorty has to bypass to place the finale where he wants it, in H. The interpretation of the central books, moreover, depends in part on one's reading of Aristotle's interest in biology; here again the interpretation of the genus-matter identity depends on one's sense of the intent of *Part. Anim. 1* and of the *Gen. Anim.* Professor Montgomery Furth of U.C.L.A. has been developing a most thought-provoking interpretation of the concept of the individual in Aristotle and therefore indirectly of the argument on substance in the central books, an interpretation with which I think both Rorty and I and anyone else must agree in its thesis that specification, the development of the individual as a this-such, is the *telos* of Aristotelian method and the process to be founded and so explained in Aristotelian ontology.[8] But I find Furth's use of crucial *Gen. Anim.* passages slanted (through reading what is meant of "soul" as meant of the form-matter compound—to put my point briefly and crudely) toward the genus = matter thesis, while my view, which would partly accept yet qualify this equation, would be, from his point of view, biased in another direction. Which of us is "right"? Both of us, I hope—for the depth and richness of Aristotle's theme, the theme of the $\tau\acute{\iota}\ \mathring{\eta}\nu\ \epsilon\mathring{\iota}\nu\alpha\iota$ of each kind of thing and the definition of substance, is open to an inexhaustible range of interpretations by an indefinite number of competent philosophical readers. Some readings of course are wrong, like the excesses of some Jaeger disciples who worked at taking the text apart into bits without the slightest effort to see (or hear, to follow our analogy a little further) its leitmotiv at all. But even within the range of authentic interpretations there is room for infinite variety.

The first disanalogy I have suggested, then, is itself partial. But there are also, as Plessner might put it, "Monopolies of Philosophy," which make its self-creation very different from that of musical composition.

A philosophical concept is implicitly a philosophical theme which demands thematic development and so produces its own text; but it doesn't stop there. Not only do some of the great texts permit or even need renewed interpretation, but they issue in new variants of the same theme, which either the same philosopher "upon more mature reflection" or successive philosophers may treat in new thematizations, which again produce new variants, and so on. And that is because a philosophical concept expresses a philosophical problem, the kind of problem which when resolved in one respect appears to be reopened in another. True, every art form too has its problems, which are resolved in ever new fashions both by the individual artist as he develops and by a sequence of individuals within a given tradition. The theme of a given composition, however, seems to be the theme of that work in a way that does not hold for philosophical "themes." It may be quoted or parodied, but then it is understood, if not acknowledged, as a quotation or a parody. Something like this may of course happen in philosophy too. Anyone who uses the concept of eccentric positionality ought to acknowledge Plessner, just as anyone in the tradition of substance metaphysics ought to have acknowledged Aristotle as its founder. But if, for example, Plessner gives us with his central theme new light on the mind-body problem, the latter as a philosophical theme belongs to no one in particular, not even to Plato or Descartes. Even a treatment like Plessner's or Merleau-Ponty's, which endeavors to show us why the mind-body relation is inherently ambiguous and so inherently incapable of definitive statement, leaves open by its very "solution" a range of further problems; indeed, it shows us why as embodied beings we *are* a problem. Or look at Frege's classic essays, of which Patzig is speaking in the passages quoted above. These are relatively brief tests in which, as Patzig rightly claims, we are privileged to watch the exquisite clarity of a great mind working through the implications of certain problems arising from his reflection on the basic conceptual tools of a given discipline, here mathematics: the concept of a number or of a function. But this development, though reached with irresistible logic, issues in some strange conclusions. Do sentences really refer to one of two objects: the true or the false? Philosophers of logic need not only to interpret Frege, but to go on to meditate themselves, in new *Ideenfolgen,* on his concepts of concept, thought, proposition, or truth.

   Some philosophical concepts, and therefore problems, do of course exhaust themselves in the course of philosophical history. The problem of substance was finished, it seems to me, with Spinoza's *Ethics* on the one hand and Hume's *Treatise* on the other, and that's why Kant made such a terrible muddle of substance in the first *Critique.* On this concept there was no middle way between dogmatism and skepticism; even a realist interpretation of Kant does not need to turn *Dinge an sich* back into substances. Kant's Copernican revolution was the successor to substance metaphysic, not a variant of it. But for the most part the great philosophical themes are perennial, not, indeed, in having permanent solutions, but in that they are developing and redeveloping themes from one work, one philosopher, one period to another.

This openness of philosophy, its inconclusiveness, from which I started, has at least three reasons.[9] Patzig, in the essay I have been quoting, describes philosophy as *die Wissenschaft des Selbstverständlichen*.[10] It is the discipline that reflects systematically on what is otherwise taken for granted, whether in the practice of some art or science or in some aspect of everyday life, like perception or moral choice. Such reflection is inexhaustible, partly perhaps because of the inexhaustibility of its object, partly, however, because of the self-proliferation of reflection itself. Sartre complains about the possible infinite regress of thoughts about thoughts about thoughts and proposes to cut off this danger with his prereflective *cogito*. Yet the possibility always remains—unless the process can come to rest in what Sartre calls "pure reflection" (which I believe his own premises forbid his achieving) or perhaps, as in part 5 of Spinoza's *Ethics,* in the intellectual love of God. Spinoza and some mystics excepted, however, reflection is always open. It contains the possibility of "going further" which prevents the philosophical development of a fundamental concept from coming to a close as the development of a musical theme might do. König describes the specific skill of philosophy as $\epsilon \tilde{v} \lambda \acute{\epsilon} \gamma \epsilon \iota \nu$ in the sense of a *legein* which seeks its own perfection but has not yet achieved it. This is so, one would suppose, because of the inexhaustibility, not only of the interpretive work of philosophy, but of philosophical reflection itself.

Besides, philosophy is dialogue and one can never anticipate the novelty of one's interlocutor's answers. Western philosophy is a conversation that has gone on since Thales, a conversation in which each philosophical thinker, however limited an underlaborer, must take his place. No single interlude, however beautifully developed, can wholly shut off further conversation. Take the example König used and which I discussed briefly, Aristotle's account of happiness as the good life. Aristotle, in the harmony he purports to find between the opinion of all (happiness is the highest good), of the many (happiness is pleasure), and of the wisest (happiness is an activity of the rational part of the soul in accordance with virtue throughout a lifetime), is in fact relying, I believe, on the consensus of fourth century Athenians as to the question who the wisest are, namely, the men of practical wisdom. In our society this premise is missing, and Aristotelian ethic as such, therefore, is not in any simple way acceptable to us. This insight teaches us something both about Aristotle and about ourselves, and with respect to the problem of happiness, of the highest good, of philosophical method, of basic social principles, therefore, the dialogue continues. With the exception of some repetitive and anomalous passages, the *Nicomachean Ethics* is indeed a most profound and beautifully organized work of philosophy, yet its theme remains open and in a way "undeveloped." As a historian one might just listen and interpret, but as a philosophical student even of the history of philosophy one needs, not just to understand and interpret, but to continue the debate. What is happiness, what is the good life, what is the bearing of our social structure on these judgments? Such questions must be answered ever again by each of us, but never once for all.

In recent times, finally, a further reason has emerged for the openness of philosophical themes. Philosophy used to be equivalent to knowledge. As the special sciences split off from the mother stem, however, the scope and role of philosophy as a unique and founding discipline became less clear. The separation of philosophy from science took, I suppose one could say, two principal directions, in phenomenology on the continent of Europe and in conceptual analysis in the Anglo-American tradition. But despite the richness of some phenomenological description and some conceptual analysis, the loss of content in philosophical inquiry has been a lamentable result. As the relations between philosophical and empirical inquiry have again begun to flourish, at a more reflective, and one hopes, more fruitful level, so that, as from Aristotle on it has partly done, philosophy reflects on the fundamental conceptual problems of other disciplines and in turn (in fashions more difficult to describe precisely) receives illumination for its own problems (on mind, say, on perception, on the relation of moral standards to society), from new knowledge in empirical disciplines, philosophical reflection appears in a new openness to the progress of knowledge in other fields. Whatever basic new knowledge is gained in empirical science, for instance, the discovery of the genetic code and therefore of the information-theoretical foundation of all life process, or the investigation in empirical sociology of the nature of social roles and of their role in the constitution of the individual, philosophy itself appears in the role of mediator in an unending negotiation as well between one discipline and another (between, say, anthropology and genetics) as between any one discipline and the conceptions of everyday life (between, say, sociology and morality). Thus philosophy comes to exist as the conversation that relates each discipline to its own fundamental concepts, or each discipline, or each area of everyday life, to any one other or to several others. Clearly, then, as knowledge develops, so does philosophy and so does any given philosophical theme, such as the mind-body problem, the theory of perception, or the theory of I-other relations. It is in this context, of course, that Plessner's philosophical writing most clearly illustrates the uniqueness and the openness, and the unique openness, of philosophical thought. This character of Plessner's work is beautifully expounded and illustrated in Günter Dux's Epilogue to Plessner's *Philosophische Anthropologie*; but I may perhaps add, in conclusion, a reference to one particular recent essay, "Trieb und Leidenschaft,"[11] which well illustrates—as many others would—this discipline-spanning quality of Plessner's philosophizing. The context of the essay is political and therefore practical, but it also takes into account (1) the biological nature of man and (2) the uniqueness of man, even as animal, in contrast to other "only" animals. And finally, in expounding the concept of *Leidenschaft*, the transformation of animal drives into human passions, it issues in a tribute to poetry, which alone, Plessner maintains, in contrast to science, *praxis* or philosophical reflection, can present human passion in its true nature. This tension between many disciplines characterizes not only the work of Plessner as philosopher and sociologist, as historian of ideas and social critic, but the task of philosophy in our time and in the future: philosophy as mediator, engaged in an enterprise as fundamental as it is essentially open and incomplete. Philosophy, like music, must create its own text, but philosophy, unlike art—or unlike other arts—creates texts which, for all their coherent and rigorous development, always point beyond themselves to other texts to come.[12]

Notes

1. Friedrich Schlegel, *Kritische Schriften* (Munich: Hanser, 1964), p. 87. He makes, humorously, a similar point in another fragment: "Das beständige Wiederholen des Themas in der Philosophie entspringt aus zwei verschiedenen Ursachen. Entweder der Autor hat etwas entdeckt, er weiss aber selbst noch nicht recht was; und in diesem Sinne sind Kants Schriften musikalisch genug. Oder er hat etwas Neues gehört, ohne es behörig zu vernehmen, und in diesem Sinne sind die Kantianer die grössten Tonkünstler der Literatur" (p. 64).

2. Günther Patzig, in G. Frege, *Funktion, Begriff, Bedeutung* (Göttingen: Vandenhoeck v. Ruprecht, 1962; 3rd ed., 1969), pp. 13-14.

3. Joseph König, "Das spezifische Können der Philosophie als εὖ λέγειν," *Blätter für deutsche Philosophie*, 10 (1936): 134.

4. I owe this suggestion to Professor Catherine Wilkinson.

5. König, p. 132.

6. But philosophical keys vary continuously!

7. Richard Rorty, "Genus as Matter: A Reading of *Metaphysics* Z-H," in *Exegesis and Argument: Studies in Greek Philosophy Presented to Gregory Vlastos*, ed. E. N. Lee, A. P. D. Mourelatos, R. M. Rorty, *Phronesis* suppl. vol. (Assen: Van Gorcum, 1973), pp. 393-420.

8. Work in progress; part delivered at Greek philosophy workshop, Stanford, March 1972.

9. Professor Nelson has also suggested, in the same conversation referred to above, that philosophical themes develop indefinitely because every philosophical problem involves every other. I have not added this to the reasons given here, because I am not quite convinced that it is correct. But perhaps it is, in a sense, an expansion of my third reason. In philosophy, any problem can connect with any other—anywhere!

10. Patzig, p. 15.

11. *Merkur*, 25 (1971): 307-315.

12. I am grateful to Charles Rosen for several conversations on the subject of this essay, and to Richard Swift for reading and criticizing the manuscript.

II

Philosophy In and Out of Europe:

1. The European Sources of Recent Anglo-American Philosophy

1974

Professor Dagfinn Føllesdal of the University of Oslo and Stanford once remarked, "I am interested in Quine and Husserl because Quine thinks intentionality is nonsense and Husserl thinks it's fundamental to philosophy." This contrariety characterizes not only Professor Føllesdal's two favorite philosophers, however, but contemporary philosophy in general. The Anglo-American or "analytical" tradition, in what I think it is fair to call its dominant and certainly its most domineering mode, is held within the bounds of empiricist philosophy, which seeks definite, ultimate particulars to refer to, with no nonsense about consciousness, objectives of thought, and such, while the continental tradition concerns itself mainly with consciousness, its intentional or so to speak goal-directed nature and such ethereal subjects. This is a dichotomy obvious from the makeup of philosophy departments or the journal literature or what you will. What I want to argue here, however, is that even the so-called analytical tradition has in fact developed in response to typically English or American misreadings of two great European thinkers, Frege and Wittgenstein, whose work, thus misinterpreted, has been in each case cabined, cribbed, confined within the inflexible bonds of unquestioned, and unquestioning, empiricist principles.

Now although my story is sober truth, not legend, it happened, like so many legends, in three stages. Or perhaps, for the sake of the magic number three, I want to make it seem so. For admittedly, the curtain rose on the first act of my drama in England in the early years of this century, and although its last and still, alas, unfinished phase has been enacted chiefly in America (with act two pretty equally divided between ourselves and England), I am not going to go back to the early 1900s in this country, when Dewey effected the metamorphosis of Hegel into a cheerful American progressivist. This was, admittedly, an empiricization of a German thinker: Dewey was a latter-day Hume in dialectical dress. But as we all know, the great thing about Hegel is that anyone can make anything of him, or of something in him: stand him on his head or on his feet, roll him in a barrel down Niagara Falls, or what you will. Besides, the pragmatization of German idealism is, I sincerely hope, over and done with. Despite some efforts to revive it, it remains, it seems to me, stone dead, and I see no need to invoke it, even as a prologue to act one.

So much for my non-prologue. The first act has two scenes, the first of which lasts longer than the second. The first is the development of Russell's philosophy, in which Frege's definition of number (which Russell had rediscovered independently), and, in general, Frege's effort to develop a formalism for the foundations of mathematics, played a crucial role. The second is the rise of logical positivism, later rechristened logical empiricism, which allegedly derived much of its inspiration from the early work of Ludwig Wittgenstein.

The stage set for both scenes, however (and indeed, as I have already stated, for the whole performance), is empiricism, with some changes in properties as well as in lighting between the empiricism of Hume and Hobbes. Empiricism, I said at the start, seeks definite, ultimate particulars to refer to, out of which, as out of solid building blocks, it can raise up the structure of human knowledge. If we really stick to experience, however, such building blocks—"data," as we shall see Russell calling them—turn out to be purely inner subjective units, what Hume called simple impressions or Hobbes, phantasms, those particular seemings-to-me to which, when taken literally to pieces, all experience appears to reduce. To this insistence on ultimate psychological atoms, Hume added two principles, both of which, again, seem, at first sight at least, to be undeniably correct. On the one hand, any bit of experience is separable from any other. If every Swede I have so far met is thick headed and every Frenchman entertaining, that does not mean I may not tomorrow meet a most amusing Swede or a Gallic bore. In my childhood ripe apples were red and grapefruit yellow; now ripe apples—the only good ones, indeed—are green and the sweetest grapefruit pink. Any experience can meet or part with any other. Hobbes didn't stress this consequence of his empiricist doctrine, but in terms of phantasms themselves, the stuff of all experience, he could not have denied it. Hume's third principle, however, palliates the skeptical import of the second: though nothing we experience *must* go with anything else, Hume finds, impressions and their fainter copies, ideas, do run together naturally, or through custom, to which nature determines us, by a "gentle force of association," guided by patterns of resemblance and contiguity as well as by the repetitive sequences that issue in the feeling of necessity expressed in our judgments of cause and effect. Despite the skeptical consequences of his second principle (the separability of all experienced contents, and hence our own inability to *know* with certainty that the objective world will remain as we find it, or indeed that there is any external world at all)—despite this skepticism, therefore, we do muddle through, Hume believes, in the affairs of common life, by what Russell was to call "animal inference," following the tracks we don't get shocked out of and veering off those we do. Now, as I have just indicated, Russell accepted this Humean principle also, at least in his later work, but he recognized that it didn't suffice to give us anything worthy the name of knowledge. To that end he needed the characteristic dicta of Hobbes's version of empiricist doctrine—which, so far as I know, he did not derive from Hobbes himself; rather, he declared explicitly that he was applying the tools of modern logic, that is, in effect, of Frege, to the vindication of the empiricism of Hume. Yet he needed Hobbism, which he derived, I would conjecture, simply from the intellectual milieu of modern naturalism, a position which Hobbes, the most "dangerous" as well as the most prophetic philosopher of the seventeenth century, had quite precisely foretold.

What had Hobbes included in his empiricist philosophy that Hume had omitted, or in any case played down? In the place of Hume's easygoing associationism, Hobbes insisted on a thoroughgoing materialist ontology. We *have* only phantasms, but the only *theory* we can safely build upon that flimsy foundation is a materialist one, a theory of matter in motion, since (and here Hobbes argues as does Epicurus of old) only a materialist theory will fail to be contradicted (falsified!) by sense itself.

So we have, in all, four props for our empiricist setting: (1) *data,* as Russell is to call them, that is, Hume's impressions or Hobbes's phantasms; (2) their logical separability, which Russell, following Hume, insists on, and which Hobbes would certainly have had to accept; (3) Hume's associationism, the foundation of muddling through, which, though Russell regretfully accepts it, will prove more important in the second act of our three-act story than in the first or third; and (4) the Hobbesian conception of a conventional, but inevitable, materialist theory of all there is—all human hopes and thoughts included—a principle which runs counter to the amiability of Hume but suits the rigor of our chief performers in act 1, and more emphatically, or more elaborately, the still eminent and eminently vocal characters of our act 3.

So, finally, now that the stage is (austerely) set—act 1, scene 1: Russell and Fregean Logic. Although it has been said that no philosopher changed his position so often as Russell, it is clear, both from his own statement in *My Philosophical Development*[1] and from the unfinished note by Alan Wood appended to that book, that after his early rejection of idealism Russell marched straight forward always toward a precise analytical position dominated on the one hand by his logical genius and on the other by his belief in the ultimate truth of modern physics—a creed classically expressed as early as 1903 in "A Free Man's Worship." In *My Philosophical Development* (1959), he summarized the view he finally came to hold, as follows:

> There are three key points in the above theory. (1) The first is that the entities that occur in mathematical physics are not part of the stuff of the world, but are constructions composed of the events and taken as units for the convenience of the mathematician. (2) The second is that the whole of what we perceive without inference belongs to our private world. In this respect, I agree with Berkeley. The starry heaven that we believe in is inferred. (3) The third point is that the causal lines which enable us to be aware of a diversity of objects, though there are some such lines everywhere, are apt to peter out like rivers in the sand. That is why we do not at all times perceive everything.[2]

Number two comprises the thesis common to Hobbes and Hume: the thesis that the whole of what Russell called "knowledge by acquaintance" is subjective—all I *have* directly and unquestionably as my experience are my sensations, vivid or dim, pleasant or disagreeable, but just mine. One and three are complications imposed on Hobbes's materialist theory by the demands of twentieth century physics, but they nevertheless express our empiricist principle (4): only the theories of physics, whatever they are, permit us inferential knowledge of things beyond ourselves. "We are bound to believe" modern physics, Russell declares, "on pain of death."[3] He continues:

> If there were any community which rejected the doctrines of modern physics, physicists employed by a hostile government would have no difficulty in exterminating it. The modern physicist, therefore, enjoys powers far exceeding those of the Inquisition in its palmiest days, and it certainly behoves us to treat his pronouncements with due awe. For my part, I have no doubt that, although progressive changes are to be expected in physics, the present doctrines are likely to be nearer to the truth than any rival doctrines now before the world. Science is at no moment quite right, but it is seldom quite

wrong, and has, as a rule, a better chance of being right than the theories of the unscientific. It is, therefore, rational to accept it hypothetically.[4]

That is in essence Hobbes's doctrine, and taken at its face value there seems nothing wrong with it. Of course we accept modern physics, "confused," as Russell admits, though its doctrines sometimes seem to be. But what is only implicit in the statement I have quoted, yet glaringly evident between the lines, and indeed behind all the lines of Russellian philosophy, from the early enunciations of logical atomism (1918) all the way to *Human Knowledge: Its Scope and Limits* (1957), is the thesis that, beyond our subjective data, *only* physics is to be believed, even hypothetically. There are subjective data and there is physics and that's it. And here, at last, I come to the use, and misuse, of Frege's thought in Russell's philosophy. For the mathematical logic used to articulate Russell's empiricism, and absorbed into it, so to speak, is purely *extensional* logic, that is, it deals with the relations between truth values of terms or propositions without attention to their meaning, without attention to their rational uses by rational speakers or hearers.

This logic was developed in the first instance for the formalization of arithmetic. Before Frege, Russell explains, mathematicians interested in foundations problems got into all sorts of trouble by trying to find a definition of number based on counting—but counting is something people do, and people are troublesome. What Frege, then Peano, then Russell, discovered—and what Frege elaborated in his *Basic Laws of Arithmetic*— was the definition of number as a class of similar classes. Two is the class of all couples, three is the class of all trios, etc. But for the existence—or nonexistence—of a class, it doesn't matter a whit what anybody does, like counting, or hoping, or wanting, or thinking. A "class" is determined wholly by its constituents, by the items referred to and which comprise it, not by what anybody means by it or believes about it. In terms of the distinction made by Frege himself in his classic essay "On Sense and Reference" (an essay that expresses Frege's philosophy, not only his logic, and that far outruns the empiricism of Russell), in terms of this distinction, a class is defined with respect to *reference,* and not to *sense.* This was a revolutionary insight for the philosophy of mathematics, but where do we go from there?

We proceed to the famous principle of substitutivity. In terms of an extensional, or truth-functional, logic, it must be the case that for any true identity statement any predicate truly applicable to the one term is truly applicable to the other. This is the law of substitutivity *salva veritate,* sacred to logicians of the extensionalist school. But this law fails in cases involving beliefs or propositional attitudes. Let me try to give you an example. Pat asks Jim, "Is my pig ready for market, that pig in the pen beside the road?'' ''Yes,'' says Jim, ''that pig's ready for market.'' So Jim, believing the pig in the pen beside the road to be ready for market, also believes Pat's pig is ready for market. What he doesn't know, however, is that last week Pat had stolen that pig from Alec; in fact, Pat's pig is in another pen, at the back of the haggard, sick with erysipelas, and not ready for market at all. So we have two true premises:

1. Jim believes the pig in the pen beside the road is ready for market.

2. The pig in the pen beside the road is Alec's pig.

But from these two premises we derive, by substitution, the false statement:

3. Jim believes Alec's pig is ready for market.

What in fact he believes, mistakenly, is that Pat's pig is ready for market. In the context of belief statements, or knowledge statements, or any statements involving propositional *attitudes,* in other words, substitutivity fails. Extensional logic breaks down. On the other hand, if extensional logic is good enough for arithmetic, and indeed, it has by now proven good enough for all mathematics, including set theory, so much the worse, it seems, for propositional attitudes—for beliefs, thoughts, hopes, ''intentions'' in general. If we are to specify the real (though subjective) particulars of which experience is built and to do it clearly and logically, thoughts and beliefs and such must go. Plainly, moreover, not only belief claims or knowledge claims but also ethical claims just make no sense in such empiricist-extensional terms. Russell himself once said in a letter to the *Listener* that so far as philosophy goes—and that means hard-nosed empirical philosophy implemented through extensional logic—there was no difference, so far as he could tell, between a dislike of merciless cruelty and a liking for oysters. So Russell the pacifist, Russell the humanitarian, lived a life schizophrenically at odds with his own philosophy.

On the other hand, the extensional logic imported from Frege—and amplified with necessary modification by Russell and Whitehead in *Principia Mathematica*—while it corresponded to Frege's ideal of logic and of the foundations of arithmetic, did not correspond to Frege's *philosophical* position. For Frege himself, as I have already indicated, insisted on the distinction between the *reference* of terms or propositions and their *sense,* that is, in the usual meaning of that term, their meaning. Suppose that all and only all mammals have true diaphrams separating the thoracic from the abdominal cavity; and suppose also that all and only all mammals have hair. These two properties, then, have the same reference, but surely not the same sense. To have a true diaphram is not to be hairy, even if both predicates happen to have exactly the same extension. Frege recognized the importance of this *intensional* aspect of concepts (something like what used to be called their connotation as distinct from their denotation), which Russell emphatically attempted to deny. It was the elaboration of extensional logic which Russell wished to assimilate to Humean (and, I believe, Hobbesian) empiricism in order to achieve the hard, clear philosophical position I have quoted from his own account of his own philosophical development. That means, in effect, to exile humanity, to exile epistemic claims, claims of beauty, beliefs in justice, from the cold physical world of meaningless items, which are quantifiable but bare of quality.

Now let me deal more briefly with act 1, scene 2. It was the same hope of purely extensional formalization that seemed to have motivated the early work of Ludwig Wittgenstein, the Wittgenstein of the *Tractatus* (1922), and it was indeed such a hope that motivated those who claimed to be influenced by him, including Russell himself. Wittgenstein had already spent some time in Cambridge, in the circle of Russell and Moore, before he wrote the *Tractatus*, and it appears reasonable to suppose that it was their kind of questioning that was expressed in his epoch-making work. "What *exactly* do you mean by that?" was Moore's favorite question. Exactitude of speech was the aim of philosophy, and logic (*extensional* logic) as a formalistic language was to give this aim complete and satisfactory expression. "The world is all that is the case," said Wittgenstein in the *Tractatus*, and "logic mirrors the world." Such Wittgensteinian dicta expressed the search for exactitude and factuality, the rejection of speculation and metaphysics, which impelled the founders of the Vienna circle, a European movement, to be sure, but one speedily exported bodily as well as intellectually to Britain and America. Now these philosophers, Carnap (in his early days), Ayer, Feigl, and many others, explicitly grounded their system on what they took to be the message of the *Tractatus*. Wittgenstein spoke of atomic facts to be mirrored in atomic propositions. The positivists' "protocol sentences," as they called them, were allegedly such atomic propositions, stating Wittgensteinian atomic facts. But were they? It is extremely difficult, indeed, to find a Wittgensteinian atomic fact and hence an atomic proposition. As the positivists interpreted the *Tractatus*, atomic propositions, or "protocol sentences," were reports of Humean impressions, like "here now yellow." In fact, however, as Professor Anscombe has clearly shown, there is no indication whatsoever in the *Tractatus* (and some indication to the contrary) that it was reports of such Russellian data that Wittgenstein had had in mind.[5] The austere logicism of early Wittgenstein, in short, had been badly skewed

by its transposition into the subjectivist terms of the Humean demand
for "minimum sensibles." Apart from the difficulty of interpreting
atomic facts and propositions, moreover, there is a second problem.
There is a strain of mysticism in the *Tractatus* which its positivistic
interpreters simply ignored. Wittgenstein, it is sometimes alleged, was
as much influenced by Kierkegaard and Schopenhauer as by the search
for precision of Russell and Moore. Be that as it may, his hope to find
the logic to mirror the world—or the world mirrored by that logic—
issues, with a kind of cryptic courage, in failure: in the determination to
say nothing lacking scientific exactitude and so, it seems, to say nothing
at all. But this paradoxical aspect of the *Tractatus* was quite beyond the
comprehension of its "disciples" in Vienna and eventually in Chicago
or Minneapolis or Princeton or Los Angeles. The philosophy of Russell
and of logical empiricism, in other words, was founded on a misreading
of Frege and early Wittgenstein, in which their emphasis on mathematical logic was taken over and set within the blinkers of empiricism to
the neglect of their profounder philosophical thought.

So much for act 1. The second phase of my story began with
Wittgenstein's discovery of the limits of his own early position.
Language doesn't "picture" the world, he discovered; it is rather like a
game, or a set of games, that we play in it. His *Blue* and *Brown Books,*
circulated in pirated manuscripts in the early post-war years, then the
publication of the *Philosophical Investigations* in 1953, laid the foundation for what came to be called "ordinary language" philosophy, a style
of philosophizing which dominated the Anglo-American scene for at
least a decade. Here it was our third empiricist principle, Hume's associationism, that took over. The search for Russellian "data" was abandoned, along with the insistence on hard, exact, "scientific" language
that had motivated the earlier phase.

J. L. Austin, though contrasted with Wittgenstein by most philosophers of this general cast of mind, seems to me, in *Sense and Sensibilia*
at least, to reflect the hail-fellow-well-met nonsense-dispelling mood
characteristic of this period. Not scientific, or technically philosophic,
but ordinary language is now taken as the norm for philosophical
thought. Those elusive "data" are never to be found. Fine; stop looking! We can all be hearty chaps together; nobody need worry any
longer, as Forster's undergraduates did in *The Longest Journey,* about
whether the cow was really there. Nobody need worry about "mind,"
that notorious ghost in the machine. Philosophy was to dispel its moldy
cobwebs—and itself. Instead of combining, as Russell and (early)
Carnap did, subjective data with a superstructure of physics, we
abandon those elusive phantasms (where are they anyhow, except under
drugs or anesthesia?); we abandon the dogma of the exclusive and
exhaustive truth of physics: the man on the bus finds his own way home

without reliance on differential equations, let alone indeterminacy principles or complementarity or the Schrödinger equation. This is just Humean naturalism, the reliance on custom to help us muddle through, taken as the message of Wittgenstein in the *Investigations* period. Philosophical problems were special headaches of funny people called philosophers; but who needs *them*? Forget them and get on with the job, teaching gym or chemistry, counting or ploughing or praying. Philosophy is a game which we can turn off at will, in order, as Hume put it, "to live at ease ever after."

Now that's all very well. But what had Wittgenstein *really* done in the *Investigations* and other reflections of that period? If one reads him in German, as most English speakers didn't, one gets a very different feel of what it's all about. What he did, while abandoning the traditional vocabulary of empiricism—"impressions," "sense data" and the like—was to take its problems to their logical conclusion, as no gentlemanly Englishman (or even Scot) had ever done, and to come out *beyond* them with a new spirit of philosophizing, not easy, as most dons took it to be, but difficult, cramped, and even agonizing. What is it to have toothache? No philosophical theory will tell us. But that is not to say there is no pain. What is it to see the duck or the rabbit in the duck-rabbit figure? What is it to see an aspect? Again no theory has been able to say, nor can it do so. Traditional philosophy, that is, empiricist philosophy, chased will-o'-the-wisps over such questions— as, for example, Moore asked, at great and tedious length, Is my sense datum really one surface of the inkwell? Wittgenstein did indeed seek to abandon such vain sport, but he was troubled, I believe, truly troubled, by the problems of meaning, of language use, of the human forms of life that underlay those frivolous philosophical preoccupations. This was no easy palliative, but a hard, rough way to a new style of thinking. In *Über Gewissheit,* for example, published posthumously not long ago, Wittgenstein had taken off from Moore's defense of practical certainty. Moore, before a large and suitably respectful philosophical gathering, had held up his hand and declared, simply and positively, "This is a hand." For all the ins and outs about sense data, to which he had contributed a goodly share, so much, he insisted, was really certain about the real world. Now where Moore, as always, had played a witty intellectual game, in which he turned the philosophers' arguments, including his own, against himself, Wittgenstein starts from Moore's argument and uses it, it seems to me, to very different effect. For Wittgenstein digs into the problem, turns it up and down and over, makes his reader think long and painfully with him. Granted, it is difficult to specify exactly where one comes out with such hard thinking. Indeed, both Wittgenstein himself and his friend and editor, Professor Anscombe, declared that he could have no disciples. (Or if there is work

that is really Wittgensteinian, the closest I can find to it is in essays, for
example, like Iris Murdoch's *The Sovereignty of Good* or Alan Don-
agan's piece on Wittgenstein on pain in Pitcher's anthology.) For
the most part the Wittgenstein born of the Anglicized version of his
intensely inverted thinking, was a travesty of the original, a jolly get-
together of port- or beer-drinking companions in common rooms or
pubs, a world away from the tormented questing of a single demonic
mind, thinking alone among and at the English, but never with them.

That was act 2. But then came one more. I didn't understand it when
it began, but now think perhaps I do. What happened was that the jolly
ordinary-language chaps, and others less jolly from the same general
empiricist establishment, took unto themselves the rigors of post-
Fregean logic, now greatly developed in its modern elaborations, like
those of Quine, Tarski, Church, and many others. Here Quine himself
is perhaps the most outstanding case. He was never, indeed, a so-called
"ordinary language" thinker, and one of his major philosophical
papers, "Two Dogmas of Empiricism," appeared at the time to constitute an attack on the authority of the dominant empiricist mode of
thought. What Quine has produced over the years, however, is still
empiricism of a kind. In effect he has turned Hume back into Hobbes,
skeptical or pragmatic into dogmatic or materialist empiricism. Like all
empiricists, he insists on specifiable little bits as all of what there is, but
little bits as the behaviorist or the physicist rather than the introspective
psychologist prescribes them. So he has developed what he calls a
"naturalized" epistemology in which, first, extensional logic is taken
as the model for all thinking, and, second, behavioristic psychology,
and ultimately, physics, is taken as the authoritative application of such
a logic to the world. Hence the absurdity, for him, of intentional talk,
talk of thoughts, beliefs, propositional attitudes. The *ne plus ultra* of
this position is exemplified in his paper "Of Natural Kinds," where,
seeing that not only consciousness words like "hope" or "fear," but
even property words like "blue" or "hairy" or "long," are not reducible to the extension of the classes they apply to, he argues that all such
terms will vanish when we finally come up out of the primeval slime in
which, qua humanists, or just qua human, we still are wallowing, and
talk hard scientific sense. In short, although he writes English with
seldom equalled elegance, he denies the right of any natural-language
user to behave as any natural-language user does, including, of course,
himself.

Quine is the most outstanding, because the clearest and most authoritative representative of this Hobbesian-empiricist-extensionalist position. But let me give you in conclusion two further examples of the
consequences it entails, one concerning the ultimate interpretation of
what seem to most of us to be uniquely human or at least uniquely

animate activities or capacities, the other concerning the interpretation of the laws of science, and especially the allegedly sacrosanct science of physics itself.

Both examples may be drawn from a book called *Content and Consciousness* by D. C. Dennett, published in 1969, enthusiastically received by some eminent Establishment philosophers and discussed at a meeting of the American Philosophical Association as an especially important contribution to the philosophy of mind. Dennett first takes it as read that all physical laws are purely extensional (a point to which I shall return shortly), and, second, argues that we use discourse not (at the moment) so reducible only in connection with "mental" states or activities. In other words, "intentionality," the goal-directedness of "mental" capacities or activities, is spoken of in part at least in nonextensional terms. Now admittedly Dennett declares at the close of his argument that the day when "intentional" language becomes obsolete is neither to be expected nor hoped for. Yet he does argue—as Quine does—as if such "intentional" talk were an unfortunate relic of the neolithic age. Thus, he remarks, we used to say that the river longs to go to the sea; now we talk hydraulics and don't talk of rivers wanting anything.[6] And for him this means to talk of them purely extensionally. This kind of new "scientific"=extensional discourse works, Dennett seems to believe, for biology (at least for evolutionary theory), and of course for computers. So on principle why not for persons? We *might* climb up out of the primeval slime, as Quine anticipates, and apply, theoretically and exclusively, the language of mathematics to the language of our own experience—although I must admit I don't know who the "we" who would do it would be.

But there is another question raised by the starting point of Dennett's argument. What does it mean to interpret physical—let alone biological or social-scientific—laws in purely extensional terms? There have been intensely acrobatic efforts by orthodox logicians to assimilate the concept of law to the principle of extensionality. A favorite example is that of dispositional concepts like "solubility." "Salt is soluble in water." What does that mean? How can a contrary-to-fact conditional (if I were to put this salt in water, it would dissolve) be interpreted in terms of truth values, of what *is* and *is not*? The answer is, it can't be. Either Hume is right and we just follow the constant conjunctions we've become accustomed to, and causal laws are mere matters of habit, or laws of nature, whether of physics or of any other discipline, must be given a *non*extensional form. We cannot make any *necessary* statements about the physical world, or even any rational statements of probability, or of dispositions, unless we permit nonextensional logic to enter our *physical* discourse, not only our discourse about beliefs and wants and colors and tastes and right and wrong. This point has been

made on the one hand (in his Quinine persona) by Professor Føllesdal,
in warning us that if we want to be strict ("to talk sense," he says,
though I must admit such sense appears to me to be nonsense) we
should avoid "contrary-to-fact conditionals, scientific law statements,
confirmation statements, and many types of probability statements and
disposition terms."[7] And on the other hand, the same point has been
made in the contrary sense by a host of epistemologists and modal logicians (including Føllesdal himself in his other character), who resist
the dogma I have been expounding, and who insist that even for the
interpretation of physical laws, let alone of belief or epistemic or
evaluative contexts, it is necessary to permit modal operators, like
"ought" and "should" and "might" and "must." The laws of
physics, so abjectly worshipped by Hobbesian empiricists like Russell
or Quine, are no laws at all if the extensional logic developed by Frege
for arithmetic and since expanded to apply to mathematics as a whole, is
foisted on a real world more flexible and varied in the kinds of realities
it contains than the *rigor logicae* from which they suffer allows them to
admit. There are, of course, I am happy to say in conclusion, many
respected philosophers even in the major, analytical Establishment,
who hold the latter view rather than the former: who believe extensional
logic inadequate even for the interpretation of natural laws, let alone of
more plainly human contexts. What I have been reporting, however, is
one leading and indeed almost dominant strand of analytical thought,
which even its opponents, I regret to say, take seriously, and which has
derived, as I have argued, from the misuse and misextrapolation of
Frege's logical initiative and Wittgenstein's early effort to apply it
within the confining premises of empiricist thought. To all those who
help to break the stranglehold of extensional logic and therewith the
blinders of an outworn search for least particulars—whether Hobbesian
or Humean—from which to construct a meaningless one-level universe
cleared of life, quality, responsibility, or freedom: to all such, even
outsiders like the present writer owe a vote of thanks. Yet their welcome
existence only diminishes, but does not cancel out, the scandal of a
philosophy that calls all that is human, or even, for that matter, all that
is included in the major propositions of the sciences (which do after all
express beliefs), "primeval" or "obscure." What I have been concerned with here, however, is not so much that scandal itself or the too
respectful response to it by many less simplistic thinkers, but only the
oddity that the genius of Frege and of Wittgenstein should have been so
strangely misapplied when transposed into the framework, first and
third of a dogmatic materialist philosophy, and second of a less
mephitic but still epistemologically inadequate naturalism of habit—in
effect a conditioned reflex philosophy less inhumane in its eighteenth

century than in its Skinnerian form, but still as impotent as the first or third versions to deal with the philosophical problems that face us in the late, as in the early, twentieth century.

Notes

1. Bertrand Russell, *My Philosophical Development* (London: G. Allen and Unwin, 1959).

2. Ibid., p. 27.

3. Ibid., p. 17.

4. Ibid.

5. See, for example, G. E. M. Anscombe, *An Introduction to Wittgenstein's Tractatus* (London: Hutchinson & Co., 1969), pp. 25-30. The same point is made in an article that reveals connections between Wittgensteinian and continental philosophizing quite different from those suggested here: Blanche L. Premo, "The Early Wittgenstein and Hermeneutics," *Philosophy Today*, 16 (1972): 43-65.

6. Daniel C. Dennett, *Content and Consciousness* (London: Routledge & Kegan Paul; New York: Humanities Press, 1969), p. 89.

7. Dagfinn Føllesdal, "Quantification into Causal Contexts," in *Reference and Modality*, ed. L. Linsky (London: Oxford University Press, 1971), p. 62.

III

Philosophy In and Out of Europe:

2. The Reception of Continental Philosophy in America

1974

THERE ARE TWO ESTABLISHMENTS IN AMERICAN PHILOSOPHY nowadays, a Major, or so-to-speak Establishment Establishment, which is firmly oriented to the Anglo-American, basically empiricist, tradition, and a minor, so-to-speak Anti-Establishment Establishment, engaged in reporting, developing, interpreting and assimilating twentieth century continental, that is, European, thought. *I* believe, indeed, that at least the most conspicuous branch of the Anglo-American Establishment, sometimes called analytical philosophy, itself derives from three successive stages of mistaken adaptation of the work of certain German-language philosophers within the narrow confines of British, specifically Humean, premises. The exposition of that heresy, however, I have attempted elsewhere.[1] I shall focus here on the chief permutations by which the minor, and confessedly European, Establishment has established itself. I have to divide my presentation along two different lines. First, I shall be dealing with the four major European thinkers whose work has been imported—*as* European—into America. Secondly, I want to illustrate how the form of importation has differed in each case, ranging from one extreme, the adoption both by émigrés and by Americans of a very specialized European philosophical method, to the other extreme, the thorough assimilation of European leitmotivs in the development of an American philosopher's own arguments. The four philosophers whose work has found its way most conspicuously into the Minor Establishment (as I've called it) are Husserl, Heidegger, Sartre, and Merleau-Ponty; the various ways in which the philosophies of each of them have immigrated to this country I shall try to make clear as I proceed.

Husserl, in a way, is the most fundamental of all four, since, in its origin, the work of all the other three is unquestionably indebted to him. Heidegger was his assistant, and his major work, *Being and Time,* was dedicated to Husserl (a dedication rescinded during the Third Reich). Sartre began his philosophical career by discovering Husserl's concept of intentionality during the year he spent in the prewar thirties at the German House in Berlin. Merleau-Ponty, in his major work, relies heavily on his own reading of Husserl's then unpublished *opera posthuma,* which he consulted at Louvain. It is Husserl also, as I shall try to explain presently (or rather to say, at greater length, for I can't really explain it), whose method has been most faithfully followed in work done and published in this country. Yet at the same time, I must confess in advance, his own work, and that of his best disciples, appears to me, however rigorous and brilliant, to constitute a kind of quiet and alien backwater cut off from the mainstream of philosophical problems peculiar to our place and to our century.

Husserl started from the question of the philosophical foundations of mathematics. What is mathematics about? What are its objects? He began by giving a psychologistic answer: to put it very crudely, the objects of mathematics are what mathematicians are thinking. But he soon saw that this was mistaken. That the area of a circle is πr^2, for example, has nothing to do with the question whether anybody happens to think so. Mathematics, and, indeed, every science, every aspect of rational life, he came to insist, must rest on principles free from any taint of contingency, principles which only philosophy, as distinct from any empirical discipline, can discover. Philosophy as a rigorous, presuppositionless science must lay bare, exactly, evidently, and systematically, the essential structures of consciousness which underlie all disciplines and all areas of human experience, the structures both of the possible activities of consciousness and of its possible objects. It was this discipline, this systematic and exact investigation of the essential structures of consciousness, which Husserl entitled phenomenology, and which he constantly developed and modified in a formidably technical style throughout his long career; it is this discipline that his followers have continued to preach and to develop after him both in Europe and America. Phenomenology alone provides, it was, and is, alleged, before all ontology, before all "world views," before all cultural relativities, those necessary and universal truths that other philosophers had so long sought along mistaken paths. Moreover, the necessary truths so developed can be developed, it was, and is, alleged, only by the special techniques of "reduction," that is, by putting to one side, or "bracketing," the question of empirical existence, limiting one's investigations to consciousness itself and inquiring carefully and systematically into its essential character. The field of phenomenology *is,* as Husserl's disciple Aaron Gurwitsch entitled his best-known work, the field of consciousness. If you want to know, for example, not hypothetically and experimentally, but prior to all such conjectures, what perception is, you should try, as Husserl did in *Ideas One,* to look—with the mind's eye—extremely carefully at the essential structures of this kind of conscious act. Looking at the ash tree on the hill, for instance, includes, *as* looking, the anticipation that if I walked around it I would see, in an indefinite but systematic sequence, a series of views, or "profiles," of it; while if I imagine the ash tree on the hill, I get just one view, not such an awareness of more to come. The same kind of distinction can be made for an object of perception, qua content of consciousness, as distinct from any object of fancy, as fancied. Moreover, in every act of consciousness one can distinguish the essential characters of the act as such, e.g., perceiving, from the character of its target, i.e., what is perceived (still as content of consiousness, not as a "real" thing out in a "real" world). And finally, the relation between act and target is always some variant of that pervasive relation fundamental to the very nature of consciousness itself which Husserl called *intentionality.* It is this concept which, in a very different spirit, Sartre adopted from Husserl, as did Merleau-Ponty, too, I think one can say, at least implicitly; and so did Heidegger, though under a different name (or several different names) and in a radically altered context.

But let's take that as read: the question I want to raise here does not concern the role or the transformation of Husserlian intentionality in the work of other European thinkers. What I want to ask here is, rather: What was the fate of Husserl's method in America, and what does it offer, I would have to say both in Europe and for us, as an approach to contemporary philosophical problems?

Most philosophies, it seems to me, are transformed in some degree by exportation, if only through translation in the linguistic sense, but also by cultural transposition. That had certainly been true of the earlier odyssey of Hegel, whose lofty German system had been disguised, first in the late Victorian gowns, and minds, of Oxford and Cambridge dons, then in the rosier "synthesis" of American speculative philosophy, finally in the naïve progressivism of John Dewey, which assimilated while rejecting it. In the case of phenomenology, however, the movement simply came to America lock, stock, and barrel, represented both by émigrés and by American disciples, and, within certain enclaves of American philosophy, continued, and still continues, as it had begun, to seek out the necessary structures of consciousness, the presupposition-less presuppositions of perception, of artistic consciousness, of social existence, and so on. The work so executed has persisted, with entire faithfulness and exact devotion, as pure and unsullied as were the European frescoes painstakingly transported for display at the Metropolitan some years ago. The result is paradoxical. On the one hand, phenomenological techniques can handle fruitfully many problems in philosophy which the more limited, empiricist approach can only brush aside. For example, the systematically anticipative structure of perception already referred to escapes the notice of traditional empiricism, which has to look for least bits of experience to hold onto; or when this search for least bits fails, empiricism says cheerily, look, friends, there was no problem. In this area, as in some others—for instance, in Roman Ingarden's work on the literary work of art—phenomenology really does look deeper and see farther than the alternative tradition is able to do.

At the same time, as I have suggested at the outset, the fundamental task that Husserl and his disciples had set themselves, and continue to set themselves, appears to me, in at least two important respects, tangential to the aims that twentieth century philosophy needs to set itself. First, phenomenology seeks apodicticity: it reaffirms the traditional doctrine that philosophy consists in the enunciation of necessary truths. But what philosophical reflection needs—desperately, in our confusing century—to understand is not the necessary, but the contingent, the way in which, to use Heidegger's term, we have been thrown into the world. The necessary, like πr^2, can only be eternal; we need to make sense of change, of what might be otherwise; we need to seek out the rationale of history. Husserl, in his last years, came to be interested in history, in the origin, for example, with Galileo, of modern naturalism, or in the origin of geometry. But "origin," for him, had somehow to be grasped ideally, unhistorically. In other words, for phenomenology, as for its "analytical" antagonists, conceptual structure, logic, must be prior to history. In my view, however, the major problem of philosophy throughout the twentieth century has been precisely to conceptualize the contrary thesis, that history is prior to logic. How to achieve this aim without falling either into the obscurities of a speculative metaphysic like Whitehead's or into the irrationalism of some variants of existentialist thought, for instance, indeed, the original one of Kierkegaard—how to make sense, philosophically, of the priority of history to logic seems to me to have been, and still to be, our major philosophical task. This aim, however, runs directly counter to that of phenomenology, which must *seek*, even if it never succeeds in finding, not a meaning within contingency, but pure, unsullied, necessary truth. Such a search seems to me, with all due respect for the skill and devotion of its practitioners, the purest anachronism, like the revival of some ancient Egyptian ritual at a time when philosophy is at crisis point, at a crisis point peculiar to *our* situation, where we have to reckon not only with the great Scottish skeptic whose heirs, like it or not, we are, but with the takeover of philosophical reflection by one scientism or another, whether by behavioristic psychology or physics in so-called "naturalized epistemology" or by a mésalliance with Darwinism in which the theory of knowledge is swallowed up, cobralike, by the theory of natural selection. With these monstrosities around us, the Husserlian, like the Platonic or Cartesian, quest for certainty is a luxury we can ill afford.

Second, moreover, as I stressed earlier, phenomenology restricts, and must restrict, itself to the field of consciousness. Now certainly if that were the only alternative to abandoning consciousness, to arguing, as some up-and-coming philosophers do, that there are no thoughts, or there is no pain, that the mind is the brain or the central nervous system or what you will, we would have no choice but to follow the phenomenologist's path. But again, the task of twentieth century philosophy has been, and still is, precisely to overcome this alternative, the alternative bequeathed to modern thought through the clear, arid, doomed dualism of Descartes. We have to learn to understand ourselves, neither as disembodied spirits somehow lodged for a time in pieces of machinery, nor as such machinery itself, but as the peculiar kind of living animals we are, animals who, even in our animal nature, need a culture, need to live *in* as well as *through* the artifacts of language, of ritual, of art, of science, even of philosophy itself. Husserl, too, admittedly, devout phenomenologists will at once object, thought hard and to good effect in his late works about the so-called "life world," which is after all the world of embodied beings; and so do his present successors. But this is always the life world "reduced"—to a structure of consciousness, to its essence, to the "transcendental ego" which is said to "constitute" it, as it is said to constitute every specialized area of experience. This is an elegant, and, heaven knows, a serious game for its initiates, a game, indeed, which appeals to many students just because of its aura of European solemnity, as distinct from the patent triviality of the games many "British"-type philosophers like to play. But it is a game, nevertheless, in that its rules and strategies seem to fall, for the most part, safely outside the less well-defined but more urgent philosophical problems posed by the fact and character of our embodiment. "What happens," one of my colleagues, himself trained in phenomenology, has been heard to ask, "when the Transcendental Ego drinks too many martinis?" It's not an altogether frivolous question. Once more, the point is not that mind is reducible to body, but that they can't be torn asunder. We need to learn to think them both together and to give those thoughts adequate philosophical expression. History and body: those are our categories. Phenomenology can treat them gingerly and at barge pole length, but doesn't dwell in them, as we must do; and so it remains, I can only conclude, an alien body in our philosophical life.

The other three continental imports, Heidegger, Sartre, and Merleau-Ponty, having, for good or ill, some connection in people's minds with "existentialism," and therefore with the reinterpretation of the human condition, appear more promising for assimilation to our own philosophical inquiries. And here there has indeed been assimilation of a number of varieties, which I shall try to distinguish, at least in outline, chiefly with respect to Heidegger and briefly, in conclusion, for the other two.

What has happened to Heidegger in America? Three things (at least, there may be more that haven't come my way).

First, Heidegger was imported originally along with the postwar enthusiasm for "existentialism," an enthusiasm which still persists in some places in this country, although it is pretty well a dead letter in most quarters in Europe. Now of course Heidegger was never an "existentialist": he investigated the fundamental structures of human existence, *Existentialien* as he called them, as a step on the way to "fundamental ontology" as such. Moreover, though introducing his project in *Being and Time* as "phenomenology," he so radically reworked the bent of that method as to make of it the quest for Being itself. Thus, as we shall see, his analysis of the Being of human being is but the first step in that much more inclusive and perilous task. What Heidegger taught us, despite himself, however, was indeed a number of lessons about the structure of human existence. First, he is the first great philosopher of this century systematically to evade the Cartesian alternative. "Consciousness" is not for him, as it is for Husserl, the medium in which he works. Nor, at least centrally, is he concerned with the other Cartesian alternative of "body." He describes what it is to be human as to-be-in-a-world without succumbing either to Cartesian problems or to Cartesian solutions. For this reason if for no other it is fair to say that any contemporary philosophy ought to proceed from the foundation established once and for all in *Being and Time*. Some "existential" concepts, moreover, like that of "dread" as central to human development, or the contrast between "authentic" and "inauthentic" existence, have been introduced into our thinking chiefly through Heidegger's use of them. Moreover, the principle of historicity, of human being as basically an expression of temporality, and of time as fundamentally human, before it is chronological and mathematical: this principle has made its way into the thinking of many contemporary philosophers chiefly through *Being and Time*.

Those were the first and more manageable imports from Heidegger-ian thought. Since the postwar years, however, a vast Heideggerian corpus has become available in translation. The result of this greater apparent accessibility has, I think, been twofold.

On the one hand, there are simple adorers of Heidegger who swallow the Anglicized master with total lack of criticism, and in many cases, it seems to me, necessarily with little understanding. For if "tout comprendre c'est tout pardonner," it doesn't hold, conversely, that "tout adorer (et pardonner), c'est tout comprendre." Heidegger's works, when rendered into English, are simply made into some form of pseudo-philosophical patter for the most part utterly out of touch with the original. The reason is that Heidegger's style, and therefore Heidegger's thinking, is not only German, but Germanic: he plays on and with and in his native language in a fashion that can, of course, be under-stood to some extent by aliens well trained in that language, as any foreign literature can be, but in a fashion that no one, however devoted, can transpose, word for word, sentence for sentence, into another tongue. It is not just the difficulty of rendering special Heideggerian terms, like *Dasein* or *Verfallen* or *Geviert* or *Gestell,* as is the case with Kantian terms like *Anschauung* or *Verstand* or *Vernunft.* The difficulty goes deeper in at least two ways.

First, it is not just a question of rendering terms or even phrases, but of trying to convey in English a constant use and reuse of German roots that lend themselves to subtle interactions of which our hybrid language is incapable. Note: I am *not* subscribing to the thesis, which I heard everywhere enunciated when I was studying in Germany in 1931-33, that philosophizing—or thought, as Heidegger now prefers to call it—can only go on at any depth or to any purpose in ancient Greek or modern German. The irony of Hume, for example, so different from romantic irony, cannot be assimilated, I should think, to German phil-osophy. Compare, for instance, his arguments in the *Dialogues Con-cerning Natural Religion* with what Kant (having read them in transla-tion) made of them in the Transcendental Dialectic of the first *Critique.* We have our subtleties, too. But the forgotten metaphors of our speech are much more thoroughly forgotten than those of German; they do not lend themselves so readily to the philosophical word play which, from Hegel's time to Heidegger's, has characterized a certain style of German philosophy. Such word-play may, indeed, be pretentious, vicious, or just silly. Heidegger's often is any or all of these. There is of course the famous case of "nothing noths," which may or may not be nonsense; I don't know. But what Heidegger has to say that unques-tionably makes sense, up to a point at least—for instance, his attack on the notion of "the technical" as the governing principle of philosophy—is said so thoroughly through the manipulation of German roots and compounds that it just can't make sense to hand it out in English to students eager for philosophical bread; if it isn't stones they get it must be cotton candy. Let me give you just two examples out of a myriad, both from the "Letter on Humanism." Near the beginning there is a paragraph devoted to describing "the element of thought." The passage in question begins:

> Das Element ist das, aus dem her das Denken vermag, ein Denken zu sein. Das Element ist das eigentlich Vermögende: das Vermögen.[2]

How does one render this? "The element is that from which thinking is able to be a thinking. The element is the genuinely enabling . . .," so far, so good; we can make it to "able" and "enable," but what is *das Vermögen*? The power, the capacity? We have lost the essential pun. And then the passage continues to play on the stem *mögen* of *Vermögen*, which means to like, or be fond of, as well as to be able—and still further on with *möglich* and *Möglichkeit*, possible and possibility. It concludes:

> Wenn ich von der "stillen Kraft des Möglichen" spreche, meine ich nicht das possibile einer nur vorgestellten possibilitas, nicht die potentia als essentia eines actus der existentia, sondern das Sein selbst, das mögend über das Denken und so über das Wesen des Menschen und das heisst über dessen Bezug zum Sein vermag. Etwas vermögen bedeutet hier: es in seinem Wesen wahren, in seinem Element einbehalten.[3]

"If I speak of the 'quiet power of the possible' [where has the "able"/ "enable" link got to?], I do not mean the *possibile* of a merely represented *possibilitas*, not the *potentia* as *esse* of an *actus* of *existentia*, but Being itself, which [*mögend*, loving? . . . *vermag*, controls, has power over?] the thought and over the essence of man, and that means, over his relation to Being. To be able [to do?] something means here: to cherish it [*wahren*, the root is *wahr*, true] in its essence, to hold it within its element." One may of course read this even in German and find it sleight of hand; but bereft of its rootedness in the turns of meaning the original permits, I really don't see how it is to be understood.

A second, briefer example, a few pages later: Heidegger has been lamenting the degeneration of language, which in its essence, he holds, is "the house of the truth of Being." Now, however, he tells us, language allows us to manipulate it as "an instrument of the power over what is [*das Seiende*]," that is, over beings (little b). This little-b being, ("Dieses selbst"), he continues, "erscheint als das Wirkliche im

Gewirk von Ursache und Wirkung."[4] Shall we say, "appears as the real in the interaction of cause and effect?" What becomes of the *wirk* in *Wirklich-Gewirk-Wirkung?* It's a game we just can't play.

But there is a second, and even more deep-seated difficulty, and that is the spirit of Heidegger's whole enterprise, from the preliminary existential analysis of *Being and Time* to the "thought" of Being paraded in the later works. This is not the time or place to go in any detail into the question of Heidegger's politics, which indeed is not a question but a fact; but politics apart, his very being is so utterly German, so unquestioningly grounded in "blood and soil," that with the exception of some texts like the later Kant book, *Die Frage nach dem Ding,* it seems quite incapable of exportation as the more cosmopolitan thought of philosophers like Kant or Husserl or Frege is exportable, at least within the limits of particular linguistic difficulties, to other shores. Not for nothing did Heidegger call his disclosure of authentic existence in *Sein und Zeit* a tribute to the German patriots Dilthey and Count Yorck von Wartenburg. Not for nothing did he turn, when *Sein und Zeit* proved incapable of completion, to the great lyric poets of the German language, Rilke, Trakl, George, and above all Hölderlin, for intellectual sustenance and solace. Not for nothing did he declare, in a text composed in the thirties and published in the fifties, that Germany is the bearer of Thought and of Being, caught between the two barbarian giants, America and Russia. For even though he insists elsewhere that his smugly chauvinistic rhetoric was not nationalistically intended, or that, for instance, Hölderlin's "Homecoming" is not addressed to Germans qua Germans, this can only mean that "German" for Heidegger is synonymous with "rooted in Being," just as "Americanism," though a phenomenon stemming from Europe, stands for whatever has lost such rootedness and given way to the superficial and the technical. Poetry, for Heidegger, is the primal language in which a people founds Being, and philosophy, for him, is the handmaiden of poetry, seeking to turn us back from our cyberneticized strayings to the still sound of Being itself. But poetry belongs to *a* natural language, not, like mathematics, to all languages at once, and Heidegger's allegiance to the poets of his native language ties his thinking inevitably to the German tongue. I do believe, incidentally, and in this Heidegger's reliance on the sayings of poets about language may be salutary, that one can defend philosophically some kind of thesis of the priority of poetry. One can argue that there is something fundamental to the very possibility of language itself which is uniquely exhibited in the power of poetic discourse, in what Jakobson has christened "poeticity," something more fundamental than the syntactical rules of prose or the exactitudes of mathematical formalism. But I believe also that one can defend this thesis without surrendering oneself to the poetry of one's own language as the only poetry on which such a philosophical principle could relay. Indeed, I have tried myself elsewhere to suggest a starting point at least for such an argument.[5] But that is not, it seems to me, what Heidegger has done. He is a thinker rooted in his own place, in his own landscape, in his own language; neither the poetry he relies on nor the word-play he works through can be simply transplanted, as, for instance, phenomenology was, to the sidewalks of New York. It is wrong, I believe, for any student of philosophy to venerate, without any critical reflection of his own, any single thinker. It is wrong, in the light of his political record, to venerate Heidegger in particular. To venerate an Americanized version of the Heideggerian opus is utterly lamentable—or, if you prefer a lighter tone, utterly laughable. But it *is* done.

On the other hand, as I have already suggested, *Being and Time*, with its truly post-Cartesian thinking, with its basic concepts of being-in-the-world and of temporality, also Heidegger's early Kant book, with its stress on finitude and on the productive imagination, even perhaps (though I'm less sanguine about this) some later essays, can serve English-speaking readers in the development of their own reflections. There are many American philosophers, including the present writer, for whom this is the case. Ted Kisiel of Northern Illinois, for example, has made good use of the clues Heidegger gives in *Being and Time* for a hermeneutical philosophy of science. But the most interesting instance of this kind is that of Professor Hubert Dreyfus of Berkeley, who purveys *his* Heidegger, not wholly uncritically, but with deep intellectual passion and undoubted pedagogical brilliance to all—hundreds each year—who come to listen, and uses that Heidegger, in turn, for his own philosophical purposes, purposes with which, indeed, I find myself almost wholly in accord. In the long run what he is after, I believe, as I am too, is a reassessment of the human condition which can make sense of the whole of what it is to be human, which can exhibit the distinction between the sciences and the arts, the limits of technology, the dependence of each area of human life on the whole structure of being-in-the-world, without succumbing, as it is now so fashionable to do, to the lure of one science or another, whether natural or social, as a cure-all for our philosophical troubles. Yet at some crucial places I really don't think that Dreyfus's Heidegger, though elegantly articulated, is Heidegger himself. Thus, for example, Dreyfus takes *das Man,* the "who" of everyday existence, as a kind of reservoir on which the rare human being who has achieved authenticity may draw. Now of course it's true that, in Heidegger's view, even the man of destiny *also* lives an everyday existence; but surely the shift from living as *das Man* to living one's "proper" Being-to-Death is of a very different, and more radical, kind than Dreyfus's reading would suggest. Or, while using *Being and Time* to good effect in his own thinking, he nevertheless holds that Heidegger has later rejected *all* his earlier work, including *Being and Time*. But strangest of all, Dreyfus equates the Being Heidegger by his own admission has constantly been searching for with the *world* of Being-in-the-World—that is, the human world, the world-as-we-live-it and live in it. Yet Heidegger, according to his own proud pronouncement, investigated human being as Being-in-the-World only because human being is the only being whose Being is in question for its Being; so it is there he starts on the long quest for Being itself. Now admittedly *our* Being is Being-in-a-World; but World is not therefore identical with Being; far from it. We in our world, he keeps insisting, have forgotten Being, fallen out of Being and into nihilism. We need to seek, according to Heidegger, not cheerful adjustment to our own degraded culture, but the hard road of return to the first beginnings of Western thought, to pre-Socratic rootedness in Being. Heidegger, as philosophers as different as Jacques Derrida and Dorothea Frede have pointed out, is still firmly based in the great ontological tradition. The Being he seeks is not world, surely not "culture," but the Being of Parmenides, already lost in good measure by the time of Plato's *Republic,* still further with Aristotle, and finally in our day, so far lost from view with the triumph of technology, cybernetics, and Americanism, that only Thought—a lifetime of Heideggerian Thought—can give some slender hope for its recovery.[6] Admittedly, Dreyfus knows the details of McQuarrie and Robinson's translation of *Sein und Zeit* much better than I do the original; but whenever I protest at some, as I think, bowdlerization of the text, he says, "But I've checked the German." To check the German, however, is not to steep oneself in it or to grasp the tenor of the thought behind it. Admittedly, in teaching foreign texts in translation, as we all have to do, this is always a danger. I have been caught out myself relying on Cornford's *Theaetetus,* which I taught for years in Belfast, "checking the Greek" occasionally, but not knowing it as a professional classical philosopher ought to know it. It is a difficult situation, especially for those of us who teach contemporary European philosophy. Our students, surfeited, and rightly so, with the language- and logic-chopping of many (I did *not* say "all"!) analytical philosophers, long for philosophy in the more soul-searching continental strain. What they get in the case of Heidegger is, as I have said, either adulation, which is not philosophy at all, or an ingenious philosophy which, Americanized, is only partly Heidegger.

I shall deal with the other two cases more succinctly, for the facts with respect to Sartre are readily accessible, and for Merleau-Ponty, easy to find once one knows where to look.

In the case of Sartre there has been an effort, less ingenious but more widespread than in that of Heidegger, to transpose his central concepts of "authenticity," of freedom, of bad as against possible good faith, into blander American terms, so that we may have a viable "existentialist ethic," or "ethics of authenticity." But Sartre never wrote his ethic, for the very good reason that his philosophical principles forbade him to do so. If you start, as he did, from consciousness as for-itself, as the negation of its objective target, the in-itself, concepts like "good" or "right" are either pure negations or bad faith. There is no foundation available to him on which an ethic could be built. He made a half-hearted effort in his weakest piece, *Existentialism and Humanism,* to do something of the kind, and presumably he set Simone de Beauvoir to try it in her equally unsatisfactory *Ethics of Ambiguity.* In his major philosophical writings, however, he has necessarily swung, so far, between the impasse of man as useless passion on the one hand, in *Being and Nothingness,* and an abstract and unreal pseudo-Marxism on the other, in the *Critique of Dialectical Reason.* There has been good reporting and criticism of Sartrean philosophy by a number of English and American writers, but the attempts to assimilate him to middle-class morality constitute a truly unnecessary misuse of major philosophical texts. French philosophy, being Latinate, shouldn't be *so* hard to render in, and understand through, our largely Latinate professional language. I needn't speak, I hope, of the much greater abuse of Sartre and other "existentialist" writers by so-called "existential therapists," who make of anxiety a neurosis to be wheedled away, rather than the only gate, if such there be at all, to integrity and freedom.

What, finally, of Merleau-Ponty? Here we come to a case of the influence of European thought so thoroughly assimilated that it can be taken up, not only by students of continental philosophy as such, but even by so-called "analytical" thinkers without their recognizing the European source of the arguments they use or comment on.

A fashionable concern of fashionable philosophers in the past decade or so has been something called "action theory," the problem of what human action is, as distinct from mere motion or from behavior behavioristically interpreted. It is difficult to explain just what this topic amounts to, because, although there has been very good work done in its name, there has been (and still is) also a good deal that is trivial. It is basically a question of the distinction between "reasons" (Why did he want to go to town?) and "causes" (Why did the car skid?). Perhaps it is easiest to see how philosophers managed to make an issue of this distinction if we put it in the context of the philosophy of law. What does it mean to say X murdered Y? It used to be thought by many philosophers, and legal theorists, that one had to be able to pinpoint, in an unbroken sequence of causes and effects, the moment when X pulled the trigger: that was the *act* that killed Y. But clearly a murder, or any purposeful action, is not just a moment in a chain. To be first-degree murder, for instance, it must be premeditated. What does that mean?

Not some black-box operation in the murderer's mind, as people used to suppose, but a complex and integrated nexus of processes and actions theoretically explicable in terms of reasons (motives) as well as means, opportunity, and at one moment in the whole sequence, actual trigger pulling. An action, many philosophers have argued, therefore, follows from an intention differently from the way a physical effect follows from a cause. Others, in turn, have attempted to refute these arguments and to reduce actions again to purely causal terms, and so on.

The point I want to make about this new "specialism" is a simple one. One of the most influential works in the field of action theory was Charles Taylor's *Explanation of Behaviour,* first published in 1964.[7] And Taylor, who is bilingual in French and English, acknowledges in a number of places his indebtedness to Merleau-Ponty's major work. Now Merleau-Ponty not only appropriated to his own ends and in his own way what he considered (probably mistakenly) to be Husserl's message in the then unedited posthumous fragments, he not only appropriated in his own way Heidegger's fundamental concept of Being-in-the-World, but he also developed these themes, in his *Phenomenology of Perception,* as no previous thinker had explicitly done, in terms of the conception of a basically ambiguous, yet unified psycho-physical being-in-the-world. He not only bypassed Descartes, as Heidegger had, but tried to reckon with him, as any French thinker must, in order to come out beyond the Cartesian alternative. That reflective, intended conquest of dualism is precisely the necessary condition for any adequate theory of action, which must recognize at one and the same time the biological and the intellectual-emotional dimensions of our existence, which, in other words, as I said earlier, must take as its fundamental concepts *body* and *history.* And it is Merleau-Ponty's way of starting on this enterprise that has made his work seem to many of us a foundation on which we could build in our own efforts to see man and man-in-nature in a new light. Taylor's book was, in part at least, inspired by this impression, as he himself openly declares.

Yet insofar as Taylor's argument was taken up by "action theorists," his indebtedness to Merleau-Ponty went unheeded. The book was, after all, based on an Oxford dissertation; Taylor is an admired member of the British Establishment, of the Establishment Establishment, as I've called it, and no one, or hardly anyone, with the honorable exception of the author himself, acknowledged the acknowledgment of his European source. Scores, perhaps hundreds, of little people in big or little institutions have written about Taylor, glossed Taylor, taken off from Taylor in their vocation of hairsplitting, without ever noticing that the text they are respectfully commenting on is, if not the statement of a French philosophy, a work inspired by French philosophy. For them, it is the philosophy of a Canadian from Oxford; that is all they know or care about.

Since then, Taylor's work has also been influenced by that of Paul Ricoeur; I can't go into that now. But let me conclude with an anecdote which illustrates the kind of assimilation of one tradition to another that I am trying to exemplify as the contrary extreme to the faithful adoption of Husserl and his method by American phenomenologists. Some years ago the then president of the Yale Philosophy Club told me they had two visitors at succeeding meetings. First came Charles Taylor, who publicly avowed his debt to Merleau-Ponty; then came Miss Anscombe, now Professor of Logic and Metaphysics at Cambridge, who remarked, as I'm told she often does, "Of course everybody knows everything written on the continent is just gas," and when asked if there was anything important going on in *British* philosophy, declared, "Yes, there is one young man who is really a philosophical genius, and that's Charles Taylor." Perhaps after all that's the best fate that can befall a philosophy when it goes abroad. It has borne fruit, some sound, some wizened, but no one, except for the importer himself and a few like-minded colleagues, notices the tree from which it came.

Notes

1. See Chap. II above.
2. Martin Heidegger, *Wegmarken* (Frankfurt: Klostermann, 1967), pp. 147-148.
3. Ibid.
4. Ibid., p. 150.
5. See Chap. XI below.
6. For Dreyfus's interpretation of *das Man,* see his "The Priority of *The* World to *My* World: Heidegger's Answer to Husserl (and Sartre)," in *Man and World* (in press, 1975). The second and third points arose in discussions at the U.C.S.D. conference on Heidegger in the spring of 1974. To my third point Dreyfus replies, "But Being is still active, it appears in a distorted form. Or, put another way, we have also forgotten what world means" (personal communication).
7. Charles Taylor, *The Explanation of Behaviour* (New York: Humanities Press, 1964).

IV

A Note on the Philosophy of Heidegger: Confessions of a Young Positivist

1938

TEN YEARS AGO MARTIN HEIDEGGER PRESENTED TO THE WORLD, IN the first volume of *Sein und Zeit*,[1] his introduction to a novel type of metaphysics. His work was said to constitute a uniquely effective wedge into the ontological problem; with its approach through an "existential" analysis of human nature, it purported to set philosophy at last upon the highroad to the fastnesses of being—with a key to their most secret chambers in her hand. On the face of it, Heidegger's method seems to consist in the familiar handling of metaphysical problems through a prior analysis of human nature. He begins, it is true, not with the epistemological question, what can I know, but with a more inclusive problem, very inaccessible to simple statement. Perhaps it is the summation of Kant's three questions: What is man—or, more aptly, *how* is man, what is his *modus essendi*? Still, that is but another variation of the approach to nature through human nature; and even though every familiar term—man, person, human being, human nature, experience—is denied us as inadequate, it would certainly appear to the uninitiated that some such analysis is the theme of *Sein und Zeit*. To its author, however, and to the sympathetic audience that greeted the appearance of his work, no such superficial interpretation is in any way permissible or relevant. Heidegger's method, and especially the philosophical earnestness fundamental to its application, achieved for the philosophical public of Germany a new Copernican revolution in speculative thought.

If one takes that judgment seriously, one should expect, therefore, that a more considered study might reveal, within the framework of an anthropocentric approach to metaphysics, some unique insight or some new tool of philosophical analysis. As a matter of fact, I cannot make any such discovery either in Heidegger's published works or in oral expositions of his views.[2] A close examination seems rather to expose, within the ponderous sentences of essay and lecture, a very insubstantial basis for a flimsy superstructure. Heidegger's philosophy is unique only in its rampant misuse of language and in its own emphatic claim to uniqueness. I should like to support that thesis by a brief analysis of its method and content.

1. There are two essential preliminaries to the application of Heidegger's method. The first of these is a return to original insights through the "destruction" of traditional philosophies. One might speak of primitivism in this connection, were not the term "primitive" in some of its connotations so emphatically eliminated by Heidegger's own exposition of the process denoted. The intuitions to which he wishes to return are, indeed, temporally primitive; they are primitive, likewise, in the sense that they are said to be the original, uncorrupted, and therefore peculiarly immediate insights of man into metaphysical reality. But they are not to be regarded as primitive in the sense of being simple, naïve, less self-conscious or less sophisticated than later speculations. Such notions Heidegger denounces roundly; and with them he would certainly reject the title of primitivist. He wishes to return, not to first faltering footsteps, but to hard-won heights long neglected by wanderers on the level plain of professional philosophy. He wants to plumb forgotten depths, not to wade in obscure shallows. It is, to be sure, characteristic of Heidegger, not only here but throughout his system, to reject in vehement terms all "isms" that might possibly be applied to his thought, so that one may perhaps call him a primitivist in his historical approach, with the reservation that he shuns that or any title. Whatever one calls the method, however, it is clear that Heidegger is attempting to effect a return to some first insight uniquely profound and difficult of attainment. He effects that return, in part, by a "destructive" analysis of philosophic tradition. I may cite a few illustrations of the destructive method, without going too far into the impassable jungles of Heideggerian vocabulary.

In his lectures on truth,[3] Heidegger subjected the long-suffering correspondence theory to scathing criticism—not because of its logical inconsistencies or factual inadequacies, but because it had falsified the early Greek intuition—an intuition lost in part as early as the *Theaetetus*. Starting out with an exposition of Aquinas' definition of truth, he pronounced its central error to lie in the fixing of judgment as the locus for truth. Truth is a property of Being, not of judgment. Truth cannot rightly be said to reside in judgments, since judgments, as one kind of being, already reside "in truth"—and also, as we shall see, in untruth. To attain this relocation, Heidegger turns to a literal interpretation of the Greek ἀλήθεια. Truth is unhiddenness, the unhiddenness of Being. Being discovers itself. "Unhiddenness," however, suggests not only the being unhidden, but the coming out of hiding. If it is un-hidden, Being must have been or must be in some manner hidden. The hiddenness of Being, or untruth, is likewise a factor in the medium of all existences. Perhaps this is but a topsy-turvy way of saying that knowledge involves the possibility of error, or that empirical judgments are probable only, or the like. It very emphatically asserts itself, however, to be no such thing, but rather a reachievement of a primary intuition historically antecedent to the establishment of anything like an epistemology. An exposition of the *Republic* and the *Theaetetus*, where the genuine (Being) notion of truth and the degenerate (judgment) concept are said to appear in hybrid form, is used to substantiate this interpretation.

For the original intuition of Being itself, second, it is necessary to go farther back than Plato—to the Presocratics. Heidegger's interpretation of Anaximander illustrates admirably his historical method. Let me sketch, quoting from lecture notes, the procedure followed in the lectures of the summer semester, 1932, entitled "The Beginning of Occidental Philosophy."

The introductory lecture began with this statement:

> Occidental philosophy began among the Greeks in the sixth century before Christ. It has been falsified by Rome, Judaism, and Christianity. We shall seek out the unfalsified beginning. We therefore examine the first extant fragment, namely, two sentences of Anaximander.

The longer fragment[4] is then analyzed phrase by phrase, with ample philosophical and philological detail. I shall quote a portion of the exposition of the first clause: ἐξ ὧν δὲ ἡ γένεσίς ἐστι τοῖς οὖσι . . . . The question is: Of what is Anaximander speaking? "He is speaking," Heidegger answers, "of τὰ ὄντα."

> τὰ ὄντα means that which is [*das Seiende*]. It is being considered as a unit—as appears from the fact that the neuter plural in Greek governs the singular verb.

> What, then, do we mean by "that which is"? What does Anaximander mean by it?

> We could mean some such thing as the sea, the land, the sky, plants, animals, people, man-made things, human history. All those things are something [*Seiendes*]; they are particular existents [*vereinzelte Seienden*]. But

here it is τὰ ὄντα that is spoken of, *that* which is [das *Seiende*]. So it is not particulars that are indicated, but somehow everything together.

Does Anaximander then perhaps mean the whole count of particular things, their total sum? Can one know all things, can one count up every single one? No. τὰ ὄντα cannot be used in this sense either.

Let us begin again. Let us try to count up particular things. What kind of undertaking is this? We withdraw the individual from its environment; but *before* we begin to count we have in each individual *more* than an individual. This more is not all (in the sense of a sum), and yet it is more than all.

There follows an exposition of the whole as more than the all (or sum total), and it is concluded that being considered as a *whole* likewise fails as the denotation of τὰ ὄντα.

That which is thus eludes us when we want to lay hands on it. It is neither particular things, nor the sum total of its existents, nor the whole of being. What is it then?

We say "being as a whole," and distinguish the meaning of that phrase from our meaning when we say "the whole of being." What do we mean by being as a whole [*das Seiende im Ganzen*]?

Being as a whole is what we have continually before us and around us. It does not matter how much of this being we *know*, i.e., whether or not we have scientific knowledge of it. The peasant has being as a whole immediately before him, while the city man with his fluttering multiplicity of things does not have it in the same immediate proximity. Being as a whole always has completeness in some degree; everything about us is interlocked with everything else. All things have a character of belonging together. This wholeness is familiar to us, so that something new, in making its appearance, appears out of a familiar background.

The next question is: What is said about this "being-as-a-whole"? Similar questions, with similarly detailed answers, work through the whole sentence.

Especially crucial is the retranslation of δίκη, ἀδικία, and τίσις, in which Heidegger stresses the foreignness to the Greek mind of moral terms like justice, injustice, retaliation. Presocratic philosophies are not "nature" philosophies, in which "moral" analogies can be drawn. The separation of being into "natural" and "moral" spheres is a later and degenerate phenomenon. The new amoral translations, to be sure, are most difficult to grasp, not because the original is "naïve," primitive, hesitant, but because "we do not see the greatness of the beginning since we have grown small." "Only what is itself great or concerned with greatness can come into contact with greatness." From this proposition it is easy to infer that, small as we are, we need some gradual initiation into the beginning and its problem; and so we are introduced to Heidegger's interpretation of that problem itself (*die Seinsfrage*), and to the core of his own philosophy.

The occult and exalted nature of the *Seinsfrage* forms a central strand in Heidegger's thought; and such is the arrogance with which its lofty position is proclaimed, that one wonders whether there are not ulterior motives involved. It seems sometimes to be for the greater glory of Heidegger that all thinkers of the past twenty-five hundred years are found to have been so tragically off the track. Heidegger's procedure seems to be especially dubious, for example, in that part of *Sein und Zeit* in which he rejects, with his usual emphasis, the Hegelian definition of time in its relation to spirit.[5] By snatching Hegel's words out of their context, his critic creates the impression that *Geist* and *Zeit* have been artificially drawn together in a vacuum, and then identified—as if, to use Alexander's figure, a relation had descended upon them like the cover on sleepers in a common lodging house. Such an artificial relationship is then shown to falsify the actual situation; and a new description of the relation between time and personal existence is set down—a description that is strongly reminiscent of the original Hegelian text, so rudely dismembered for purposes of criticism. Heidegger's primitivism, together with his "destructive" analysis of later concepts, appears sometimes to be a function of his determination to be philosophically indebted to no man.

2. Beside clearing the road of the encumbrances of traditional theories, it is essential, secondly, to forestall any interventions that might arise from science, logic, or common sense.

Two objections are made to the point of view of the scientist or scientific philosopher. The categories he uses are barren and distorted; and the objectivity he boasts of is illusory. The category of "nature," as the interpretation of the Presocratics suggested, is an artificial and second-hand concept, introduced at a point in history at which the profound insight of the true philosopher gives way to the verbal stereotypes of the academician. It is Being as a whole, not nature or morality or God or some such arbitrarily hacked-off segment of being, that is the object of genuine philosophic reflection. Such terms must be abandoned altogether from the vocabulary; they are not even permitted, in Hegelian fashion, en route to a final synthesis. Especially vicious is the conceptual corollary of "nature," *Vorhandenheit*. *Vorhandenheit*[6] seems to mean the passive thereness of extended objects. Perhaps "simple location" best renders the term; but such is the insularity of Heidegger's thought that he steps forward as the sole exponent of that concept or the "fallacy" involved in its usage. Nor does he consider the possibility that science itself may have outgrown the simple spatio-temporal categorizations of the seventeenth century; the science he criticizes is still thoroughly Newtonian. Taking something like a Newtonian world view, then, as his object, he speaks of it as distorting and falsifying, by its oversimplifications, the true nature of Being. Being is not primarily out there, passive, mechanical; it is here-at-hand, ready for use, organically related in a living whole. Such criticism is, of course, reminiscent of Bergson; and Heidegger does actually acknowledge a certain kinship with the French intuitionist, stressing, however, the inadequacy of Bergson's analyses.[7]

If one asks why the scientist wastes his time in the futile manipulations of falsifying concepts, Heidegger answers that the key to the scientific attitude may be found in the illusory purpose of "objectivity," which the scientist sets up as his goal. The mere fact that perspectives enter into the cognitive and perceptive processes seems to Heidegger to cancel the possibility of objective thought. Objectivity, we are told, means "point-of-viewlessness"—unmediated approach to bare fact, totally independent of the knower's perspective. It is evident, however, not only that there is no bare fact, but that if there were any, no point-of-viewless approach to it would be possible. "There is no point-of-viewlessness," Heidegger declares, "there is only choice of point of view, strength of point of view, and courage of point of view."[8] Objectivity, since it is, on Heidegger's definition, equivalent to point-of-viewlessness. is thus rendered illusory; and science or scientific method, whose essence is to seek just such objectivity, is set aside as philosophically impotent.

Any claim for logic as a tool of philosophical analysis is likewise refuted by an argument similar to the above. The categories of logic are as dead as those of natural science. That fact is especially useful in the course of Heidegger's own arguments. Should the logician venture to point out a fallacy, or suggest that logic cannot follow the philosopher's line of inference, "so much the worse for logic."[9] The logic-chopping faculty cannot be expected to find its way into the labyrinth of Being.

Common sense, finally, is likewise silenced by its own inability to follow the workings of the philosophic mind. Heidegger uses to its extreme the principle of philosophical aristocracy. Philosophy is the task of the few, of the great, the genuinely human in a normative sense. The analogy of the cave is grist to this mill.[10] That apparently solid, close-to-earth faculty that we name common sense is in fact the communicant of shadows. It is only the brave philosopher—for dullards, madly brave—who dares the steep ascent and the bright glare of the sun; it is only he who comes to know the sunlight and its workings, and to recognize in their true character the shadowy figures of the cave. To deny all this is to render oneself suspect of being among the captives, a knower of shadows only. Thus any protests from the side of common sense, like those from logic, refute themselves by virtue of their own inadequacy.

It should be added, perhaps, that the forcefulness of Heidegger's "aristocratic" arguments depends in large part on the personality of the lecturer. One is caught as in a political rally by the slow intensity of his speech. The contemptuous epigrams with which he dismisses the protests of logic or good sense sting the listener's ears with their acidity; and his prophetic solemnity when he invokes the quest for Being ties one as spellbound as if one were a novice taking his first step into the rituals of the Eleusinian mysteries. One sits on the edge of one's chair and agrees breathlessly: no point-of-viewlessness, only courage of point of view—and oh, were one but among the blessed few who have it!

3. With the path cleared of all objections from logic, science, or common sense, a start may be made in the analysis of personal existence through which the new ontology is to be approached. The method is a phenomenological one. Here again, however, the title must be applied with reservations. Heidegger was nurtured in the school of the phenomenologist, Husserl, and as late as *Sein und Zeit* he acknowledges his indebtedness to the master, and the importance of the phenomenological attitude for his own explorations.[11] He has since, however, disclaimed that relationship, and has been as acid in his critique of phenomenology qua school or system as in any other historical judgment.

His method, notwithstanding, is at the outset akin to that preached by his teacher. The purpose, in fact, of the rigorous discarding of traditional or professional phraseologies is to come to a face-to-face view of the phenomenon itself. The game, one might say, is to outstare the phenomenon, dubbing it with no familiar titles, but waiting until in the moment of divine madness a new one occurs. The phenomenon is in this case any everyday happening. Heidegger stands for twenty minutes at the casement window in the seminar room,[12] asking: What am I doing when I turn this handle? Would a dog eating a bone be doing the same kind of thing? What is the essence of my action? What is the difference between man-opening-window and dog-eating-bone? What am I doing when I walk down the street? What is the relation of my foot to the sidewalk? I don't actually touch it, and yet I feel it. How is this possible?

There is something in all this very like the temper of Bradley's analysis of relations, even though the outcome be rather different. Immerse yourself in the phenomenon until it becomes practically impossible to extricate yourself sufficiently to analyze it in any sane perspective. Then, instead of escaping to the Absolute, subject the phenomenon to a novel terminology: make it connote the essence of Being as temporality, or the inner nature of some occult type of relatedness.

4. There follows upon the first baptism of the phenomenon the tor-

tuous series of impenetrably involved definitions that is most distinctive of Heidegger. Professor Carnap has pointed out that Heidegger's arguments in *Was ist Metaphysik?* depend to a large extent upon syntactical misconstructions.[13] The phrase, "nothing nothings," for instance, is a meaningless analogy to such a sentence as "rain rains." The same holds of the similar proposition, "world worlds."[14] Nouns as well as verbs, moreover, are invented—or at least receive startlingly new denotations—in the course of Heidegger's reasonings.

In contrast to the natural or common-sense category of *Vorhandenheit*, for instance, the notion of *Zuhandenheit* is introduced to suggest the *modus essendi* of things within the world of the personal existent.[15] Things are not primarily out there, lying passively in a neutral space from moment to moment. They are at hand, there to be used, grasped, worn, eaten, played with, admired, or shunned. They threaten, beckon, elude, offer themselves for use or for neglect. A hammer is primarily a tool, something to pick up and hammer with, not just a thing of such a shape and size and hardness. A tree is first of all something that offers shade from the noonday sun or shelter from the rain, not a straight stick with arms that sprout green. Things exist fundamentally in the mode of at-handness, not of simple thereness. They appear to us basically in terms of their function in our world. It is only by abstraction—and falsification—that we transform them into pieces of stuff, there in themselves and only posteriorly approached for our uses.

We, moreover, in our world—immersed in the Being-as-a-whole known to Anaximander—are said to have "existence" in a very special sense. Just that special kind of self-conscious (the term is forbidden, but its denotation is at least similar to that intended here) relation to our environment and history which characterizes our experience (a term also forbidden) is called "existence."[16] The distracted losing of one's selfhood in the petty cares of every day is "a special mode of existence" called "insistence"[17] or, in *Sein und Zeit*, *Verfallen*.[18] The self-anticipatory character of personal existence, finally, is its "transcendence."[19] In the development of these concepts, moreover, we find a host of new terms like *Auffälligkeit, Aufdringlichkeit, Aufsässigkeit,*[20] *Weltlichkeit, Umweltlichkeit, innerweltlich,*[21] *Bewandtnis, Bedeutsamkeit,"*[22] etc., etc. On the first analysis of existence there follows a recapitulation in terms of temporal concepts—terms that bear no relation to any notion of time as an ordered series, but are said to introduce a new and more fundamental concept of temporality, of which the "vulgar" concept is the everyday or *verfallen* offshoot.[23] *Innerzeitigkeit,*[24] *Gegenwärtigung, Gewesenheit, Geschichtlichkeit,* and *Geschichte* as opposed to history[25] are among the terms that meet us at this juncture. In short, a page of *Sein und Zeit* on which novel definitions are underlined is likely to be very completely covered with pencil marks. Let me quote one typical sentence, the like of which occurs on every page of the treatise:

> Das Gewärtigen des Wobei in eins mit dem Behalten des Womit der Bewandtnis ermöglicht in seiner ekstatischen Einheit das spezifisch hantierende Gegenwärtigen des Zeugs.[26]

Perhaps the climax of the whole occurs in a central portion of *Sein und Zeit* in the definition of *Dasein* (personal existence) as *Sorge* (care). Existence, it turns out, is essentially care; and care is *Das Sich-Vorweg-Schon-Sein-In (der Welt) als Sein-bei- (innerweltlich begegnendem Seienden)*[27] Paraphrased, this gnarled definiens states the platitude that human nature participates through anticipation in the future and through memory in the past, and at the same time is bound by indissoluble ties to the insistent cares of the present.

5. It is not, however, solely linguistic tours de force that make up the content of the new ontology and its propaedeutic. There is in almost every philosophic system some little truth of psychology or epistemology that makes the thing seem plausible up to a certain point. And here there is, sometimes taken over bodily from Kierkegaard, sometimes originally phrased, description of certain states of mind common to the experience of many individuals. Central, for instance, to *Sein und Zeit* as well as to the little treatise, *Was ist Metaphysik?* is the "concept" of "dread."[28] Everyone, I suppose, knows in some variation the nauseous feeling of a vague undefined dread—whether as fear of death, or simply as an undenotative anxiety toward nothing in particular. The feeling of being on the verge of nothingness is certainly a bona fide psychological datum in most experiences. And as older rationalistic idealisms converted the exhilaration of intellectual enjoyment, the thrill of understanding a mathematical principle or of intuiting the scope of a philosophical generalization, into a cosmic sensation, reading Reason into the structure of the Really Real, so the venerable idealistic arrogance reasserts itself here, taking a more avowedly emotional phenomenon as the center of a new solution of the *Seinsfrage*. From dread we pass to "Being to Death,"[29] which takes the stage as the central factor in existence, the genuine meaning of "care"; and being to death in turn leads us to those mystic temporal categories cut off from the understanding of the vulgar concept of time. From this new and higher temporality, finally, we are ready to move on in our search for Being—we shall find it within the horizon of an existential notion of time.

The categories of transcendence, insistence, and genuine historicity—boundness to one's past—likewise reflect familiar aspects of human nature. Planning ahead, worry about petty details of the day's routine, dependence on one's youthful conditionings for attitudes and opinions: those are obvious features of our experience, good solid starting points in matter of fact. If the beginning is so plausible, should we not give ear to the amplifications that follow; should we not climb with the philosopher from such solid stepping-stones to what should be equally solid heights of speculation? And so we find ourselves plunged suddenly into the Being of Being with its tangle of neologisms—and yet the exact spot at which we passed from sense to nonsense is hard to mark. Once we begin, it seems we are bound to follow.

Heidegger's new variation on the idealistic theme, his playing up of my emotional experience (dread, *Verfallen*, etc.) as the key to the center of Being, purports, of course, to have left far behind it the old strife of realism-idealism. But it exhibits in fact the temper of dogmatic philosophy in its worst form, taking as its basis a certain experience, say, of psychological dizziness, and embroidering on that field the pattern of a new ontology. And the psychological existence of the field, the joy of recognition with which we greet the description of a phenomenon from our own experience, helps to render plausible the subsequent plunge into profundity.

Beside its basis in the data of introspection, moreover, the new ontology includes some half-truths of epistemology, anthropology, etc., which likewise serve to render it palatable at first taste. The first portion of *Sein und Zeit* contains, for example, an interpretation of knowing as subordinate to doing which is strikingly reminiscent of Dewey. Let me cite one instance. A little pointer that shows when the bus is going to turn—used in Black Forest tourist busses—serves as a graphic representation of the function of the concept, emphasizing the pragmatic function of thought in opposition to older correspondence theories of knowledge.[30] The new doctrine, to be sure, will not admit to being a theory of knowledge, that is one of the old useless categories. Its sentences belong to a new propaedeutic to a new insight into the nature of Being. No such stereotype as "theory of knowledge" is allowed. And yet, disguised under a new title, the doctrines of knowledge as predictive, of cognition as originating from practice and subordinate to its ends, are distinctly visible, rendering the system, again, plausible in contrast to the straw men of sterile correspondence epistemologies. Some quasi-scientific anthropological doctrines likewise occur in the form of a contrast in the behavior of civilized and primitive men. One considers the picture of a savage and a modern European faced for the first time with the sight of a new machine,[31] and draws a conclusion about the difference between *Benommenheit* (takenness), and *Verhalten* (taking an attitude), "insistence" and "transcendence," mere environment and true "world." But such terms as "routine habits" and "intelligent habits" would seem, actually, to fit the case as well as the more cryptic pair *Benommenheit* and *Verhalten* with their ontological retinue.

These, then, are some of the elements in Heidegger's philosophy: the repudiation of traditional philosophy in any but a radically novel interpretation, the rejection of the scientific attitude, the immersion in phenomena, the consequent baptism of these phenomena with new, tongue-twisting titles, the construction on their base of towers of mystifying dogmata, and the founding of such systems, finally, upon plausible descriptions of psychological and epistemological phenomena and reasonable generalizations about experience.

Notes

1. Martin Heidegger, *Sein und Zeit, erste Hälfte*, 3rd ed. (Halle: Max Niemeyer, 1931). Reprint from *Jahrbuch für Philosophie und phönomenologische Forschung*, vol. 8.

2. Texts for this criticism are: *Sein und Zeit; Kant und das Problem der Meta-Physik* (Bonn: F. Cohen, 1929); *Was ist Metaphysik?* (Bonn: F. Cohen, 1929); *Vom Wesen des Grundes* (Halle: Max Niemeyer, 1931); notes on lectures by Heidegger at the University of Freiburg, "Vom Wesen der Wahrheit," winter semester, 1931-32, and "Der Anfang der abendländischen Philosophie," summer semester, 1932; notes on discussions, seminar on Plato's *Phaedrus*, summer semester, 1932.

3. Winter semester, 1931-32.

4. H. Diels, *Die Fragmente der Vorsokratiker*, Anaximander, frag. 1.

5. *Sein und Zeit*, pp. 428 ff.

6. Ibid., pp. 49, 59, 61, 81, etc.

7. Ibid., p. 433n.; p. 333.

8. Summer semester, 1932.

9. Ibid.

10. Winter semester, 1931-32.

11. *Sein und Zeit*, pp. 27 ff.

12. *Phaedrus* seminar, summer semester, 1932.

13. Rudolf Carnap, "Überwindung der Metaphysik durch logische Analyse der Sprache," *Erkenntnis*, 2 (1931-32), 219 ff. Cf. esp. sec. 5, pp. 239 ff.

14. Summer semester, 1932. *Vom Wesen des Grundes*, p. 101.

15. *Sein und Zeit*, p. 69.

16. Ibid., pp. 42, 53, 117.

17. Summer semester, 1932.

18. *Sein und Zeit*, p. 175. Summer semester, 1932.

19. *Sein und Zeit*, pp. 363 ff. *Vom Wesen des Grundes*, p. 79. Summer semester, 1932.

20. *Sein und Zeit*, p. 74.

21. Ibid., pp. 65, 66.

22. Ibid., pp. 84, 87.

23. Ibid., pp. 420 ff.

24. Ibid., p. 412.
25. Ibid., pp. 359, 365, 375.
26. Ibid., p. 353.
27. Ibid., p. 192.
28. Ibid., pp. 184 ff.
29. Ibid., pp. 235 ff.
30. Ibid., p. 78.
31. Example used in discussion, proseminar, summer semester, 1932.

V

Authenticity: An Existential Virtue

1952

ETHICS, PEIRCE HAS SAID, DEPENDS ON AESTHETICS, I.E. JUDGMENTS of ought depend on the delineation of an ideal, of what is admirable and what is not.[1] Existentialism has given to the admirable a new location—and hence by implication has relocated judgments of moral value. What the existentialist admires is not the happiness of a man's life, the goodness of his disposition, or the rightness of his acts, but the authenticity of his existence. This is, I think, the unique contribution of existentialism to ethical theory. There are, of course, other ethical principles involved in existential philosophy, but they are principles that it has in common with other ethical systems. For example, the existentialist denies the practical supremacy of reason, he denies the universality of moral values, he asserts the all-importance, ethically, of the historical individual in his unique situation—all these tenets the existentialist shares with numerous other moralists, past and present. They are tenets that will appear obvious truths to those who believe them and obvious falsehoods to those who disbelieve them; in either event they are not unique. But the stress on authenticity is, I think, a unique existentialist emphasis—and an important one.

There are, in contemporary existentialism, two principal versions of this new ethical concept. For Heidegger, genuine existence is existence that dares to face death: it rises from the dissipating and deceptive consolations of today's concerns to the inner realization that its own past must take shape and significance in relation to its inevitable last tomorrow. Contrasted with such genuine existence is *Verfallen*, the distraction or scattering of one's freedom in the cares of everyday, where not the true individual, but *das Man,* the indifferent "they," is sovereign. In Sartre, on the other hand, genuine existence is conceived of as free, not in facing death so much as in facing the meaningless ground of its own transcendence, that is, the fact that the values by which I live depend not on divine fiat or metaphysical necessity but on myself alone. Contrasted with such awareness is bad faith, the stultification of freedom in the enslavement to an "objective" truth or a consuming passion.

In both versions, the concept of authenticity is rooted in the existential interpretation of freedom. We live from birth to death under the compulsion of brute fact; yet out of the mere givenness of situation it is we ourselves who shape ourselves and our world. And in this shaping we succeed or fail. To succeed is not to escape compulsion but to transcend it—to give it significance and meaning by our own projection of the absurdly given past into a directed future. But such shaping of contingency, such imposition of meaning on the meaningless, is possible only through the very recognition of meaninglessness— of the nothingness that underlies our lives. Such recognition means, for Sartre, the awareness, in dread, that the values by which I live are totally, absurdly mine; the contingency, the compulsion I must face, is the irrevocable givenness of my own creation. In the more radical conception of Heidegger it is not the absurdity, the nothingness, of life which must be faced but the ultimate nothingness, the last and total contingency of death, which must inwardly determine as it outwardly delimits my existence. Thus for Sartre it is a peculiar attitude toward freedom in its relation to value that defines authentic existence; for Heidegger it is the orientation to the end of life, the resolve to death, that is essential to authenticity. In both cases authenticity is a kind of honesty or a kind of courage; the authentic individual faces something that the unauthentic individual is afraid to face.

If, in authentic existence, freedom can inform necessity and give meaning to the meaningless, it may also fail of its transcendence, it may succumb to the multiplicity and absurdity of fact, it may seek escape in the fiction of a supporting cosmic morality or in the domination of a blind passion or in the nagging distractions of its everyday concerns. In other words, freedom is not an abstraction to be generically applied to "man" as such, but a risk, a venture, a demand. In a sense we are all free, but we are free to achieve our freedom or to lose it. There are no natural slaves, but most of us have enslaved ourselves. Existentialism is, in this, a kind of inverse Spinozism. Like Spinoza, it sees man as bond *or* free; only unlike Spinoza, it finds reason not a liberator but one of the possible enslavers, and in imagination of a sort the source not of enslavement but of emancipation from it.

It should be noticed, however, that in Heidegger's conception the sphere of the nonauthentic, of *Verfallen*, is always with us. There is no easy distinction between those who, leaving the fraudulent behind them, achieve the level of genuine existence and those who do not. We are all, always, a prey to the cares of here and now; of a thousand and one trivialities all our days are made. Yet there is an essential, qualitative, recognizable difference, a total difference, morally, between the existence for which the trivialities are the whole and the existence for which the manifold of experience is transcended in a unity not, like the Kantian, abstract and universal, but intensely personal and concrete.

What does it mean to say, as Heidegger does, that what constitutes this unity is a "resolve to death," that it is "being to death" or "freedom to death" which emancipates the individual from bondage to the "they"? The arguments by which Heidegger develops this thesis cannot be taken seriously as arguments. Like most of his arguments they consist principally in inversions of ground and consequent and in the kind of word play in which German philosophy from Hegel on abounds. For example, if empirically it is found that various peoples and individuals face death in various ways, he can define personal existence as "being to death" and say that it is not the case that death is essential to existence because people die and face the fact of dying, but, much more profoundly, people die and face the fact of dying because existence *is* being to death. In other words, a posterioris are turned into a prioris: and, presto, there is the philosopher posssessed of a foresight far finer than the hindsight of the ordinary man. Or, for instance, he can play, much as Aristotle does with *telos* in the *Politics*, with the meaning of "end": death is the end of life, and therefore the end of life, etc.

Yet, although *Sein and Zeit* is a tissue of this sort of pseudo definition and redefinition, there is in its central thesis a serious truth. For the individual deprived of supernatural support, cast alone into his world, the dread of death is a haunting if suppressed theme that runs through life. What is more, if at all times communication between men is tattered and fragile, it is in the face of death that each man stands most strikingly and irrevocably alone. For this Everyman there is after all no guide in his most need to go by his side; and therefore, more intensely than for his medieval counterpart, his relation to death marks as nothing else does the integrity and independence of his life. Thus, if authenticity is rare, authenticity in youth one may expect to find extremely rare, for it is a virtue that flowers only in and through dread, in the living presence of its own mortality.

Yet whether "being to death" is the sole content and meaning of existential authenticity, as Heidegger makes it, is another question. That the awareness of death is a significant factor in any conscious life is certain, and to have shown this is an extremely important service of *Sein und Zeit* to contemporary thought. For this is, so far as I know, the first time since Plato that death has been given central philosophic significance in the interpretation of life. In the case of Lucretius, for example, the fear of death, and in that of Hobbes, the fear of violent death, are hinges, so to speak, on which their philosophic systems are hung; but they are not, like Heidegger's "resolve to death," internal to the analysis of life itself. Whatever moralists wish to do hereafter with this concept, they must certainly reckon with it.

On the other hand, in the fashion in which Heidegger presents it, the emphasis on death involves an inescapable narrowness which warps the total conception of the authentic individual. It is *only* a man's death, Heidegger says, which is irreplaceably his own, which is not interchangeable with the experience of others; and therefore it is only in "being to death" that he escapes the claims of the public and corrupting "they" and is genuinely himself, genuinely free. His "freedom to death," the confrontation with this one fact that is really his own, is the whole content and meaning of his freedom, and the existence of other selves as of the world is for him only a means to the achievement of this grim and lonely triumph. But this is not only emancipation from the bewildering distraction of the anonymous "they"; it is emancipation from all that might, by our own creation, be made meaningful. It is indeed a transcendence of the meaningless manifold, but a transcendence too dearly bought, for the very oneness and intensity of the achievement make it itself almost empty of meaning. This is again the *Nullpunktsexistenz* of Kierkegaard, from which even God himself has vanished. Personal authenticity is a significant ethical concept, and the relation of the individual to death is an essential aspect of it, but it is not an aspect that can stand alone as Heidegger makes it do. If nothing else, some relation to others in *their* authenticity, some living communication or the attempt at it, must play a part. But Heidegger's authentic individual wanders his solitary "dead ends," and they are not after all very admirable roads to follow nor is it a very admirable sort of man who follows them.

If, then, Heidegger's definition of authentic existence is inadequate, that of Sartre may at first glance appear more fruitful. For Sartre, again, the honesty of the authentic person consists in his facing the nature of his own freedom. This description, since it is tied to life rather than to its cessation, does not seem, essentially, to entail the same narrowness as does Heidegger's version. Yet as the French existentialists have developed their theory they have, I think, impoverished as much as they have enriched the concept of authenticity.

For one thing, instead of amplifying the concept of *das Sein zum Tode* or proceeding from it, Sartre has, in his theoretical statements, dismissed it rather cavalierly. My death, he says, since it can never become part of my own experience, is more real to others than to me. It is true, of course, that the death of others, of those near to me in particular, forms an essential part of my experience in a fashion that

Heidegger ought to but does not recognize. But my own relation to my own death does also, in its paradoxical fashion, constitute an essential element in my experience. Sartre himself has given a brilliant account of the most dramatic and visible kind of "being to death" in his moving tribute to the Resistance, *The Republic of Silence:*

> Exile, captivity, and especially death (which we usually shrink from facing at all in happier times) became for us the habitual objects of our concern. We learned that they were neither inevitable accidents, nor even constant and exterior dangers, but that they must be considered as our lot itself, our destiny, the profound source of our reality as men. . . . Thus the basic question of liberty was posed, and we were brought to the verge of the deepest knowledge that man can have of himself. For the secret of a man is not his Oedipus complex or his inferiority complex: it is the limit of his own liberty, his capacity for resisting torture and death.[2]

And he has, though perhaps less successfully, dealt with similar themes in such works as *The Wall* or *The Unburied Dead.* But theoretically, it seems, he is too much interested in what is called the "open future"—or perhaps the indefinite extent of open futures which the existential revolutionary needs to envisage—to be much concerned, philosophically, with the individual's awareness of death. Yet the concept of authenticity needs this sharp edge to mark it. Genuine existence is revealed for what it is in relation to what Jaspers called *Grenzsituationen,* and the dreadful awareness of my own creation of myself is indeed such a situation. But my death is the most dramatic of such boundary situations, and in fact it is more than that: it is the essential and determining boundary situation. If it is terrible that I am responsible for what I have become, it is always hopeful to reflect that tomorrow I may do better. But what is most terrible is that I cannot do so forever, that in fact if I have bungled and cheated and generally made a fool of myself, there is only a little while, perhaps not all of today even, in which to do it over. Kierkegaard's favorite maxim, "over 70,000 fathoms, miles and miles from all human help, to be glad," is an essential constituent of existentialism and in particular of the concept of the authentic individual.

And perhaps one may call on Kierkegaard to support a second criticism of Sartre's conception of authenticity. This time it is the "knight of infinite resignation" whom I should like to recall. It is not necessary here to attempt to understand this character, let alone to endorse him, so to speak, as a moral model, but there is this about him which is important: though he is extremely different from the ordinary sort of person, he may, Kierkegaard says, look and act just like him. That, we have noticed, is true also of Heidegger's authentic person. In the case of Sartre, however, those who live by *mauvaise foi* are marked off from an elusive but admirable sort of individual who presumably has left bad faith behind and lives entirely in the separate and distinct area of authenticity. Now the concept of bad faith has in fact served as a key for some brilliant portraits of various sorts of depravity, as, for example, in the *Portrait of the Anti-Semite*. Yet if one looks, for instance, at the masterly picture of life by *mauvaise foi* painted in the opening episode of *The Room*, one gets the feeling that the life of bad faith is the conventional one and, by implication, that of good faith unconventional. In fact this is, implicitly as least, the theme of the whole story—the story of a young woman who chooses to share the life of her mad husband, even to try earnestly and tragically to share his hallucinations, rather than return to the vacantly respectable existence of her horrified bourgeois parents. And here again, if one equates convention with bourgeois convention, the interest of the existential revolutionary demands such a view. Liberation is the existential keynote all along the line. It is the shackles of convention, of beliefs imposed from outside, that bind us personally, just as the economic interests of those who foster the conventions bind us socially. To cast off the expressions of false privilege in our private lives is to become authentic, to become ourselves, just as political revolution will, in this view, cast off for us the shackles that bind us in our economic and political lives.

Now of course it is true that the authentic person is seldom a conventional person. The concept of authenticity is not a concept of adjustment—in fact with respect to the current ideal of the well-adjusted member of society, it is truly and deeply a heresy. One can even say that some societies almost demand rebellion of a sort as the price of authenticity. Yet there may be authentic individuals who live all their lives, like the knight of infinite resignation, as highly respectable members of highly respectable societies. Elizabeth Bennett is an authentic individual, though she never did anything more unconventional than walk three miles on a rather muddy day. Sartre's authentic existent, on the other hand, deprived of all the trivialities *and* all the substance of *Verfallen* and given only a highly mechanical un-Marxist Marxism by which to live, remains a mere ideal, or a ghost of a person. Mathieu, for example, who in *The Age of Reason* is a real person, has not achieved authenticity but is constantly and desperately seeking it. He is unable to survive the *Grenzsituation* which the French existentialists in their own persons met so courageously. Absurdly and defiantly, he is killed (or so it seems) during the fall of France in 1940. The trouble is that an authentic existent, as Sartre conceives him, has no end given him *except* his own authenticity; but authenticity is not so much an end of acts as a value that is realized as a by-product of acts. The failure to recognize this essential complexity of the ethical situation is a serious lack of existentialism, as it is of most other systematic moralities. Moralists seek to describe *the* end of human action, but many values, and perhaps the highest, are produced, as Hartmann puts it, "on the back of an act." The self-consciousness involved in seeking them makes them impossible to find. And authenticity is such a value. Those who attain it are doing and seeking what others are doing and seeking; the unique and in a sense timeless value their life exhibits is a quality of, but not an end for, that life inself.

But this lack of complexity reflects a deeper lack, for the central difficulty underlying all these errors or omissions of existentialism is the narrowness of the existential view of the free act. It is because of that narrowness that the existential hero has nothing to seek *but* his own authentic act. The existentialist has rightly seen that, "thrown into the world," always already "engaged," we are nevertheless each totally responsible for our own destinies. But by singling out the act alone by which a man faces his own "condemnation to be free," the existentialist isolates part of a complex situation which cannot in fact be so isolated. It is true that it is *I* who have-always-already-chosen the values by which I live. But I have chosen, not created them; if they were not in some sense there to be chosen, if they did not somehow compel me to choose them, they would not be values at all. I could not even, like Kirillov, choose suicide as the negation of all values. Sartre says that values "start up like partridges before our acts." That *is* how it looks in the reflective moment of dread—but the aspect of total responsibility is only one aspect of a more complex situation. The choice is my choice, yet it is also the choice *of* something, and of something that obliges me to choose it. For Sartre, however, there is a crude and absolute disjunction between the free act of genuine existence and the bad faith of belief in values as metaphysically self-existent or supernaturally revealed. Either I myself, all alone, simply act, or I enslave myself to a falsely hypostatized being; hence the desperate endeavor to make of the act itself—of my freedom as such or the honesty to face to freedom—the whole end and object of the free man. But there are no pure acts. An act involves a reference to values which in some way make a claim on the agent and perhaps, at least indirectly, bind him to other agents or to those affected by his acts.

It is probably in some such context, moreover, that the problems of the relations between individuals need to be treated. And that brings me to my final criticism, that is, the all too familiar but necessary objection that the authentic individual, while facing with admirable courage the ultimate loneliness of human life, is nevertheless even lonelier than circumstances warrant. To be sure, Sartre and, presumably with his knowledge and assent, Beauvoir have tried in various ways to meet this common objection, but, in my opinion at least, with very little success.

They try to relate one self to others in accordance with two favorite maxims (each of which is the slogan for a Beauvoir novel): Hegel's "Every consciousness wants the death of another" and Dostoyevski's "We are all responsible for all." The Hegelian maxim serves as a guiding principle for Sartre's detailed analysis of the circle of conflicts in *L'Être et le Néant*, and it also serves as a basis for the description of class consciousness and therefore as a bridge to his theory of revolution. That it is not an adequate principle for a complete or essential analysis of human relationships has been said often enough, and that some uneasiness is felt about it even at headquarters is evidenced by the extremely crude arguments with which Beauvoir has since attempted to dismiss it in *The Ethics of Ambiguity*. The first view one takes of another, that the other consciousness wants the death of mine, is naïve, she says, for one at once realizes that of course, as we all know, if anyone takes anything away from me, he is really giving it to me all the while. This is undoubtedly one of the worst philosophical arguments ever penned—not to mention the shocking fact that there are in this case four hundred pages of naïveté in the master's masterpiece. Nor have other attempts to get from the first to the second maxim had better success. Sartre and, following him, Beauvoir repeatedly argue from my concrete, intensely private freedom to freedom as a universal end, but always with curious sophistry—except perhaps in the argument that I cannot be free unless others are so. It is true that minimal requirements of civil and economic freedom are the sine qua non of my freedom. Yet we believe in freedom for others not *only* because it facilitates our own. This argument, though valid, is insufficient. And what is worse, the politics that is developed on this basis has, despite its opposition to dialectical materialism, the same lifeless and mechanical quality as the article it seeks to replace. One need only instance the long series of articles called *What is Literature?* in which, after a rather ingenious analysis of the differences between the arts, Sartre embarks on a completely stock Marxian account of the functions of the prose writer, in which Richard Wright becomes the greatest American novelist and Flaubert is no good because he did not take his political responsibilities seriously, and so on.

Yet it does seem likely that somehow and in some sense the concept of authenticity does involve not only the winning of freedom but the respect for freedom, not only the achievement of dignity in the individual but the acceptance of the Kantian maxim of the dignity of all individuals. Some such connection does seem to exist; one cannot imagine an authentic individual who really has no respect for the liberty of others, and one cannot imagine the existence of authenticity where some sort of liberty does not exist, in idea even if not in fact. But there has been, so far as I know, no convincing philosophic statement why this should be so. Certainly to take away substantive values as *mauvaise foi* and then to put freedom back in as a substantive value is not good enough. But on the other hand, like Heidegger, to view the existence of others only as a means to my freedom is worse than not good enough— it is positively evil. Yet it is difficult, at least in existential language, to say why.

Perhaps this failure of existentialism—its failure adequately to relate my freedom to freedom in general—is connected with the more limited or more concrete problem that it equally fails to treat, that is, the problem of the manner in which authenticity is determined or defined or influenced by the direct relation of one individual to another *in* his freedom. Both Jaspers and Marcel have introduced concepts of communication into existentialism, but in both cases the treatment is so vague and sentimental as to contribute little. Yet it is here, in the question of communication as well as in the implications of the concept of authentic existence for the general concept of liberty, that more needs to be said.

Is it wholly in loneliness that authenticity is achieved? If genuine existence is transcendence successfully accomplished, giving form and meaning to the meaningless succession of hours and needs, does it not, in transcending contingency and nothingness, in some sense transcend loneliness as well? Is not—sometimes, at least—the transcendence of loneliness needed for the very achievement of authenticity? True, authenticity itself, the core of genuine existence, is a value that must center in the individual who bears it; the inner dissipation of the self in seeming devotion to other selves is, existentially speaking, deeply immoral. Even the "self-sacrifice" of an authentic person perfects and dignifies the individual and inalienable person that is himself. Yet, if one can distinguish between a fraudulent and an authentic aspect of the self, may one not distinguish also between a fraudulent and an authentic relation between selves? The quality of the concern with others on the distractive level is evident in all gregariousness; its most extreme expression, perhaps, is the cozy friendliness of radio announcers to their disembodied audience. But, in the projection toward one's own freedom which focuses distraction into authenticity, the bewildered and bewildering diffusion of everyday sociability would seem likewise to be, if not replaced, at least reoriented in the direction of a genuine and decisive reaching-out to the few others whose existence shows a significant kinship to one's own. Even if authenticity is in an essential aspect "being to death," it is in that very aspect, in the light of the ultimate dissolution of the person loved or loving, that the urgency and the reality of communication are most strikingly exhibited. In short, between the two Beauvoir maxims, between the sadism of the Hegelian master and the sainthood of Zossima, there lies a whole range of kinds of and endeavors at communication—of times and places in which, fleetingly and in devious ways, perhaps, but still truly, minds do meet. And, without the actuality and possibility of such meetings, the irrevocable loneliness of human life, however authentic, would be indeed too great to bear.

But whether existential philosophy as such can produce an adequate solution for this problem—whether it can build again the bridge it has broken—is another question. Every philosophy "explains" only such phenomena as its premises already include; it can only amplify what its basic beliefs already assert. So, for example, Descartes's failure to understand the living—both animal life and human passion—is determined by the concept of "clear and distinct idea" with which he starts. If, then, for the existentialists, the beginning is the individual in loneliness and peril, the whole content of their doctrine is the elaboration and expansion of this same theme; and, to go further, to describe the ties of men as well as their momentary decisions, demands at least, as we have suggested earlier, a recognition of the complexity of the free act, of the element in every act of submission to a claim as well as responsibility for choosing to submit.

This is not to deny the significance of the existential insight but to demand its interpretation in a wider, other than existential, setting. Without some such immersion in a more inclusive view of man's nature, existentialism remains a significant but static insight into one aspect of human consciousness. True, it is an aspect peculiarly descriptive of the crisis of our time. But it is the kind of philosophy which sees something that must be seen and goes no further. And to go further, or rather to go back, to make a new and richer beginning, is no longer existentialism. Yet if, for the existentialist, freedom is transcendence, he should perhaps be willing to acknowledge that, in the projective creation of the future, existentialism itself is among the data to be transcended.

Notes

1. C. S. Peirce, *Collected Papers*, vol. 5, par. 36 (Cambridge: Harvard University Press, 1934): "We cannot get any clue to the secret of Ethics . . . until we have first made up our formula for what it is that we are prepared to admire. I do not care what doctrine of ethics be embraced, it will always be so. . . . Ethics must rest upon a doctrine which, without at all considering what our conduct is to be divides ideally possible states of things into two classes, those that would be admirable and those that would be unadmirable, and

undertakes to define precisely what it is that constitutes the admirableness of an ideal. . . . I call that inquiry Esthetics, because it is generally said that the three normative sciences are logic, ethics and esthetics, being the three doctrines that distinguish good and bad; Logic in regard to representations of truth, Ethics in regard to efforts of will, and Esthetics in objects considered simply in their presentation."

2. Jean-Paul Sartre, "The Republic of Silence," in *The Republic of Silence*, ed. and trans. A. J. Liebling (New York: Harcourt Brace & Co., 1947), pp. 498-499.

VI

Heidegger: Philosopher and Prophet

1958

HEIDEGGER'S RECENTLY PUBLISHED WORK, *Der Satz vom Grund,* concludes with this exhortation:

> . . . does not the essence of man, does not his belonging to Being, does not the essence of Being itself remain ever yet and ever more overwhelmingly what befits thought? . . . That is the question. That is the world question of thought. Its answer will decide what becomes of the earth and of the existence of man on this earth.[1]

On this same note he had opened, thirty years earlier, his greatest and most influential work, *Sein und Zeit.* It is the nature, the vocation of man, Heidegger believes, to ask the all-important question: What is it to be? And yet we fail to ask it; and it is our nature, equally, our responsibility, our guilt, that we so fail. To summon us to our vocation, to warn us of our failure, has been his single aim.

What has this Heidegger, the prophet of the *Seinsfrage*, to say to us? That is hard to assess. German philosophical thinking speaks a language doubly different from English: different not only in the language itself, but in its conception *of* language. British philosophers are haunted by Berkeley's distrust of words; yet distrusting words as guides, they limit themselves happily to the study of words as instruments. A German philosopher is much more inclined to trust to "the wisdom of language," to allow words to tell him their meaning, and guide him, beyond themselves, to an understanding of what they mean. For British philosophers, equivocal words are, philosophically, bad words. For German philosophers, and especially for Heidegger, who like all prophets, delights to puzzle and confound, they are the only words of interest—words to be cherished, caressed, submitted to in wonder and ectasy. Can there be any communication across such a gulf?

There have been points of contact, and perhaps we may begin with one of them. The present Waynflete Professor of Metaphysical Philosophy at the University of Oxford published, at a youthful stage of his career (in *Mind*, in 1929), a review of *Sein und Zeit*. In the construction of his new and alarming terminology, Professor Ryle quite rightly said, Heidegger was attempting to penetrate behind the technical terms of science and philosophy to more "primitive Meanings." This was, on Ryle's view, perilous: "For it is at least arguable that it is here, and not in the language of the village and the nursery, that mankind has made a partial escape from metaphor." I shall not try to imagine the village and the nursery that could speak the language of *Sein und Zeit—Sich-vorweg-schon-sein-in-(der Welt) als Sein-bei-(innerweltlich begegnendem Seiendem)*," "Ahead-of-oneself-being-already-in-the-world as Being-with-beings-meeting-one-inside-the-world"—only the genius of a Bosch could conceive it. But I should like to consider the implications, vis-à-vis Heidegger, of Ryle's statement that in the language of science and philosophy "mankind has made a partial escape from metaphor." Precisely. It is from the hope to escape from metaphor—which is in fact a form of despair and not a hope—that Heidegger would call his listeners to escape.

What is it to escape from metaphor? It is, obviously, to escape from poetry. "Poets are liars by profession." From the point of view of literal meaning, or the striving for literal meaning, poetry is pseudo-statement; poetic language exhibits seven, or six, or a hundred and thirty-seven types of ambiguity, all mildly amazing and amusing to the normal, i.e., unpoetic, mind. And philosophy, being an academic subject, is itself literal, dealing in literal language with literal language—if not with the language of science, then with the language of car drivers and cricket players, not with that of poets. Yet, Ryle admitted, the escape of science and philosophy from metaphor is but "partial." What if that very partiality, the retained metaphorical quality of their language, were after all their saving grace, their residue of meaning? If we cannot sometimes say *A* is *B*, when in some sense it is, yet in some sense it isn't, then we can say only *A* is *A*, which is to say nothing. What if language is poetry, and literal language but a desiccated and residual poetry? That is Heidegger's view:

Poetry it is that founds and names the being and nature of all things—no arbitrary talk, but the talk through which alone all that we then discuss and manipulate in ordinary language is first laid open. Thus poetry never picks up language as an available implement; on the contrary, it is poetry that makes language possible. Poetry is the primal language of a historical people. So . . . the nature of language must be understood out of the nature of poetry.[2]

True, this view is "perilous." This statement of it comes from Heidegger's essay on "Hölderlin and the Nature of Poetry," which comments, in part, on the saying:

Darum ist der Güter Gefährlichstes, die Sprache, dem Menschen gegeben . . . damit er zeuge, was er sei. . . .

For that reason, the most perilous of goods, language, is given to man . . . that he may bear witness, what he is. . . .[3]

Yes, speech rooted in poetry, speech as metaphor, is dangerous: it may betray, may lead, as Ryle in his review predicted for Heidegger, to "windy mysticism." But speech conceived as literal is, in the last analysis, speech as precise; and speech as precise, like Kant's "concepts without images" (to which in fact, or rather metaphorically, it is equivalent), is empty.

Well, then, supposing we let in metaphor. Was Ryle saying, or am I saying, that *Sein und Zeit* is a poem, or that it is about poetry? Surely not the former. In all the history of all the schoolmen, there was never a more crabbed and cacophonous, a less 'poetic" text. Nor the latter; for the theme of the book is my being-in-a-world. It deals with the relations essential to such being, including, it is true, forms of language like gossip or explanation, or, in the latter part of the argument, history, but not especially poetry. That was rather, on the face of it, a theme to which Heidegger turned when *Sein und Zeit*, Part II, eluded him; he turned to the exegesis of poetry because philosophy failed him, or he it. But such an account is not quite fair. If philosophy is neither poetry nor about poetry, it ought nevertheless to serve poetry. At least to try to reach, as Heidegger tries to do in *Sein und Zeit*, beyond the language of science or of philosophy ruled by science—even of common sense—to a root language, to "primitive meanings" as Ryle called them, is to move in the direction of making philosophy serve poetry: of escaping from the escape from metaphor.

That is, in terms of modern philosophy, to move out of Kant's shadow: away from the interpretation of nature as phenomenal and objective, as objective because phenomenal, and intelligible because objective, and therefore intelligible because phenomenal; to allow play again to the mind's urge somewhere somehow to penetrate reality, to *understand* once more, even if in metaphor and in peril. One sees, for example, in the recent first steps of Oxford philosophy back toward metaphysics, how powerfully Kant's prohibition has been operating all this time. The conception of an objective world of appearances, within which analytical philosophy could safely move, was Kant's creation. No reaching through to reality, Kant had said, no thing-in-itself, but a well-regulated set of objects for science, among them the empirical mind, itself in a tenuous and subjective way an object for science. This limited and impersonal knowledge—the concept of objectivity, *Gegenständigkeit*; of things as simply and substantially there, spread out in a meaningless spatio-temporal order, *Vorhandenheit*; of man as a thing there among other things—all this Heidegger would demote to second place. He gives these conceptions, almost, the place Kant gave to metaphysics: they flow from an inevitable but mistaken impulse of human being to dissipate its proper understanding, to fasten here and there and everywhere on the things that are, in neglect of its truer task, to seek Being—which it must, yet would rather pretend not to, understand. But that, of course, is precisely the task Kant denied it. Thus the second volume of *Sein und Zeit* was to have contained a "destruction" of traditional ontology, starting with Kant and going back, through Descartes and Aristotle, to what Heidegger considers the first and authentic source of ontological insight, in the pre-Socratic beginnings of Western thought.

"Poetry founds and names the being and nature of all things": the escape from metaphor is an escape, also, from Being, the return to metaphor, to poetry, should be a return to the "nearness and shelter of Being." But surely this is mere obscurantism: did sorcerers and astrologers and purveyors of witchcraft bring us closer to the knowledge of what things are than do physiologists and physicists? Whatever there is—though we needn't call it by such a misty name as "Being"—surely we know more about it than we used to. In *Der Satz vom Grund* (his university lectures for the winter semester, 1955-56, together with a public lecture given in 1956 on the same subject), Heidegger answers "Yes" and "No." The Law of Sufficient Reason, he says, can be heard in two keys. As the law which governs the search for causes, the calculation of effects, it presides over our science-ruled age, issuing, out of a single passion for analytical thought, in atomic fission and the construction of electronic brains, in the dehumanizing of humanity, perhaps the end of human life on earth. This is what happens to us when we think about *das Seiende*, the things that are. Call it "knowing more" if you like. But the Law of Sufficient Reason may be heard in another key. So heard, it would summon us, not to the endless calculation of causes, but to *das Sein*, to Being, the groundless root of all grounds. And it is the choice between the two ways of hearing this ambiguous principle that is "the world question of thought."

The escape from metaphor is an escape from Being. An escape from Being, for Heidegger, is an escape from history. Or rather, it *is* our history, and at the same time our forgetfulness of that history. The resultant *Weltverdüsterung*, the darkening of our world, is Heidegger's constant theme. This is the age of research, that is, of the planned, systematic coordination of intellectual tasks. What sort of tasks can be planned and coordinated? Neat, limited, manageable tasks: tasks, primarily, that demand inventiveness rather than understanding, tasks for engineering know-how rather than theoretical insight. Heidegger draws no line between pure and applied science. Science is research; research *is* a procedure for solving well-packaged problems; such problems are, in general, problems of manufacture, of inventing new and better gadgets. *Das Herstellbare*, the class of gadgets, is what we're after. That is what specialization, the rigid departmental structure of expertise in our society, amounts to. And all this, all this vast proliferation of technical skills, has nevertheless its inner unity, its historical and metaphysical unity: it had to happen this way. It had to happen this way *because* we have fallen out of Being. We are more concerned with beings, from genes to spaceships, than with our true vocation, to be shepherds and watchers of Being. So we are lost, and Being itself has become, in Nietzsche's words, "a haze and an error"—nothing.

In the *Introduction to Metaphysics* (lectures delivered in 1935 but published in 1953) Heidegger describes the stages in this alienation of the mind from its true ontological root. First, mind is misunderstood as "intelligence," the faculty of logic. Next, it comes to be considered as purely practical, an intellectual gadget for the manufacture of more gadgets. Further, its products are organized and "cultivated" alongside other such devices:

> As soon as this misinterpretation of mind as a tool sets in, the powers of intellectual and spiritual activity, poetry and fine art, statesmanship and religion, move into the sphere of a possible *conscious* cultivation and planning. At the same time they are split up into areas. The spiritual world becomes Culture, in the creation and maintenance of which, at the same time, the individual person tries to procure his own fulfillment. Those areas become fields of free activity, which sets itself standards in whatever significance it just happens to achieve. These standards of validity for production and use are called values. Cultural values are assured of meaning in the whole of a culture only by limiting themselves to their validity for themselves: poetry for poetry's sake, art for art's sake, science for the sake of science.[4]

Nor is this the last step. There is finally the Palace of Culture, the last inevitable step to Marxism. The works of mind have collapsed out of their artificial isolation into trimmings of a ruthlessly practical, metaphysically alienated state. From this doom there is but one path to turn aside into: the path to Being.

Heidegger is, of course, by no means alone in his critique of our "needy time." What distinguishes his view of modern decadence is the notion, to which he returns again and again, that the whole story is told, essentially, in Greek philosophy. For him, a reflective reaffirmation of liberalism would be meaningless: the liberal conception of a free society, with its "culture," its "values," its "ideals," is a helpless gesturing, a last foolish gasp before the total negativity of Marxism engulfs us. And an older authoritarianism would be just as impotent. The damage was done, wholly done, so very long ago: Christianity, too, was at its very start, as Nietzsche saw, doomed not to redeem but to destroy. What was it that happened between the time of Parmenides and Aristotle? Much of Heidegger's answer is tied to sleight of hand with Greek phrases—his fantasies in translation and etymology are notorious—but the gist of it is, again, the loss of Being. One section of the *Introduction to Metaphysics* is called "Being and Thought." This is a dichotomy, Heidegger explains, which did not exist for the first and greatest thinkers of the West. For Parmenides, Being, *einai*, and *noien*, what Heidegger calls *Vernehmen*, what we may perhaps call in a very general sense "awareness," were one. And human existence, according to Heidegger, was rooted in this oneness. Man was deep in Being, drew his life from the appearance of Being, which was truly appearance, not illusion, from the becoming of Being, which again was at one with Being, not the mere flux that the misinterpretation of Heraclitus has led us to think it was. *Logos*, which is the same as Being, held man, rooted and at home. But by the time of Aristotle man had broken loose from this first great anchorage and floated out upon that tide of nihilism on which we are still adrift. Man had become "a rational animal," the animal that "*has* logos," the animal that can calculate, that knows its way about, the most successful animal—but the animal, torn from its ground in Being, whose very being is *unheimlich*, uncanny, literally unhomely, not-at-home. Heidegger's theory of truth tells the same story. For the Presocratics truth was *aletheia,* the unhiddenness of Being. By the time of Aristotle it had become a property of propositions: their "correspondence" with "facts." This loosening of truth from Being led on then directly, in Heidegger's view, to Nietzsche's dictum that truth is a form of error, and Being itself an error, a haze.

So we come back, once more, to the *Seinsfrage*, the need to awaken an understanding for the sense of the question: What is it to be? Was Nietzsche right? Is Being "a haze and an error"? Or is it in ourselves, in our historical destiny, that the nothingness of Being lies:

Is Being to blame for its confusion, and is it the fault of the word that it remains so empty, or are we to blame if with all our bustle and pursuit of things that are, we have nevertheless fallen out of Being? And is it not especially the fault of us today, not only of our nearest and remotest ancestors, but of a happening which runs from the beginning through the history of the west, a happening to which all the eyes of all historians will never penetrate and which has nevertheless been happening and is happening, and will happen in the future? What if it were possible that man, that nations, in their grandest activities and power designs, should have to do with things that are and yet have long ago fallen out from Being without knowing they had done so, and that this should be the deepest and mightiest ground of their decline?[5]

This—the loss of Being, the alienation of the mind from Being—is the "spiritual destiny of the West," "historicity," to which the *Zeit* of *Sein und Zeit* was meant to point. When Heidegger said that his book was intended to serve the spirit of Yorck von Wartenburg and Dilthey, this, it seems, is what he meant. Yorck von Wartenburg distinguished between the "ontic" and "historic," that is (for Heidegger), between all those detached and distorting manipulations of the things that are that constitute our misguided intellectual tradition, and the one true, decisive historical task of facing truly the true nature of that tradition, turning back, the long hard way to its beginning—to before its beginning—and beginning again.

It is to this task that Heidegger calls his people: to face, to assimilate, and to transcend the destiny of the West.

This Europe, wretchedly blinded, forever on the brink of self-slaughter, lies today in the great pincers between Russia on the one hand and America on the other. Russia and America are, from a metaphysical point of view, the same: the same frenzy of technology unleashed, and of the rootless organization of the Average Man. When the furthermost corner of the globe has been technologically conquered and opened to economic exploitation, when any event whatsoever has become accessible with any speed whatsoever, when we can "experience" simultaneously an attempt on the life of a king in France and a symphony concert in Tokyo, when time is no longer anything but speed, momentariness, and simultaneity, and time as history has vanished from all the life of all the nations, when the boxer passes as the great man of a people, when the millions numbered at mass meetings are a triumph—then, yes, then, the question still grips us like a ghost through all these phantoms: What for? Where to? And what then?

We lie in the pincers. Our people, standing in the center, feel the sharpest pressure from the pincers: the people richest in neighbors and so the people most imperiled and, withal, the metaphysical people. But out of this calling, of which we are certain, this people will be able to achieve for itself a destiny only if it first forms *in itself* an echo, a possibility of the echo of this calling, and understands creatively its own inheritance. . . .

To ask: How is it with Being?—that means nothing less than to reiterate the beginning of our historical-spiritual existence, in order to transform it into the new beginning. Such a thing is possible. It is indeed the decisive form of history, because it originates in the most basic events. But a beginning is not repeated by screwing oneself back to it as something that once was, and is now familiar, and has simply to be imitated. No, the beginning must be begun again *more radically* and with all that a true beginning brings with it—all that is strange and dark and unassured.[6]

We started from poetry. Where, in all this, have we left it? As philosopher, Heidegger's aim is, and has always been, to turn the human mind again to Being. That was the aim, in *Sein und Zeit*, of the phenomenological analysis of human being, and that is the intention of the prophecies with which for thirty years he has dominated the German philosophical scene. But this historic task—to turn the mind again to Being—is also, and first and foremost, in his view, the task of the poet. "Poetry is the primal language of a historical people"; only the poets can teach a people their proper ear for Being—can bring them, in resonance to Being, to their historical task. Philosophy analyzes away the barriers of our everyday, routine, technique-bound lives, in order to clear the way to Being, to turn us toward Being. But the poets are the "more daring ones" who "speak Being," who "name the holy":[7]

Einzig das Lied überm Land
heiligt und feiert.[8]

I began by asking: What has Heidegger to say to us? So far I have been trying to make out what Heidegger has to say. Now, in Heideggerian fashion, I must change the emphasis, and ask again: What has Heidegger to say to *us*?

In a sense, nothing. "Poetry," says Heidegger, "founds and names the being and nature of all things." Yet if poetry rather than literal language is the source of understanding, still language, even poetic language, does not *make* what it understands. Though it names the being and nature of all things, it does not *found* them. "Words and language," Heidegger wrote in the *Introduction to Metaphysics*, "are not shells in which things are simply packaged for the commerce of speech and writing. It is only in the word, in language, that things become and are."[9] But that is to make of the poet and his acolyte, the philosopher, a maker in a sense in which he is not. A poet makes poems, and through them understanding; but he does not make that *of* which the poems are, or bring, the understanding. If he (or his philosophical interpreter) pretends to do so, he becomes a false maker, a maker of illusions, a magician and a mountebank. That is Heidegger; that is his arrogance and his failure. His tricks of language, which appear to elucidate, are tricks only.

Historically, also, the story Heidegger has to tell is false. It is false prophecy, as his word-magic is false poetic. If we are to take the first step beyond nihilism, to transcend despair, we will not do it so sweepingly as by putting the source of nihilism back to Aristotle or Plato. To expound a line of Parmenides as if it *were* the history of Western thought, to expound *this* history of Western thought as if it were the history of humanity, and even, as Heidegger does, to expound this history as if it were the history of Being: "the destiny of Being . . . to become a haze and an error"—this is not history but hubris.

Yet there is something in it. Heidegger's prophecies are haunting, and only live ghosts haunt. What there is in them of truth is negative, but still a truth: analysis, logic, is not enough. Philosophy is not poetry, but it must flow from the same source, from a comprehensive vision, which precedes, supports, and at the same time transcends analysis. And once one thinks of it that way, even in that fantastically distorted, and insupportable history there is something; for it is after all Aristotle who is thought to have invented a detached and self-supporting logic. Where we are alienated from ontological rootedness, where we are drifting and astray, it is the spirit of Aristotelianism that has misled us. It is the dream of method, of *logos* as portable property, that has become our nightmare.[10]

A brief statement, to convey the teachings of thirty years. But the question it raises, Heidegger would insist, is not just any question, not even one of a number of questions. It is *the* question. Some twoscore volumes are not too much to devote to summoning up *the* question, to calling us to "the spiritual destiny of the West," even "the destiny of Being itself." That's as may be. But look back over the twoscore volumes, compare, for example, *Der Satz vom Grund* with *Sein und Zeit*. There is a striking change, a change in the proportion of trickery to truth. The earlier book is full of word play, of endless intricate distortions of German roots and endings, in the worst tradition of the worst German philosophy; yet through the bizarre and twisted labyrinths of its language it is after something: it is after the structure of human finitude, and in and through finitude the hope, even, of human dignity. Finitude: being held down into nothingness, on to the brink of the abyss—that is our ground. Only at the dizzy edge of nothing can we take our stand. This is the root concept of all existentialist literature, which received in *Sein und Zeit* its definitive philosophic expression. This is what Heidegger has shown us, and on this insight we must not turn our backs.

True, it is in itself a powerless insight. Alone, it can lead the lonely consciousness only to the hate-filled subjectivism of Sartre. But if insufficient, it is nevertheless a necessary insight. If we are in truth to renew the "infinite question of being," it is with "the finite powers of man," and in the aching awareness of that finitude, that we must ask it. The alternative—Sartre is right in that—is metaphysical bad faith. But on that indispensable insight Heidegger himself has turned his back. He was, he says himself, never an existentialist. Certainly he is one no longer. Where in the latest of the twoscore volumes is "world"— my world, not made by me, yet world through what I make of it? Where is the absurd givenness of personal facticity; where are dread, death, conscience, resolve? They have drifted away on a tide of easier eloquence, of the tricks in trade of a practiced lecturer:

> The Law of Sufficient Reason and its history don't attract us to linger with them. We have enough else to excite us: for instance, the discovery of new elements in natural science; for instance, the discovery of new clocks for calculating the age of the earth; or, for instance, a book about "Gods, Graves, and Scholars," or a notice about the construction of a spaceship.[11]

Behind the cheap rhetoric, what is there? The ghost of the Quest for Being fencing with the ghost of Aristotle. Something, but by no means enough.

Notes

1. Martin Heidegger, *Der Satz vom Grund* (Tübingen: Neske, 1957), pp. 210-211.

2. Martin Heidegger, "Hölderlin und das Wesen der Dichtung," in *Erläuterungen zu Hölderlins Dichtung* (Frankfurt am Main: Klostermann, 1951), p. 40; 4th ed. (1971), p. 43.

3. Ibid., p. 31; p. 33.

4. Martin Heidegger, *Einführung in die Metaphysik* (Tübingen: Neimeyer, 1953), p. 36.

5. Ibid., p. 28.

6. Ibid., pp. 28-30.

7. Martin Heidegger, "Wozu Dichter," in *Holzwege*, 5th ed. (Frankfurt am Main: Klostermann, 1972), pp. 248-295, see esp. pp. 293-294.

8. Ibid., p. 253 (from Rilke, *Sonnetten an Orpheus*, pt. 1, 19).

9. *Einführung*, p. 11

10. Note as of July 1975: I would stand by the last sentence, but the interpretation of Aristotle is of course mistaken; see, for example, my *Portrait of Aristotle* (Chicago: University of Chicago Press, 1964), chap. 3.

11. *Der Satz vom Grund*, p. 15.

VII

The German Existentialists

1959

WHEN I WENT TO GERMANY AS AN EXCHANGE STUDENT, NEARLY thirty years ago, I was told that there were only two serious philosophers to be met there (or anywhere, for it was axiomatic that there were no serious philosophers outside German-speaking countries): Martin Heidegger and Karl Jaspers. They were both acknowledged to practice a kind of philosophy derived at least in part from Kierkegaard and called *Existenzphilosophie*. There was also a theologian, Paul Tillich, with similar interests. Heidegger and Jaspers still rank as the two outstanding philosophers of the German-speaking world, and Tillich is certainly in the forefront of contemporary theological philosophers. But of the three, only Tillich accepts the term "existentialism" as meaningful; both Heidegger and Jaspers reject it. On the other hand, both Heidegger and Tillich have linked what we should call their "existentialism" with ontology, a step that so far as I know is not taken by Jaspers. For him it is to "reason" and "philosophical faith" that we must turn to supplement our acknowledgment of the structure of individual existence, with its tragic finitude.

Let me fill in this very abstract comparison by looking briefly at the thought of these three men in some of their recent writings.

Jaspers is right in a way in disclaiming the title "existentialist," since the concept of the inner, concrete existence of the person has formed one current only, though a persistent one, in the development of his thought. Basing his conception of scientific knowledge on the example of Max Weber and his *wertfreie Wissenschaft*, he takes an almost positivist view of the nature of science within its proper sphere: confined always to a segment of the phenomena, never reaching to the whole or to the ultimate. The personal, existential sphere of life, where, Jaspers believes, we may reach through sometimes to true, living communications with one another, supplements but does not contradict the claims of science. Nor is personal existence in its turn self-sustaining. It is supported, whether in achievement or in failure, by its reliance on a higher reality; it depends upon a transcendence that it can never know, as the logical mind knows cause and effect in science, or confront, as the loving person confronts the person beloved, but can only adumbrate, forever incompletely, in the symbolisms of fable or ritual or creed. This threefold structure runs consistently through all of Jasper's thought: it is as clear in his recent book, *The Atomic Bomb and the Future of Mankind,* as in his three-volume *Philosophy* of 1932.

Yet if we look at the book on the atom bomb, we do find, I think, that the greatness of Jasper's philosophical method resides in its *existentialist* character, and that his weakness, for most English-speaking readers at least, lies in the means by which he attempts to overcome the paradox of individual, historical existence as he sees it. It *is* as an existentialist that he succeeds, and as a nonexistentialist that he fails. Again, let me fill in a little this rather sweeping contrast.

Jasper's best-known contribution to existentialist philosophy was his conception of the "boundary situation," the kind of situation in which the ultimate motives and values that govern an individual's life are brought dramatically into focus by the necessity for making a fundamental choice. We are all faced with this kind of situation, eventually by the way we meet death, but by implication, daily. This has always been so: as much when Jaspers first introduced the *Grenzsituation* as now—as much, for that matter, when Socrates argued with Crito about the obligations of citizenship. But with the H-bomb not only every man, but man as such, stands before the boundary. Mankind collectively exhibits today, on a global scale, the validity of Jasper's basic conception. Every political decision is weighted with the possibility of the total destruction of human life, of life itself. Not only that. The decision entailing life or nonlife is but one aspect of the boundary we stand on. The world has divided itself into free and unfree, exemplifying again, despite the ambiguities on both sides, the inescapable dilemma of human life: the dichotomy of freedom and slavery: of the power of man over machines or the mechanization of man. For again modern industrial society with its power for total tyranny—for 1984—has brought to huge and dramatic realization a boundary situation that was always inherent in man's relationship with man.

Nor is it only the overall boundary situation—of peace vs. H-bomb, the free world vs. totalitarianism—that Jaspers pictures. Within this overall dichotomy he looks at each major problem or phenomenon—colonialism, nationalism, increase of population, changed military techniques, the United Nations, and so on—with an immense serenity, clarity, and passion, takes it to *its Grenzsituation,* and leaves it there. In his sense of situation, of what it is, politically, ethically, historically, to stand here and now within this predicament, in his command of the logic of predicaments, his integrity in facing them, his immense command of relevant facts, his assessment of the value of "historical substance," or traditional rootedness (in his appreciation of so un-German a character as Burke, for example, or of the basic problems of contemporary political democracy)—in all this he is undoubtedly one of the great thinkers of our time. And such thinking is very deeply rooted, it seems to me, in the existentialist heritage. Jaspers is applying the powers of a penetrating philosophical mind to the analysis of the ways in which it matters to men's decisions to be where and how and why they are, seeing the points of choice where they come, the contradictory responsibilities where they arise. He is ferreting out the logic *within* our history, discovering the structure of our being *in* our becoming. This is quite recognizably, and magnificently, existentialist thought.

But for Jaspers this is only half the story. The answer to the tragic perplexity of our existence, personal and political, lies in human dignity itself, in the intrinsic worth of human freedom. That this is so is clear from the very story he tells: of Gandhi's victory, of world response to the Hungarian revolution, and the like. In such occurrences we recognize a humanity, local and historical in its roots, but greater than history or than parochial loyalty; we meet here, even in destruction, humanity itself. By what instinct, by what power in ourselves do we know this? It is, if you like, freedom speaking to freedom; but for Jaspers it is something more. In the word of a venerated German tradition it is *Vernunft,* intuitive reason, understanding; it is *philosophical faith* that conveys the saving truth. What is *Vernunft?* Try as I may, I cannot tell. It is not unrelated, apparently, to faith in God, which we seek and find only through the *Chiffreschrift,* through myth and symbol, but it is certainly, in Jaspers' view, not the same thing. It is not in most respects what we usually call "reason." It is not "rational" in the sense of "logical" or "demonstrable"; it is not, for example, what we would say the Enlightenment characteristically believed in—almost the contrary. But on the other hand, it *is* reason as *against* revelation: it is *philosophical* faith, not religious faith. That *Verstand*—the objective reckoning of thinking machines—if it exists at all, must be borne by a higher and deeper kind of understanding seems to me incontrovertible. But it is quite another thing to suggest there is *one* such "higher wisdom," which can be, as apparently it is for Jaspers, identified with the works of great philosophers and of a few poets who come close to being philosophers. With all good will, I can find in this only an empty, if a noble, gesture.

As far as systematic philosophy is concerned, Heidegger's contribution to existentialism is more massive, for his *Sein und Zeit* is the definitive expression of the existentialist's vision of life, of the structure of finitude and the resolve to face finitude, in and of itself. But his leap into the infinite is more massive too.

It is not a leap, of course. He was there all the time; it was always the *Seinsfrage,* the quest for Being he was after. From the start he was castigating mankind for our foolish concern with things, with beings, which distracts us from the concern for Being itself that is our proper task. True, the resolve by which his rare and lonely hero was to rise above the hurrying crowd has, on the face of it, little to do with Being. It was, indeed, the existential resolve par excellence: the resolve to face squarely the nothingness of life, to live unflinchingly with guilt and dread and to live thereby with destiny. Yet Heidegger's hero was not, like Sartre's, simply seeking "his own act"; he was, so Heidegger suggests, turning from the "ontic," the many things that are, to face in his authenticity the authentic question, the "ontological" question, the question of the Being that makes things be. He was trying to penetrate from beings through nonbeing to Being. In this context, then, Heidegger's analysis of existence would be no more than a necessary step in the approach to Being, much as, in Descartes's view, the proofs of God in the *Meditations* had to be disposed of in order to proceed to the safe construction of a universal mathematics.

But where and what is the ontology that was to come? The more one reads of Heidegger's later writings, the more one finds that the theme of *Sein und Zeit,* the phenomenology of finitude, was his one true theme, and that in turning away from it to a more direct confrontation with Being he has left tortured and repetitious but genuine philosophical argument for hollow rhetoric. Compare, for example, Heidegger on our present world situation with Jaspers. For example, as I have argued elsewhere, the concluding pronouncement of *Der Satz vom Grund,* except for the implied reference to the bomb, echoes the opening statement of *Being and Time.* It is the quintessence of Heidegger's ontology:

> . . . does not the essence of man, does not his belonging to Being, does not the essence of Being itself remain ever yet and ever more overwhelmingly what befits thought? . . . That is the question. That is the world question of thought. Its answer will decide what becomes of the earth and of the existence of man on this earth.[1]

Put this beside Jasper's weighing of the moral and political issues before us. There is no need for comment. Except for some etymological excursions about Being as "permanence" or "constancy" this is all Heidegger ever has to say about that elusive concept. Most of the time, in the score of volumes published since *Sein und Zeit,* his chief concern is to tell us not what Being is (a task beyond telling, except for the poets who dare to "speak Being" and to "name the holy"), but how far away from our home in Being, from the "nearness and shelter of Being," we have come. That "nearness" was present in Parmenides, as is evident, for Heidegger, from the line that reads, in his rendering, "Thinking is the same as that for whose sake there is thought." This Presence has been lost and our history is the history of that loss.

But what kind of "history" is this? The history of the West, the history of mankind, the history of Being, read into one fragment of Parmenides? Jasper's sensitiveness to "historical substance," to the way in which circumstances do indeed matter and matter deeply to human beings, contrasts strangely with Heidegger's bombastic leveling of the centuries. Was it really Heidegger who told us what time was like, whose central theme was "historicity"? It seems hard to believe. If this be ontology, how right are they who would have none of it!

"The essence of man is his existence." This Sartrean aphorism condenses into a few words the many-vectored ramifications of Jaspers' "boundary situation," or, equally, the central conception of Heidegger's "being-in-the-world." The leap beyond this to *Vernunft* in Jaspers or to Being in Heidegger is a leap from firm ground into an abyss. It is precisely to the extent to which their thinking *is* "existentialist" that, to this writer at least, it conveys important meaning—and I think I am not alone in this view. Is existentialism, then, a dead end, a source of insight into one aspect of our lives, but, as I called it myself a long time ago, "a new expression of an old despair"—or not so long ago, a "floating philosophy, like autumn leaves, unable to take hold again upon the parent branch"? I used to think so, and, again, I was certainly not alone in thinking so, but I am by no means certain any longer that I was right.

For, paradoxically, the third of the three German existentialists I mentioned at the start, Paul Tillich, the only one who *admits* to being an existentialist, and who makes a great deal in his writings of the term "existentialism," does in fact use the characteristic existentialist analysis of finitude as the first step in the construction of a substantial and luminous ontology—an ontology, more surprisingly still, which draws some of its substance and clarity not only from Heidegger's analysis of human being but from Heidegger's ontology itself. It is a most amazing distillation, and I find it very hard to say how it is done. Tillich is a theologian, and concepts like "finitude," "dread," "resolve" are of course relevant to a theological enterprise—but that takes us no way at all. Existentialist philosophy—or theology—is more than a sequence of "concepts": it is either live thinking or it is nothing. And once one is dealing with live things, differences—especially the differences that matter—are very hard to put one's finger on. But, with considerable hesitation, let me try.

Consider Tillich's Terry lectures, *The Courage to Be* (1952), as an example. It is a good example, since the theme of existentialism looms large in it, existentialism as "the expression of the anxiety of meaninglessness and of the attempt to take this anxiety into the courage to be as oneself."[2] This is a fair, and familiar, description of the existentialists's theme. Resolve, decision, integrity, the denial of *mauvaise foi*—all these belong to the existentialists's authentic person, the person who can live with and transcend nothingness and dread. And does not this amount to courage? Moreover, in the phrase "the courage to be," Tillich is stating an ontological reference like that of *Sein und Zeit*. Courage, the virtue most conspicuous in the face of nonbeing, is the virtue that most deeply expresses the relation of man to his ground in being. "Courage can show us what being is, and being can show us what courage is." Why does this kind of thing make sense—as I find it does—in Tillich, but not in Heidegger?

One is inclined to say, in the first place, because Tillich's lectures are written in clear and simple English; and I do suspect that the necessity to think in a less "philosophical" language may have been a factor in the development of his thought. Only a native German speaker who has adopted the austerer medium of English could so simply grasp and convey to us the positive meaning of *Sein und Zeit*. But there is certainly more in it than that. Language molds but does not make the thinker. Where does the difference in the thinking lie?

Perhaps the simple historical sketch of Tillich's first lecture, on courage in Plato, the Stoics, Spinoza, and Nietzsche, may give us a clue to it. Tillich seems to accept and build on the intellectual history of the West, where Heidegger must go back to that mysterious first beginning in Anaximander and Parmenides, and throw all else away. True, Heidegger too reveres Nietzsche; yet even here his reverence tends, it seems to me, in a different direction. Not so much Nietzsche's love of life, of self-affirmation, as his hatred of all else, his massive contempt for almost everything we ordinary people feel is human, is, I suspect, what ties Heidegger to the philosopher of the Superman.

Perhaps there is here a clue, also, to another novelty in Tillich's theme. *Sein und Zeit* does, as Tillich says, describe "in philosophically exact terms" the courage of despair. But somehow Heidegger's "resolve" already carried the contemptuous ring of his later rhetoric. His hero is not only lonely, he is essentially alone: for him no other human beings exist. Can one really take "the courage to be as *oneself*" to this extreme and still meaningfully call it "courage"? And can one meaningfully make a bridge from "courage" to "being" without its other aspect, what Tillich calls "the courage to be as a part"? Spinoza, Tillich reminds us, saw "generosity" as flowing from the fuller meaning of courage. But here we are back at the old and obvious failing of existentialism: in the version of Heidegger or Sartre, the most rigorous versions, there is no place for love. That is, proverbially by now, one reason why existentialism looks so like a dead end—it gives us no bridge from person to person, but only the inner topography of the separated subject. Turned toward others, the subject in total separateness can only hate. The question is, then, how does Tillich, taking the existentialist's theme as far as he does, yet contrive, in his account of courage, to unite *generosity* with *self-affirmation*, the courage to be as a part with the courage to be as oneself? He does not simply *add* it, as Jaspers does "communication"; the two aspects of courage belong integrally to one another and to his theme. What bridge has he found from loneliness to encounter?

The answer is in one sense quite simple. For, Tillich holds, existentialism is an analysis of the human predicament, and the answers to the questions implied in man's predicament are religious. Or as he puts it in these lectures: "Every courage to be has openly or covertly a religious root."[3] It is the explicit acknowledgment of this root that permits in Tillich's concept of courage—as in Spinoza's—its double import of self-affirmation *and* generosity. Either aspect taken alone, Tillich argues, leads to tragic failure: the one to the loss of the world in existentialism; the other, just as disastrously, to the loss of the self in collectivism and conformism. "Is there," he proceeds to ask, "a courage to be which unites both forms by transcending them?"[4] The answer is, only through the power of being which is the source of all power and all courage. That is to say, only in faith, for faith is "the state of being grasped by the power of being-itself."[5] Here is the ontological root, the "being" Heidegger talks so much about: it is the ground effective in every act of courage. From it flows the more than resolute, the truly courageous quality of the lonely self-affirming will, as well as of the courage of giving, the courage to be as a part.

Yet this answer, it appears, is so simple as to be no answer. For one thing there are other "theistic" existentialists, Gabriel Marcel, for example, or Jaspers himself with his *Chiffreschrift* and his *Transzendenz*. Again, what is the difference? One can only fall back, I am afraid, on the old-fashioned criteria for philosophical truth: coherence and adequacy. Jaspers is eminently wise about this and that, but there seems somehow to be no shape to his thought, no concentrated momentum that carries one along with him. In Tillich's best writing, on the other hand, one feels an overarching single-mindedness: for him everything is a theophany. And yet there is richness and amplitude within that single aim. This is not a revivalist theology; on the contrary, it is infinitely flexible, human, and modern. (See, for example, in his *Systematic Theology,* the use he makes of Freud.) And, in our present context, it *is* genuinely an existentialist's theology, and a fortiori an existentialist's approach to being. The courage to be is rooted in the power of being, that is, of God, but of "the God who appears when God has disappeared in the anxiety of doubt."[6] Thus the courage of doubt, of despair, is always with us; it has become an essential aspect of faith itself. It leads to, because it flows from, being. And flowing also from that same source, and leading to it, is generosity, the other "courage to be," which belongs just as essentially to our human situation, but which can grow in harmony with the spirit of resolve and independence only out of their common root. The existentialist tradition turns out to be much richer than it seemed.

Notes

1. Martin Heidegger, *Der Satz vom Grund* (Tübingen: Neske, 1957), pp. 210-211.
2. Paul Tillich, *The Courage to Be* (New Haven: Yale University Press, 1952), p. 139.
3. Ibid., p. 156.
4. Ibid., p. 154.
5. Ibid., p. 156.
6. Ibid., p. 190.

VIII

Karl Jaspers: A Philosopher
of Humanity

1963

DEATH, SUFFERING, CHANCE, GUILT, CONFLICT: ONLY IN SUCH boundary situations do human beings come to awareness of what they are. But if we can approach the understanding of what we are only in these lonely limits of existence, it is in communication, in the rich and rare togetherness of persons who love in honesty and openness, that we become truly human. Only in another's being have I my being, only in another's freedom, my freedom.

These two thoughts, of the boundary situation, and of personal communication, are constant themes throughout the writings of Karl Jaspers, and, seen from this year of his eightieth birthday, throughout his life.[1] That they are constant themes in his voluminous publications he himself said, ten years ago, in his "Philosophical Autobiography." But that is to say, at the same time, that they are constant themes in his life; for it is yet another constant theme of his that there is no Philosophy as such, no once-for-all system of Ideas or clever technique for dispelling paradoxes. There is only philosophizing, reflective thought absorbing the whole person of the thinker, thought directed first and last to that most puzzling and most urgent of questions, the Socratic question: What is it to be a man?

Even in this sense of philosophy, moreover, Jaspers hesitates to count himself a philosopher. Philosophy being literally the love of wisdom, he, as a lover of philosophy, is, he says, at two removes from the possession of wisdom itself. He would guide us, as in his *Great Philosophers*, to fructifying contact with their vision; he does not count himself among them.

Yet if we look back at the panorama of his career we must feel that it is something not unlike wisdom that marks his life and work, one as they are. Or if wisdom must be reserved for the giants of philosophy, perhaps the right word is, humanity. Jaspers's philosophical works, indeed, are long, long-winded, repetitive in the extreme, as it seems to English readers only German professors know how to be. And the dead earnest of his philosophizing, unleavened by the slightest spark of lightness or humor, is often too solid and too vaporous at once, if that be possible, for English stomachs to digest. Looking at it as so very many words making over and over the same solemn pronouncements, we *want* to find it pompous nonsense. But give Jaspers a concrete issue, a moral issue with intellectual implications, or an intellectual issue in a moral context, give him, in short, a boundary situation, and you find an integrity, a moral rightness of argument and decision, a luminous clarity, sometimes even economy, of expression that can only evoke our unqualified assent and respect. So, over the years, he has spoken, for example, on the nature of mental illness, on the intellectual crisis of our time, on academic freedom, on the "total falsehood" of National Socialism, on the responsibility of all Germans, and all men, for that calamity, on the bomb, on the meaning and prospects of German unity, on the role of the churches in the modern world—and there may be more such themes to come.

Shall we then in our reading of Jaspers stick to his treatment of limited issues and leave the broader sweep of his philosophy alone? In a sense translators and publishers have done this, for although there have been a surprising number of his works published here and in America, no one has produced an English version of his three-volume *Philosophie* or of his 1,100-page work on truth, itself the first volume of a projected philosophical logic. Yet if his work and his life are one, so, a fortiori, is his work itself a unity, and in the particular judgments that command our admiration his fundamental philosophical concepts, Truth, Freedom, *Vernunft*, Transcendence, are never far removed. The best guiding line, perhaps, for trying to understand him, is the philosophical autobiography, recently republished in an eightieth-birthday *Festschrift* (*Karl Jaspers: Werk und Wirkung*), as well as in the collection *Philosophie und Welt*. (It was originally written for *The Philosophy of Karl Jaspers*, a volume in an American series, where it was, unfortunately, badly translated.)

Karl Jaspers has lived since boyhood in and with a boundary situation of his own. He suffers from an organic bronchial and heart condition which was diagnosed when he was eighteen, the prognosis being death in the thirties at the latest. His life has been organized around this illness, but—as is plain from his activity as writer and teacher—in such a way as to control it rather than let it have control of him. The impact of his personality derives partly from the courage and discipline necessary to such a life. Seeking within these limits for the greatest possible contact with human reality, he chose medicine, and in particular psychiatry as a career.

Although his active clinical work had perforce to be restricted, his pioneering achievements in this first profession were of such importance that his *General Psychopathology*, first published in 1913 and now in its seventh edition, is still in use, and, happily, has now been made available to the English-speaking public by Manchester University Press. Here, as ever after, it was the respect for human beings as such which basically motivated Jaspers's reform of psychiatry. The Heidelberg school, when he joined it, interpreted mental illness almost wholly as physically caused. Jaspers approached each patient, instead, as an unfathomable human person, to be encountered, and understood, as such.

After the *Psychopathology* his next major work, *Die Psychologie der Weltanschauungen*, was transitional to his future, more speculative interest. It has the philosophical importance of introducing the concept of the boundary situation. But it was not until December 1931 that his first considerable philosophical work, the three-volume *Philosophie*, was published, and as he says himself, his own understanding of and critical reflection on the great philosophers was even then and has been ever since in process of development. Contributing to this development, and central to all his thought, as he repeatedly says, was the influence of his wife, formerly Gertrud Mayer, whom he had married in 1910. His emphasis on communication is often explicitly, always implicitly, bound to this nearby instance of what he calls "loving conflict in total honesty." His interest in biblical religion, in particular, he owes to his wife's Jewish upbringing.

The other major influence which must be mentioned in any account of Jaspers's work is that of Max Weber. Jaspers's conception of the objectivity of science and its abstractness—that is, its necessary confinement to selected, almost artificially limited, problems—is deeply Weberian. And as his stress on human togetherness is linked to his own marriage, so, one suspects, his deep reverence for human greatness reflects his feeling for Weber, the great man whom he himself in his youth knew and revered.

In the *Philosophie* it is the first of the three volumes, *Weltorientierung,* which clearly shows Weber's mark. Jaspers's conception of natural science is an almost positivist one, plainly stamped with the ideal of *wertfreie Wissenschaft*. The other two volumes show how his scientific naturalism is supplemented by concern for the other essential, and deeper lying, aspects of human experience, *personal existence* and *transcendence*. The concept of *existence* derives from Kierkegaard, but the stress on communication is scarcely Kierkegaardian. Nor is the almost Kantian emphasis on *Vernunft*, that more than ratiocinating German Reason, which has moved more and more to the center of Jaspers's thought, as, for example, in the lectures on *Vernunft und Existenz* (1935; *Reason and Existence*, Routledge & Kegan Paul, 1955).

Transcendence for Jaspers, in contrast to the use of that term by Heidegger, retains its traditional meaning. It is ultimate mystery, which we can grasp only through image and symbol, through deciphering, *das Chiffrelesen*. It is not, however, the faith of any church to which Jaspers is turning here, but what he calls "philosophical faith," a concept that again he has continued to develop in his later writings. In his most recent book, *Der philosophische Glaube angesichts der Offenbarung*, he contrasts the self-closing circle of revelation with the circle of philosophical faith, which by its very nature remains open for and beyond failure and suffering. But these later elaborations retain, as it were, the shape already adumbrated in the three volumes of 1931-32.

Jaspers was Professor of Philosophy at Heidelberg from 1921. As a philosopher, as an active participant in the administration of a great university, dedicated by its nature to the free pursuit of truth, as the husband of a Jewish wife, as a German thinker steeped in the humanism of Goethe and of Kant, he stood from 1933 to 1945 in the second great boundary situation of his life. He was deprived of his chair in 1937; working patiently but, of course, quite privately, and without hope of a future, at his "philosophical logic," he heard in 1945 that he and his wife would be taken away on April 14. The Americans occupied Heidelberg on April 1, and so rescued, if not the greatest, certainly the best of living German philosophers from destruction at the hands of his fellow Germans. Quickly reinstated by the occupying forces to lead the resuscitation of the university, he accepted three years later a call to the University of Basel and there retired from active lecturing in 1961.

Hitler, it has been said, made Jaspers a political thinker. This is not quite true, for politics had long concerned him, and his well-known *Geistige Situation der Zeit* (1931; *Man in the Modern Age*, Routledge & Kegan Paul, 1933, 1951) is not without its political implications. But it is since the Second World War that he has produced his most important political works: *Die Schuldfrage* (reprinted in the DTV volume, *Lebensfragen der deutschen Politik*; *The Question of German Guilt* [New York: Dial, 1947]), and *Die Atombombe und die Zukunft des Menschen* (Piper, 1958; *The Future of Mankind* [Chicago: University of Chicago Press, 1961]). In both these works the philosopher of the boundary situation shows his power.

In everyday circumstances, in a reasonably fortunate life, ordinary "rule-bound behavior" goes smoothly on its way. We may pride ourselves on subjecting to enlightened criticism the rules of our society, but in the main we follow them without undue concern, and follow by implication the ultimate ideals on which in turn they rest. But most of us do come some few times, even in such a cushioned life, to turning points at which we must go one way or the other, yet on neither course can we say, serenely, that was what the rules prescribed. At places where the rules massively collapse and our freedom stands glaringly alone in all its peril and ambiguity, there we stand at a boundary. Life in the French Resistance, as Sartre expounded its meaning in the "Republic of Silence" and dramatized it in *Morts sans Sépultures*, was life at such a boundary. For every decent and sensitive German, life under National Socialism was life at such a boundary, and Jaspers in *Die Schuldfrage* probes the complex levels of responsibility implicit in such an existence. This little work can stand alongside the *Crito* for its illumination of the human condition as such, arising out of reflection on a concrete situation.

Germans under Hitler lived at a boundary, and so did we all indirectly. So *do* we all when the threat of total injustice, the boundary situation of tyranny as Thucydides and Plato first pictured it for us, has been transmuted by the power of technology to its radical totalitarian form. The total threat to freedom is with us constantly and forever. But the threat to life itself, in the nuclear age, has been similarly magnified. Not only each of us singly must learn, in Kierkegaard's phrase, to "rejoice over 70,000 fathoms." The human race itself stands in every moment at the verge of annihilation.

This global boundary situation, where freedom and life are equally imperilled, Jaspers turns to in the "bomb book." Originally a broadcast, this shorter version is also reprinted in the *Lebensfragen*. Published in much expanded book form, it became a bestseller in Germany, gained for its author the German publishers' peace prize (Friedenspreis des deutschen Buchhandels) and is now out in two paperback editions as well as in an American edition. The book contains, again, much practical wisdom on such topics as colonialism or the United Nations, or such figures as Roosevelt or Gandhi. And yet the concluding part of the argument brings us once more into the quagmire of *Vernunft* and *Wahrheit*.

This is distressing. When Jaspers speaks, for example, in an address called "Volk und Universität" in the DTV *Lebensfragen* about the nature of the university as the place of the untrammeled pursuit of truth, we know what he means by freedom, by truth; his thesis is brilliantly clear, his argument impeccable: the whole piece is a classic. Why, then, when "truth" and "freedom" and "reason" get out on their own do we find ourselves floundering? Why are the particular consequences so plain and so true, yet the general premises so formless and so cloudy?

Can it be the case, as so many German speakers have believed, that the English tongue is unsuited to philosophizing? Or can it be that even the profoundest insights, left too much scope for expansion, tend to dissipate themselves, somehow, out of sheer bulk?

Jaspers writes by accumulating jottings on slips of paper, which gradually work themselves into a book. The leading ideas, he believes, are less important than the detailed expositions they were meant to stitch together. These accumulated musings, in the case of his first book, his great text on psychopathology, took on their final shape *un*revised! Since then, he says, he has always read through his manuscripts and corrected them; and his publisher and friend Klaus Piper pays tribute to the beautifully finished state in which the manuscripts are received. Yet one cannot help feeling that in this revision there is little pruning. Perhaps it is not so much a limited subject matter as a limiting occasion, like a broadcast or a public lecture, that is needed to make Jaspers intelligible to those not used to the diffuseness of German thought and speech.

Be that as it may, not only his political pronouncements but also his vast philosophical projects have still continued to proliferate. Three of these later projects should be mentioned in a general survey of Jaspers's work. First, there is *Vom Ursprung und Ziel der Geschichte* (1949; *Origin and Goal of History* [Routledge & Kegan Paul, 1953]), a massive work singling out the "axial period" in which the roots of our culture were laid down. Related to this view of history, with its emphasis on the significance of biblical Christianity, is, secondly, the recent work already mentioned on philosophical faith in relation to revelation. Jaspers recognizes frankly the impotence of the churches as a force in contemporary culture, and he has no easy prescription for rethinking the traditional image of God to suit the secular disposition of modern man. Rather it is, as so often in his thought, a fundamental tension in our nature which he hopes to illuminate.

The philosopher, he believes, comes inevitably to awareness of a transcendent medium, which forever draws but forever eludes his knowledge. This endless code-reading, groping through and beyond symbols for the ultimate, the philosophical thinker knows to be his task, but he knows it to be in principle incapable of fulfillment. The person who believes out of piety, on the ground of revelation, though not, it is to be hoped, in conflict with the philosopher, does stand on a different foundation in his relation to the being that surrounds us. And Jaspers doubts whether these two, the way of broad philosophical vision, and the way of prayer and worship, can be united in a single life. Again we come to the boundary, and take one path or the other. Those going the one way or the other are to be honored each by the other, but there is no ultimate synthesis, no one human way that can assimilate all differences.

Last, and perhaps the best avenue of approach to Jaspers for English readers, is his grand project for a study of *The Great Philosophers*. Volume 1, which was published in 1956, has now appeared in an excellent English version. The framework of the whole work, announced in the Introduction, is, once more, alarmingly elaborate and overschematic. The philosophers are sorted out into such groups as "the seminal thinkers, the great disturbers, the creative orderers." No such classification, Jaspers would be the first to admit, is fixed and final; but the sheer complexity of it, and the air with which it is announced, might make one hesitate to embark on the first leg of the journey—for this should be the first of numerous volumes.

The work itself, however, is intended not as a formidable work of categorization, but as an introduction, for the ordinary reader, to the great thinkers of the world. It is just that. In this volume there are, first, four chapters on what Jaspers calls the four "paradigmatic individuals," not philosophers, but men who have served as models to hosts of others: Socrates, Jesus, Buddha, and Confucius. Then follow three studies of as many "seminal thinkers": Plato, Augustine, and Kant. These are the thinkers who, Jaspers believes, best help men in their own thoughts. His own thinking is closest to Kant, and perhaps for that reason his exposition of Kant is less accurate as a rendering of his original. In particular he is too eager to make the sage of Königsberg wise in the knowledge of "life." But there is still much to be learnt from his exposition. And the introductions to Plato and Augustine are magnificent.

For precisely what Jaspers hopes to do, he here succeeds in doing, that is, to bring the reader to an enriching *encounter* with a great mind. This kind of "introduction" is out of fashion in Great Britain. It is more usual to dissect particular passages for their "logic" or lack of it than to attempt to understand the mind that conceived the passage, or better, conceived the work from which the zealous analyst has extracted it. What frequently emerges from such logical exercises is not an understanding of the philosopher in question but an admiration for one's own cleverness. For most of us, however, it is more rewarding to listen to Plato or Augustine or Kant than to ourselves.

Not that Jaspers presents these thinkers as authorities we ought blindly to follow: quite the contrary. But if we are to wrestle with the perennial problems of philosophy—to ask who we are, what kin "mind" is to body, what it is to live justly, what "time" and "history" mean, how general concepts are related to the particulars of sense—if we are to ask these questions, responsibly, in and of ourselves, we must ask them when and where we stand within a long tradition of such asking. So out of our own reflective seeking we should turn to confront the great minds who in the past have asked these same root questions and by their answers, or even sometimes their reasons for not answering, have helped to shape our questioning and our answers. In this sense it is at least as basic for our education to "live in the company of the great philosophers" as it is to live with the great poets or composers or discoverers. To read *The Great Philosophers* would be an excellent way to begin, both to meet the great thinkers of the past and to meet the contemporary philosophizing of Karl Jaspers.

Notes

1. This article appeared as a review in the *Times Literary Supplement*, 12 April 1963, of the following books: *Karl Jaspers: Werk und Wirkung* (Munich: Piper); *The Great Philosophers: The Foundations*, ed. Hannah Arendt, trans. Ralph Manheim (St. Albans: Hart-Davis); *Philosophie und Welt* (Munich: Piper); *General Psychopathology*, trans. J. Hoenig and Marian W. Hamilton (Manchester: Manchester University Press); *Der philosophische Glaube angesichts der Offenbarung* (Munich: Piper); *Lebensfragen der deutschen Politik* (Munich: Deutscher Taschenbuch Verlag); *Die Atombombe und die Zukunft des Menschen: Politisches Bewusstsein in unserer Zeit* (Munich: Piper Paperback; abridged paperback, Munich: Deutscher Taschenbuch Verlag).

IX

The Aesthetic Dialogue of Sartre and Merleau-Ponty

1970

MERLEAU-PONTY'S DISCUSSIONS OF PAINTING, TOGETHER WITH HIS criticisms of Sartre, show up strikingly the contrast of their philosophies. I shall use the comparison of the two philosophers' views on art to illuminate their treatment of four basic existential concepts. These are: first, being-in-a-world; second, the concept of the lived body; third, communication; and fourth, freedom.

Let me first recall the biographical background of the aesthetic dialogue I propose to examine. Sartre and Merleau-Ponty belonged to the same generation of students at the Sorbonne and the same circle of friends; Merleau-Ponty is mentioned occasionally in Simone de Beauvoir's autobiography. He is the only one of this circle (unless Raymond Aron is included) who became an academic: he was professor at the Sorbonne from 1949 and held the Chair of Philosophy at the Collège de France from 1951 until his death in 1961. In 1945 he had joined with Sartre in founding the literary and philosophical review, *Les Temps Modernes*, but resigned a few years later over the issue of Sartre's relation to the Communist party. His attack on Sartre was formulated in a chapter of his *Adventures of Dialectic*, ''Sartre and Ultra-Bolshevism,''[1] to which Simone de Beauvoir replied in a counter-attack, ''Merleau-Ponty and Pseudo-Sartrism.'' The breach seemed to be complete; but the former friends were in fact reconciled: Sartre recounts their meeting in this connection, in the issue of *Les Temps Modernes* published in memory of Merleau-Ponty after his death. Indeed, the first essay in Merleau-Ponty's book, *Signs*, published in 1960, is dedicated to Sartre, and the Preface to that collection suggests that the renewal of their friendship was at least in part occasioned by

Sartre's moving introduction to the posthumous work of a mutual friend, Nizan. In fact, the bitterness of Merleau-Ponty's attack on Sartre was the measure, in my view, of the depth of his admiration for him and for Beauvoir. Merleau-Ponty was a philosopher for whom artistic creation was a central theme, the paradigm, as we shall see, of the human condition, and they were *his* artists; it was they who, in their novels and plays, exhibited concretely the common philosophical concern of all of them. He had said as much publicly and eloquently on a number of occasions. And then they let him down.

The quarrel, on the surface, was political; but, as Merleau-Ponty himself said in the ultrabolshevism essay, their difference went much deeper. It was, he said, both as personal as possible and as general as possible: it was philosophical.[2] Their quarrel brought to the surface, in other words, a very deep-seated difference in their ways of looking at the world. One can put it briefly by saying that while Sartre is *a man of words*, Merleau-Ponty is *a man of vision*. It is this contrast that I want to elaborate, starting from the problem presented by Sartre's literary criticism and working back to the foundation of the problem in the premises of his philosophy.

The existential approach to literature involves trying to see a writer's work as expressive of his "project," his fundamental way of being human. Every one of us, in his life, is engaged in making of his given situation a composition, an organic whole, that is uniquely his; an artist does this in and through his work, which therefore speaks to us of his particular style of being-in-the-world. Now this approach in criticism can be very illuminating indeed, trying, as it does, to achieve, and to speak from, an understanding of the artist as a whole man, deeply engaged in a human task. An example of successful existentialist criticism, for instance, is Sartre's account of Flaubert in his *Question of Method*.[3] Flaubert's origin in the middle class does not make Mme. Bovary, neither do his particular circumstances, his domineering father, his brilliant elder brother, his own effeminacy: but all these circumstances, both general and particular, are the conditions upon which, the limits within which, he, freely and uniquely, created his own being in his work. They are, to put it in very un-Sartrean terms, the matter to which he, by his own act, gave unique and significant form. In highlighting this relation between life and work, the remarks on Flaubert scattered through *Question of Method* add a new dimension to one's understanding of *Bovary*, and that is the final test of significant criticism.

Yet if one looks over the pages upon pages of Sartrean critical writing, which proliferate as only a review editor's publications can, such passages as the Flaubert ones seem to represent an unstable equilibrium between two apparently incongruent extremes. On the one hand, Sartre often falls back, in his evaluation of literature, into a perverse *inwardness*, an extreme subjectivism where all relation to the world is vehemently renounced; and on the other hand, in his lengthy and equally vehement pronouncements on committed literature, he evaluates other writers exclusively for their *external* significance, for their "social message." In the former mood he elevates Genet, thief, homosexual and narcissist, to sainthood; in the latter, Marxist or quasi-Marxist frame of mind, he finds in Richard Wright's *Black Boy* the greatest American literary work, simply, one must suppose, because of the social wrongs with which it is preoccupied. Now of course one might say that these two opposite tendencies, one wholly subjective, the other wholly objective in its critical standards, are at one in their Marxist affiliation, that is, they both express admiration for a literature of rebellion against the emptiness and stupidity of bourgeois society. But this is an indirect and superficial unity. It is not only the fact that Genet is a reject of his society, a prisoner and a pervert, that attracts Sartre to him—though that helps; Sartre really wallows in Genet's total isolation, *as such*. For him, Genet represents a last, inverted transformation of the medieval ordered universe. G. K. Chesterton had said, Sartre reminds us, that "the modern world is full of Christian ideas run wild." And *Our Lady of the Flowers*, he is confident, would have confirmed Chesterton in his. view: "It is an 'Itinerary of the Soul toward God,' the author of which, run wild, takes himself for the creator of the universe. Every object in it speaks to us of Genet as every being in the cosmos of St. Bonaventura speaks to us of God."[4]

When Sartre wrote, in *Being and Nothingness,* that man is a useless passion, for he tries to become God and fails, he had not yet met Genet. For Genet has succeeded in precisely this Sartrean task, the task of Sartrean man; and it is the total rejection of the world that enables him to succeed: "This absence of connection with external reality," Sartre says, "is transfigured and becomes the sign of the demiurge's independence of his creation. . . . In the realm of the imaginary, absolute impotence changes sign and becomes omnipotence. Genet plays at inventing the world in order to stand before it in a state of supreme indifference."[5]

And what is this self-created world in which Genet is God? It is the last phase of what Plato in the *Gorgias* calls a plover's life, savoring endlessly the only material left to a human being who has cut off the whole external human world from any relation to himself, i.e., those physical pleasures devised by the most ingenious devotion to the stimulation of his own body by itself. Such a life has little to do with the concern for social justice that is supposed to characterize "committed literature": indeed, it is its very contrary.

Why this strange seesaw in Sartre's critical writing? The first step on our way to an answer to this question we may find in his theory of the imagination.[6] The imaginary, for Sartre, is pure negation. I stand, as a consciousness, over against the world; to *imagine* is to cut myself off from the objects that confront me, to deny them. Imagination therefore is simply denial, an emptiness. That is why Genet, outcast, imprisoned and denied all instruments but his own ingenuity, so dramatically embodies Sartre's ideal of the imaginative life. But if, out of such an empty inwardness, I project the world again, envisage action in the world, a relation to others, this projection is itself deformed and distorted by the emptiness of its source. The denial of a denial does indeed produce assertion of a sort, but a mechanized, abstract assertion, not an insight into concrete situations. It is literature committed on principle, not immersed in history. What Sartre looks for in committed literature is "totalization," the full swing round from the void of imagination as he sees it. But history is *never* total, and his theory of committed literature remains as unreal, as remote from the feel of concrete action, as the void of imagination itself. So Sartre swings, in his literary theory, as in his ontology, between the two abstractions, nothingness and being, being and nothingness. If he does occasionally, as in the passages on Flaubert, halt at a midpoint between the two extremes, he manages to do so *despite* his philosophical method, not because of it.

But Sartre himself is a novelist and playwright. Why should he hold so strangely abstract a theory of literature? To take the next step in our answer, we must look back briefly at the course of his philosophical development. Sartre spent a year in the early thirties at the French House in Berlin, studying the phenomenology of Husserl. One of Husserl's central concepts, which especially impressed him, is the concept of *intentionality*. Every thought, Husserl had insisted, is by its very nature directed toward an object—not necessarily an external, physically existent object; indeed, for the phenomenological study of thought it is irrelevant whether the object in fact exists or no. But what is essential is the *directedness* of thought. The pure "I think" of Descartes is not, as he had thought it, self-contained, but turned outward beyond itself to that of which it is a thought. But the conscious mind, the ego, is therefore, Sartre argued, *nothing but* this relation to its object. In itself, it is empty. If A consists in a relation to B, and B is subtracted, what is left is *nothing*. And that is just what happens when I subtract the outward direction of my thought. If I turn inward to myself, if I look for the content of my own subjectivity as such, what I find is just exactly *nothing*.[7] The same message, applied this time explicitly to the visual arts, is conveyed by Sartre's essay on Giacometti, the artist who was obsessed by vacuum—the very contrary, as we shall see, of Merleau-Ponty's Cézanne. Thus Sartre writes:

Ironic, defiant, ceremonious and tender, Giacometti sees empty space everywhere. Surely not everywhere, you will say, for some objects touch others. But this is exactly the point. Giacometti is certain of nothing, not even that. For weeks on end, he has been fascinated by the legs of a chair that did not *touch* the floor. Between things as between men, the bridges are broken, and emptiness seeps in everywhere, every creature concealing his own.[8]

It is this fascination with emptiness, with nothing, that, for Sartre, marks the imagination and all its work, in the visual arts as well as in the literary. Imagination is the denial of the full, the out-there; what it makes, in here, is—nothing.

Why this all or none attitude? The answer lies yet another step back in Sartre's philosophical history. Beauvoir, in her memoirs, remarks of herself and Sartre in their early days together, "We were Cartesians; we thought we were nothing but pure reason and pure will." This is quite literally true of Sartre's thinking: his Cartesian premises fix irrevocably the limit of his thought.[9]

For Descartes, the mind was wholly self-explicit, luminously aware of each clear and distinct idea in turn, the sum of which taken together composed the totality of knowledge. And over against this area of pure intellectual transparency, the material world was equally explicitly there to be known. Both of these, mind and matter, Descartes believed to be substances, independently existent, though dependent at every moment on God to recreate them. Now Sartre has certainly abandoned the seventeenth-century conception of substance, of independent self-existent entities, as well as the conception of an all-powerful, non-deceiving God to support our knowledge of them. All that is left him, then, of the Cartesian heritage, is the demand of total explicitness, the refusal to see any lurking opacity behind what can be clearly formulated, thoroughly apprehended, arbitrarily chosen. Add to this shrunken remnant of Cartesian reason the vector of intentionality, the tie of thought to its object, and you have the truncated dialectic that is Sartre's philosophy, the unending oscillation between a meaningless other out-there and an empty center in-here.

However Sartre has elaborated the relation of the self, and, in particular, of the writer, to society, he has never abandoned or broadened the limits of his philosophy. Take the relation of my consciousness to my body. My body, says Sartre, is the necessity of my contingency, the stubborn flaunting by myself to myself of the limits of my project, of my fancy. We have here subjectivism versus its denial, sheer being versus the subjectivity that is *its* denial. This is but the first stage of the irresoluble conflict that is to follow. Beyond this most intimate otherness, all contact with external things or agencies equally represents their threat to myself. For if my self-consciousness is but the denial of them, they are the denial, the annihilation of my self-consciousness. Thus the chestnut root nauseates Roquentin. Thus, a fortiori, every other person, himself a denier of the world of which he makes me part, threatens me with extinction. And Sartre's social perspective, finally, the perspective of committed literature, looks out, not on any concrete I-thou relationship, any communion in submission to a common cause; that would be the self-deception of bad faith. On the contrary, his social perspective looks out upon a great web of such I-other conflicts, where each is entangled by the threat of all the others; and so, despite themselves, they weave themselves into a society. Union here can be only indirect, through common hatred: "Hell is the others."

All this follows closely and clearly from Sartre's philosophical starting point. In arguing that this is so I have, as I mentioned earlier, been restating in large part Merleau-Ponty's criticism of Sartre. But Merleau-Ponty also reproaches him in another way. He is, he says, too much of a writer.[10] This is at first sight a puzzling statement. What seems to be wrong with Sartre is that he lacks the breadth of starting point needed to allow communication with his fellow men; but surely writers do want to communicate. How is it then *as a writer* that Sartre conceives the self as so isolated, the world of imagination as a dimensionless void? Ironically, Sartre himself, in the first volume of his autobiography, published since Merleau-Ponty's death, has both illuminated and amply justified his friend's reproach. The book, of course, is called *Words*, and the title is brilliantly chosen, for he shows us there how from early childhood he lived in a fictional world, a world made by himself in and through romancing, in and through words, taken not as a means of reaching out to others, but as a means of hiding himself from them and building inwardly an imagined kingdom all his own. It was a kingdom where, as Merleau-Ponty said, "all is significance,"[11] but luminously, unequivocally, significance, where the ambiguities, the silences, the unsayable realities that underlie all living speech could be forgotten or denied. This strange unchildlike childhood already expresses the quality of existence Merleau-Ponty was describing by the phrase "too much a writer," or that I was trying to convey in calling Sartre "a man of words."

It is this quality, too, that strains and stultifies Sartre's use of existential concepts in philosophy. Consider briefly the four concepts listed above. First, Heidegger's *being-in-a-world* becomes for Sartre not so much being-in as being-over-against; it is confrontation, not indwelling, I *against* the other. The *person* as mind and body, second, is, as we have seen, but the narrowest arena of this opposition. Third, *communication,* the relation to other persons, remains forever the expression of contradiction and antagonism. Strictly speaking, there are only my words, but no hearer to address them to. And finally, what of Sartrean freedom? Plainly, on Sartre's premises, in terms of the dialectic of being and nothingness, we are *indeed* condemned to be free. Freedom is unqualified and absolute but impotent. The Sartrean hero seeks his own act but, unless in the perverse inversions of a Genet, he can never find it. For like Sartrean imagination, and indeed as the very being of the imaginer, it is essentially denial over against, never within, the world, that world which alone could give it concrete embodiment.

Merleau-Ponty begins, according to his own statement, where Sartre leaves off, not with the imaginary, sundered from the real, but with the union of real and unreal, of affirmation and denial, that marks our living experience.[12] This statement, however, is not quite accurate, since Sartre, starting from the two bare abstracts, being and nothingness, is unable to achieve a viable synthesis between these contraries. What Merleau-Ponty's statement does truthfully convey, however, is, for one thing, the kinship of his thought with Sartre. They both move intellectually within the sphere of influence of the phenomenology of Heidegger and Husserl, and, as I have already suggested, Merleau-Ponty's thought often resonated closely to Sartre's own literary work. But Merleau-Ponty's statement also puts, if not precisely, the very sharp opposition that does in fact separate the two. Merleau-Ponty begins, not where Sartre *does* leave off, but where he ought to arrive and cannot, i.e., with the concrete situation of the individual person, projecting, not an abstraction, but himself. For the phenomenon Merleau-Ponty starts from and remained with as *his* problem is not the emptiness of Sartrean imagination, but the fullness of real, embodied, ongoing perception, perception not over against the world, but in it.

It was visual perception, in particular, that especially concerned him (hence my slogan "man of vision"); and for him the paradigm case, the activity that uniquely shows us what perception is, was the activity of the painter. Not the writer making fables for himself, but the artist making a world—*our* world—through eye and hand and canvas: that is the person we should look to, to learn both what the world is and what we are. In his earliest book, *The Structure of Behavior*, he had already suggested that it is through art that human transcendence, our way of being in the world, can best be understood.[13] And in an essay, *The Eye and the Mind*, written the year before he died, he was still haunted by this theme. For the painter, he believed, withdraws behind the world to make the world afresh. It is not, Cézanne said, a picture the painter is trying to create, but a piece of nature itself. And of Cézanne, who is for him the painter *par excellence*, Merleau-Ponty says: "His work seems to us inhuman because it is making humanity, going behind the everyday human world, creating the hidden handling of experience through

which we make our world the world it is, through which we people it
with objects.'' He does this, Merleau-Ponty says, by using the impressionists' discoveries, and then transcending them to restore the object.
Impressionism, he says, ''was attempting to reproduce in painting the
effect objects have as they strike the eye or attack the senses. It represents them in the atmosphere where we perceive them instantaneously
with absolute shape bound to each other by light and air.'' Now to get
this effect, it was necessary to use only the seven colors of the prism,
eliminating ochre and the earth colors, and also to take into account the
reverberation of complementary colors. Thus if it was a question of
grass, not only green but its complement red had to be hinted at as well.
And further, of course, the impressionists conveyed the airiness they
wanted by breaking up the local hue itself. So, Merleau-Ponty says, ''a
canvas which no longer corresponds to nature, point by fine point,
restores by the interaction of its parts the general truth of the impression.'' But Cézanne went further than this. He used not only the seven
colors of the prism, but eighteen colors: six reds, five yellows, three
blues, three greens, one black. ''And this use of warm colors and of
black, show,'' Merleau-Ponty argues, ''that Cézanne wishes to represent the *object*, to rediscover it behind the atmosphere.'' ''At the same
time,'' Merleau-Ponty continues, ''he renounces the division of hue and
replaces it by graduated mixtures, by an unfolding of chromatic
shadows on the object, by a color modulation which follows the form
and the light received by he object.'' But the fact that color dominates
the pattern, does not, he says, have the same meaning in Cézanne as in
impressionism: ''The object is no longer obscured by reflections, lost in
its relations with the air and with other objects; *it is as though a secret
light glowed within it, light emanates from it, and there results an
impression of solidity and matter.*'' [14]

Yet if modern painting has wrestled with such problems with new
theories and new techniques, the task of the painter through the ages has
been a constant one: to reveal and remake the achievement of visual perception which in our routine lives we perform without focal awareness
or reflection. ''The visible in the layman's sense forgets its premises,''
he remarks in *The Eye and the Mind*. [15] The painter recalls these
premises, and so exhibits them to us explicitly, at a reflective level, as it
were, yet immediately, in our perception of the painting, so that we see,
not simply the object, but the object *as* we see it: we reenact our seeing.
In the *Night Watch* the hand pointing at us in the center of the painting is
caught again in profile as shadowed on the captain's body. It is this kind
of fusion of nonfusible aspects, Merleau-Ponty argues, which make us
''see things and a space.'' But in perception *of* things and space we see
through such play of contrary aspects: perception points *to* the thing,

and does so by its own self-concealment. To see the thing, says Merleau-Ponty, it was necessary not to see the very premises on which in fact our vision rests. It is this act of seeing *from* the play of aspects *to* the thing in space that the painter reveals to us.

But in the act of vision so revealed we have found the world not so much over against us as around us. Seeing is not only a confrontation, but an indwelling. It is "having at a distance," and this "bizarre possession" too the painter reveals to us. Merleau-Ponty rebukes Berenson for praising Giotto's "evocation of tactile values"; painting "evokes" nothing, he insists, "least of all the tactile." On the contrary, "it gives visible existence to what lay vision believes invisible, it brings it about that we have no need of a 'muscular sense' to possess the voluminousness of the world." The vision of the painter, doubly mediated—indeed, triply, through our seeing of it—this "devouring vision," as he calls it, "beyond the 'visual data,'" opens upon a texture of being whose separate sensory messages are but the punctuation or the caesuras, and which the eye inhabits, as a man inhabits his home."[16]

"The eye inhabits being, as a man inhabits his home": a very tissue of "category mistakes," yet a true, and, for the philosophy of perception, a revolutionary statement. However complex an achievement vision may be—and if we think of its neurological foundation it is immensely complex—in its phenomenological being, in its "what," it is immersion in the world: a distanceless distance, a living *in* that extends the existence of the seer to the outer limits of his seeing, and concentrates the seen in him as its center. Our visual perception is the most striking example of what Plessner calls "mediated immediacy." And this immediacy of the mediated, necessarily forgotten in the pragmatic use of sensory input, is, again, just what the painter is striving to demonstrate. He reverses the ordinary direction of outgoing, practical vision: the world fascinates him, draws him to it. Thus a painter confesses: "In a forest I have sometimes felt that it was not I who was looking at the forest, I have felt on certain days that the trees were looking at me. I was there, listening."[17] Merleau-Ponty inserted in the original edition of *The Eye and the Mind* a print of Klee's *Park bei Luzern* which vividly exemplifies this mood. Yet at the same time, *through* this receptivity, the painter creates the visible world, and himself, its viewer and inhabitant: "I expect to be inwardly submerged, buried. Perhaps I paint in order to rise up."[18]

Out of this immersion in the world, then, the painter makes the world, and shows us how, through "making" it, we have immersed ourselves in it. This interpretation of the painter's task is illustrated, for example, in Merleau-Ponty's discussion of Cézanne's "return to color" in his later work. Cézanne himself said of color: " it is the place where our brain and the universe meet." What did he mean by this? It was not, Merleau-Ponty assures us, a question of finding colors "like the colors of nature"; it was a question of seeing, and working, in "the *dimension* of color, which creates, of itself for itself, identities, differences, a materiality, a something." Not that this gives us a "recipe for the visible": there is no such recipe, not in color any more than in space. But "the return to color has the merit of leading a little closer to the 'heart of things'"—though it is "beyond the color envelope as it is beyond the space envelope."[19] The color technique of the *Portrait of Vallier* illustrates Merleau-Ponty's point here: the whites used among the colors, he says, "have . . . the function of shaping, or cutting out a being more general than being-yellow or being-green or being-blue." But the most striking example is that of the late water-colors. Whatever the merits or demerits of Merleau-Ponty's interpretation of Cézanne in general, his description here is perspicuous: "in the water-colors of the last years," he writes, "space, of which one would suppose that it is self-evidence itself, radiates about planes which we cannot assign to any place." We have rather "the superposition of transparent surfaces," the "floating movement of planes of color which cover each other, advance and retreat."[20] Nor is it a question here, he insists, of adding "another dimension to the two dimensions of the canvas, of organizing an illusion or a perception without an object, the perfection of which would be to resemble as much as possible our empirical vision." "For the depth of a picture (and likewise its height and breadth) comes from we know not where, to present itself, to grow out of the frame. The painter's vision is no longer a looking at an *out-there*, a 'physical-optical' relation, solely with the world. The world is no longer before him through representation: it is rather the painter *who is born in the things* as if by concentration and as the coming to itself of the visible."[21] Thus the painter bodies forth the emergence of the visible as the birth of our being, the emergence of ourselves as seeing beings, and of the world as the colored, spatial sphere in which we are.

We must beware, therefore, of the sort of talk that puts qualities, feelings on the canvas. The painting, once achieved, haunts us as the world does when we have shaped it into a world. The painting is not on the canvas, nor at the place, if there is one, represented by it. It is ambiguously and embracingly here, nowhere and everywhere. Cézanne's *Mt. Sainte Victoire*, transcending the "moment of the world" when he painted it, will be always wherever people have eyes to see. "It is made and remade from one of the world to the other, differently, but no less actually than the hard rock above Aix."[22] To deny this is to misread radically the painter's gift. In this connection, Merleau-Ponty made explicit his opposition to Sartre on the theory of visual art. Sartre had written of Tintoretto's *Road to Golgotha*:

That yellow rending of the sky above Golgotha is an agony made into a thing, an agony that has turned into a yellow rending of the sky, and is suddenly submerged by . . . the qualities of things, their impermeability, their extension, their blind permanence. . . . That is to say, it is no longer legible, it is like an immense vain effort, forever stopped halfway between heaven and earth, meant to express what the very nature of things prevents them from expressing.[23]

Thus the painting is, for Sartre, in the last analysis, a thing, over against me, threatening me, like every other thing. What "feeling" it does convey is, he says, a little "haze of heat" hovering about the canvas. To this, Merleau-Ponty replied:

This impression is perhaps inevitable among professionals of language, the same thing happens to them that happens to all of us when we hear a foreign language which we speak badly: we find it monotonous, marked by too strong an accent and flavor, just because it is not ours and we have not made of it the principal instrument of our relation with the world.[24]

But for the painter, he continues, and for us too if we devote ourselves to living in painting,

the sense of the painting is much more than a little haze on the surface of the canvas, since it was capable of demanding *this* color and *this* object in preference to any other and since it commands the arrangement of the picture as imperiously as a syntax or a logic. For the whole picture is not in these little agonies or joys with which it is besprinkled: they are only components in a total sense less pathetic, more *legible* and more enduring.[25]

Merleau-Ponty illustrates his point by retelling the anecdote of the innkeeper of Cassis who was watching Renoir at work. Renoir, intently watching the sea, was painting washerwomen at a stream. "He kept gazing," the puzzled onlooker said, "at I know not what and then changed one little corner." How can one look at the sea in order to paint a fresh-water stream? How could the sea tell Renoir about the washerwomen's brook? "The fact is," says Merleau-Ponty, "that every fragment of the world—and in particular the sea, so riddled with eddies and waves, so plumed with spray, so massive and immobile in itself, contains all sorts of shapes of being, and by its manner of reply to the onlooker's attack, evokes a series of possible variants, and teaches beyond itself, a general manner of saying what is."[26] Painting, in short, embodies our openness to being. Even in speech, and more strikingly in the arts that speak through silence, it is the ineffable ground of being itself that the artist seeks to encounter and that addresses us through his work. All meaning means what cannot be said; even the most formal signs carry their significance not in themselves but in what they signify, in what we understand *through* them. And in painting we have, visible and incarnate, the concrete expression of this tension, this reverberation between sign and signified, meaning and what is meant. This is intentionality, not caught between two unattainable abstractions, but at home. The painter shows us our being-in-the-world in its original quality, drawn to being and within it, yet, within it, absent from it in our withdrawal, in our gaze. For this tension of being and distance-from-being, again, is not a seesaw like that of Sartre's being and nothingness, but a living unity-in-separation, ineradicably equivocal, bright and shadowy at once, with the opacity and the luminousness of being itself. "In this circuit," says Merleau-Ponty, "there is no rupture, it is impossible to say where nature ends and man or expression begins. For it is voiceless Being itself which comes to us here, in vision, to show forth its proper meaning."[27] That is why, Merleau-Ponty argues, the dilemma of representative versus abstract art is badly stated: no object is ever *wholly* like its "representation," and at the same time even the most abstract painting "represents" reality; it is in this sense that "the grapes of Caravaggio are the grapes themselves".[28]

Painting, then, shows us paradigmatically the character of our being-in-a-world. It does so, secondly, because, as the art of and through vision, it displays as no other activity can the single equivocal unity of the person, a unity that Merleau-Ponty expresses in the phrase *le corps vécu*, the "lived body," and which can perhaps be better expressed in English by speaking of embodiment, of the person as "embodied."

The painter, Valéry said, brings his body with him; and indeed, Merleau-Ponty comments, we could not imagine a disembodied spirit *painting*. Nor, for that matter, would speech be possible for a pure mind, detached from tongue or pen. Speech is significance *in* sound or ink or chalk; it is mental and physical *at once*. Even so, a Sartrean life of words, of a pure verbalizing consciousness, is at least a possible illusion. If thought is, as Plato said, the dialogue of the soul with itself, we can at least imagine it running on, cut off from reality, in a kind of ghost world. But every painter, however "abstract" his style, is working, with arm and hand, to shape physical material, colors and lines. The painter at work stands, for Merleau-Ponty, for the bodily rootedness of all creative activity.

But, you may well ask, why only painting? Why not sculpture? Why not music? The sculptor shapes material with his hands, much as we try, in our projection of ourselves into the future, to shape the contingent material of our lives. And even better, perhaps, the composer working with sounds shapes a temporal material, he gives significant form to successive as well as simultaneous events. The shape of a human life, surely, is much more closely mirrored here than in the quiescent two-dimensional surface of a picture. If life itself may be described as *configured time*,[29] then it is music that we should take as the art that can best teach us what we are. The ear is as truly embodied spirit as the eye. And admittedly, Merleau-Ponty did say, in the *Structure of Behavior*, that it is art in general that best reveals the way in which we fashion our biological environment into a human world.[30] But it is certainly the case of painting in particular that haunted him till the end of his life.

For it is painting that is most plainly and purely the art of vision, and for Merleau-Ponty it is visual perception that most clearly expresses the way we live our bodily lives. For one thing, vision is presence in absence: in it our very being is fused with distant objects, we become part of them and they of us. Moreover, the awareness of what is visible embraces at the same time an invisible: when I look at an orange, I see the whole round object even though only one aspect of it is strictly present to my eyes. When I hear a passing car, I hear a *car*, not just a noise of which I then proceed to judge, that is a car. My perceptive grasp of things is always already interpretative. That fact remains, whatever sense I use as my example. Indeed, Merleau-Ponty himself insists that perception in its living existence is synesthetic: we grasp, through our senses and more than our senses, through the whole complex series of transactions with the world that constitutes experience, the presence about us of other things and other lives. It is only in analysis and reflection that we separate the five senses and learn to understand their distinctive achievements. Despite this common basis of cooperation among the separate or separable channels of sense, however, there *is* a special way in which visual perception illustrates the character of the lived body. Vision exemplifies as no other sense does what we may call the mutuality of subject and object. I not only see, I am in part visible to myself, and I am wholly visible to all others. I can look at other people and they can look at me. This seems so obvious as to need no statement, let alone the tortuous paragraphs and pages that Merleau-Ponty devotes to his theme. But it is, all the same, the kind of obvious truth that has far-reaching philosophical consequences when you look at it more closely. A Sartrean consciousness gazing at another person must either make him an object or succumb to becoming one himself: there is no mutuality of gaze. Even a dumb object, Roquentin's chestnut root, by its very existence makes my consciousness absurd. But, Merleau-Ponty insists, vision is already *as such* vision *by* a visible body: it is not subject fighting to the death with object, consciousness against body, but always and in its very essence the two in one. So he says, in one of the most pregnant statements of his favorite—indeed, almost his obsessive—theme:

Visible and mobile, my body is numbered among things, it is one of them, it is caught in the tissue of the world and its cohesion is that of a thing. But because it sees and moves itself, it holds things in a circle around itself, they are an annex and a prolongation of itself, they are encrusted in its flesh, they form part of its full definition and the world is made of the very stuff of the body. These reversals, these antinomies are different ways of saying that vision takes place or develops out of the medium of things, there where a visible being sets about seeing, becomes visible for itself and for the vision of all things.[31]

Again, this paradoxical direct-indirectness, this active passivity of vision, Merleau-Ponty believes, is quintessentially expressed in painting. This system of exchanges once given, he says, "all the problems of painting are there. They illustrate the enigma of the body and it justifies them." Cézanne had said, "Nature is within." Merleau-Ponty comments, "Quality, light, color, depth, which are out there before us, are so only because they awaken an echo in our body, because it makes them welcome." And from this inner echo, "this fleshly formula of their presence that things evoke in me," springs the painter's creation: the seen at one remove, yet immediate, even more immediate, in its reflective reality, "a trace, visible in its turn, where every other eye will rediscover the motives which support its inspection of the world." The painting, in short, is "a visible to the second power, fleshly essence or icon of the first."[32]

Thus painting is far from being an "image" in the sense of an unreal copy of some prosaic reality; it has its nature in the very "duplicity," as Merleau-Ponty calls it, of perception itself. Now in fact this thesis of the ambiguity of perception and especially of the interplay of perceiver and perceived, is a favorite motif of painters. They like to present, for example, that most striking and uniquely human phenomenon, the mirrored image of ourselves, which shows us ourselves in a kind of half reality as others see us. A mirrored life is a uniquely human life; no other animal lives in this strange, ambiguous relation to its own body. Consider, for example, the complex mirrorings of Velasquez's famous court scene, *Las Meninas*. Matisse's fascination with painting himself painting expresses a kindred theme. The painter is immersed in the visible world, struggling to express its visibility, yet he himself, doing this, is visible to himself doing this. Both cases—the mirror, and the painter painting his own activity of painting—generate an infinite regress that expresses the very heart of human reflectiveness. Not a still bright center of consciousness, but an inexhaustible proliferation of level upon level of significance, constitutes human thought.

But every level, every shade of meaning, however it transcend the here and now, is, again, rooted in bodily presence. Modern philosophy, under the spell of the scientific intellect, has forgotten this truth, Merleau-Ponty argues, and the insights of modern painting can show us where philosophy has failed. Modern thought, he says in *The Eye and the Mind*, is dominated by operationalism, that is, by the belief that all problems can be solved by the experimental manipulation of precisely specified variables. But significance never floats freely on the surface of things, as a scientistic philosophy would seem to suppose it does. It is always grounded in the being of the living, embodied individual; but individual life can only be *lived*, not said; in its opacity it eludes the formalisms of science, however powerful. The archetype of an operationalist theory of vision, for Merleau-Ponty, is Descartes' *Dioptrics*, where, as one might expect, vision is a matter of pure geometry, wholly transparent to the clear intellect. Descartes, Merleau-Ponty points out, shows little interest in painting; had he done so, he would have needed a different ontology. But when he does talk about it, what interests him exclusively is line and form. He might work out a theory of engraving, though even this would be, on his view, as it is not in fact, a mere copying of the geometry of the real extended world. But color in its living nature, color as it captures us, as we dwell in it, is wholly alien to a Cartesian mentality. Consider again the play of color which the impressionists have taught us to see. This is a reality of which the Cartesian theory of perception can give no account.

Perspective, too, in its bodily reality, is something different from the pure geometrical perspective of the intellect which interested Descartes. Merleau-Ponty points out, for example, how Cézanne uses the actual distortion of a line as seen. There is a portrait of Mme. Cézanne in which the border on both sides of the body fails to make a straight line; "but we know," he writes, "if a line passes under a large band of paper, the two visible segments appear dislocated." Similarly, in the *Portrait of Gustave Geffroy*, the table at the front spreads out before us—for when the eye traverses a broad surface, its images are taken from different points of view, and so the total surface is warped. "Cézanne's genius," he says, "is through the total arrangement of the picture to make the deformations in perspective cease to be visible in themselves when we look at them in the lump; and they only contribute, as they do in natural vision, to give the impression of an order in process of birth, an object in process of appearing, of collecting itself under our eyes. There is nothing less arbitrary than these celebrated deformations."[33] Indeed they are only in theory deformations; for in fact they restore the living reality which the intellect distorts.

Merleau-Ponty's account of what I have called the mutuality of vision, moreover, exemplifies also my third point of comparison with Sartre. Our being-in-the-world is indwelling as well as confrontation; and the world we dwell in is necessarily inhabited not only by things but by other persons too, by all those who see me, just as I see them. Communication is not an insoluble problem for Merleau-Ponty as it is for Sartre, but the given from which we start: the very emergence of myself as a center of experience reveals me as one among others. However isolated the painter in his struggle with the visible, therefore, he is struggling with, he is bringing into being, a common human world. The innkeeper did not understand what Renoir was doing at the seashore, but still the work Renoir created was there to speak to him and to all of us of the human condition, of the being in which together we are all immersed. So it is, again, that Cézanne's *Mont Ste. Victoire* can speak to all men always, everywhere.

The painter's place in the history of his art, moreover, Merleau-Ponty believes, shows us, more immediately than the history of literature can do, the nature of tradition. Each generation of painters has to deny the style of its predecessors and at the same time profits by their example; yet for all the painter's efforts to renew his art, the paintings of the past are there, present to us still. The writer, on the other hand, in writing, remakes language, and the literature of the past becomes at least partly obsolete, accessible to us only by an intellectual effort. It needs a verbal as well as imaginative exertion to read Chaucer; Giotto is there still, as near at least as Padua or Florence. Literature is more contemporary but also more temporary. The problem of painting, in contrast, is a quasi-eternal one, embodying, therefore, a single unbroken tradition. It remains, Merleau-Ponty says, "an abortive attempt to do what is always still to be done,"[34] yet an attempt which, in this forever uncompleted endeavor, unites men of each generation mutely but profoundly with the whole human past. "The field of pictorial meanings has been open," he writes, "ever since a man appeared in the world." This is so just because painting so truly mirrors the embodied situation: "The first drawing on the walls of caves founded a tradition only because it inherited another, that of perception. The quasieternity of art merges with the quasieternity of incarnate existence and we have in the exercise of our body and of our senses, insofar as they insert us in a world, the means of understanding our cultural gesticulation insofar as it inserts us in history. . . . The continuous attempt at expression establishes a single history—as the hold of our body on every possible object establishes a single space."[35] Here again communication with the past, as with the present, is the very ground out of which human existence springs. Temporally as well as spatially we dwell in and come to individual awareness out of our communal being.

History is a favorite theme of existential philosophers, yet Merleau-Ponty is the first writer in this tradition to found the historical being of man in communal existence. Existentialism is known with some justice as a philosophy of the lonely, alienated individual; but for Merleau-Ponty the dimension of human togetherness, both the communication of man with man and the immersion of the individual in a communal heritage, is a presupposition of human life. The painter speaks to his contemporaries of the world they see and of the way they see it, and he echoes a voice as old as man himself. It would be irrelevant here to compare Merleau-Ponty's conception of history or communication in general with that of other philosophers like Jaspers or Heidegger. But let me just look back briefly to compare the lesson Merleau-Ponty draws from painting with Sartre's theory of committed literature. For Sartre, the ego is not only isolated from others, but is itself simply a negation of the objects to which it is, in essence, a relation: it is the amputation by itself of itself from being. In committed literature this nonexistent existent, this empty ego, projects itself outward again to form a program of social action. This produces, however, as Merleau-Ponty rightly insists, not a literature of concrete activity, a reflection of history as lived, but an abstract, and false, equation of art with politics. It produces propaganda.

Here again, Sartre's premises allow him no other issue; and once more, we can express this limitation of his thought by pointing to his fascination with words, words for their own sake, not for their meaning, i.e., for what they point *to*, but cannot articulate. Speech itself, Merleau-Ponty reminds us, is grounded in silence. Even a novel has to speak, not in words, but through them; it has to signify through speech an unspoken reality, a style of life, that transcends words: "it expresses tacitly, like a painting."[36] But it is this *tacit* ground of speech which makes communication possible. There is no good in speaking if my hearer has ears but hears not, and his hearing is silent. That is why painting so usefully exhibits the nature even of speech in its primordial functioning, of what Merleau-Ponty calls "speaking speech" rather than mere language. Painting is the struggle for expression through silence, its voice is the voice of silence; and this paradigm, cut off from the abstract explicitness of language, can effectively exhibit, therefore, both the tacit ground of each act of communication, and the communion, through the "voices of silence," of each with all. It breaks the circle of verbalization and brings us face to face with one another in the world. It points toward the resonance of those occasions when we encounter one another, and toward the shared encounter with being, potentially reflective but never wholly reflected, which constitutes our common human destiny.

I listed at the beginning four concepts I wanted to mention in connection with Merleau-Ponty's view of art. So far I have referred to three of these: being-in-the-world, embodiment, and communication. Where for Sartre we have consciousness against the world, we have, for Merleau-Ponty, indwelling as the ground of confrontation. Where for Sartre we have the conflict of mind with body, and the internecine war of self against self, we have, with Merleau-Ponty, on the one hand, the integrity of the lived body, and on the other, the organic participation of the individual in a common cultural world. Finally, there remains the contrast in their conceptions of freedom. It is here that Merleau-Ponty's discussions of paintings and painters come closest to the practice of Sartre in his best literary criticism, yet we can see plainly in this case also how far he stands from Sartre in his basic philosophical beliefs.

In his reflections on painters and their lives, Merleau-Ponty practices what Sartre had christened "existential psychoanalysis," that is, he examines the artist's life as bearing on his work, and expressing it insofar as an artist's life *is* a life becoming expression. But that does not mean that the life, even in its hidden origins, determines the work. It is the man as artist in his whole projection of himself into the world that the existential critic seeks to understand; and that means to understand the work in its intrinsic significance, for the work *is* the artist's project, his freedom realized. When Van Gogh, Merleau-Ponty says, in painting *Crows over a Wheatfield*, sought to "go further," this was not a question of going one step further in a beaded causal sequence; the "further" expresses the tension that always subsists between the man who is not yet and the one who is already.[37] This is the pull of the future, full of significance not yet realized, upon a past waiting to be made significant. It is not a question here either of a one-level series of causal determinants and their effects, nor of a pure "spiritual" meaning, subsisting in a cloud-cuckooland all on its own. Rather, there is an essential polarity between the painter's life as ground and material of his work and the work as significant expression of and through the life. Thus Cézanne, Merleau-Ponty argues, would appear to an outside observer a schizoid type; even his good friend and biographer Bernard could fail to see the relevance of his sufferings to his task as a painter, could see them as mere weaknesses or eccentricities. And yet Cézanne's life has a bearing on the work, and expresses it, since in the last analysis Cézanne's life is the life "that this work demands."[38] In his practical criticism, in other words, Merleau-Ponty shows us the same equilibrium between the artist's work and his world which Sartre also exhibits in his accounts of Flaubert or Baudelaire. For Sartre, however, as I have tried to argue, this delicate balance of work and life, of significance and sheer happening, is always endangered by the Sartrean demand of *total freedom*. In a Sartrean free act I must make, not only my decision and my act, but the very standards by which I must decide. I make the world; singly and suddenly, I become God. But in fact I do no such thing—and so I become a useless passion, fallen back from the hopelessness of my infinite demands upon absurdity and despair. The ontology of being and nothingness, in other words, cannot in fact provide an adequate theory for the practice of existential criticism; Sartre's philosophy belies his best critical insights. In contrast,

Merleau-Ponty's theory of freedom is adapted to the needs of his practical criticism, which in turn confirms his theory. First, freedom for him is not literal and final, as for Sartre, but, like the lived body whose freedom it is, ambiguous. Cézanne is both schizoid sufferer *and* reshaper of the visibility of things. These are not two legs of a seesaw, but two aspects of the inescapable ambivalence, the irridescence of the very texture of our lives.

Second, freedom for Merleau-Ponty is indirect. The painter wrestling with a problem that grips him, struggling for expression with the material of line and color, the material of his experience, is displaying human freedom *through* the demands of his determinate situation, not somewhere else, over against them. Cézanne, says Merleau-Ponty, struggled and suffered and doubted to the end his power to do what in fact he was magnificently engaged in doing. "We never see our freedom face to face,"[39] not because, like Sartrean freedom, it is an impossible ideal, but because it is so real, woven into the intricate stuff of life itself.

And finally, freedom is never finished. Indeed, it *is* that openness to the future which most deeply marks our being in the world. Painting, we have seen, is always, in Merleau-Ponty's view, an abortive attempt to say what still remains to be said. It is a continuous grappling with a problem that remains always still to be solved. The intellect, he writes in the closing paragraphs of *The Eye and the Mind*, is disappointed by this conclusion: are we to go on always asking the same question, moving in a circle, in a state of continuous stupor? "But this disappointment," he writes, "is that of the imaginary in a mistaken sense, which demands a positivity that exactly fills its void. This is the regret at not being everything."[40] This seems to be his final comment on the imaginary of Sartre. But the frustration we face here in our intellectual being is compensated by a broader view: "if we can establish neither in painting nor indeed elsewhere, a hierarchy of civilizations, nor speak of progress, this is not because in a sense the first painting of all already reached into the depths of the future." Its task was not complete, but open, resonant of the future: "if no painting absolutely achieves the aim of painting, if indeed no work absolutely achieves itself, every creation changes, alters, illuminates, deepens, confirms, exalts, recreates or creates in advance all the others."[41]

In conclusion, I should like to think of the next and final sentence—the last of Merleau-Ponty's last complete work—as a hope also for his own uncompleted task, which may well reverberate in the future in ways unsuspected by himself. "If," he says in conclusion, "creations are not an acquisition, it is not only because, like all things, they pass away; it is also because they have almost all their lives before them."[42] This is, as against Sartre, Merleau-Ponty's principal merit. His arguments lack the dialectical rigor of Sartre's, they "circle round and round the same landscape." But it *is* a landscape, not a bundle of abstractions; we can live in it, philosophically, and even build in it, with help from a few like-minded thinkers, a conceptual home.[43] Sartre is the last of the Cartesians; he shows us, brilliantly and maddeningly, the impasse to which in our time the modern mind has come. Merleau-Ponty, groping, obsessed with one paradox—the paradox of visual perception—over-rhetorical, yet speaks to us as one of the first truly post-Cartesians. He gives us, if not a philosophy—perhaps not even a philosophy of visual art—a foundation on which we can build, and equally, to echo his own paradox, a view of the horizon toward which we can hope to move. The man of words alone is by profession the man of alienation; his philosophy is incurably a philosophy of alienation. The man of vision may teach us, in contrast, how to begin to build a philosophy of indwelling. He shows how in our very distance from things we are near them; he recreates conceptually, as, for him, the painter does iconically, our mediated immediacy, our attachment through detachment, the very core of our way of being-in-a-world, the puzzle of our freedom.

Notes

1. Maurice Merleau-Ponty, *Les Aventures de la Dialectique* (Paris: Gallimard, 1955), pp. 131 ff.

2. Ibid., p. 253. In what follows I have relied heavily on a number of Merleau-Ponty's discussions of Sartre, including some of the working notes in his posthumous and incompleted work *Le Visible et L'Invisible*; but, in order not to pepper my argument with references, I have not stopped to mention at each stage the Merleau-Pontyian text that supports my own reasoning.

3. Published in *Critique de la raison dialectique I* (Paris: Gallimard, 1960); trans. Hazel Barnes, *Search for a Method* (New York: Alfred A. Knopf, 1963).

4. Jean-Paul Sartre, Introduction to Jean Genet, *Our Lady of the Flowers* (London: Blond, 1964), p. 47.

5. Ibid., p. 53.

6. See *L'Imaginaire* (Paris: Alcan, 1940); *The Psychology of the Imagination* (New York: Rider, 1940).

7. See *The Transcendence of the Ego* (New York: Noonday Press, 1957). First published, "La Transcendance de l'Ego," in *Recherches philosophiques*, 6 (1936-37): 85-123.

8. Jean-Paul Sartre, *Situations* (New York: Fawcett World Library, 1966), p. 126. Cf. on the same page, "Giacometti is a sculptor because he carries his vacuum along with him, as a snail its shell. . . ." But compare also the treatment of Giacometti as graphic artist in a contrary sense in Merleau-Ponty's *L'Oeil et l'Esprit* (Paris: Gallimard, 1964), p. 24.

9. I have argued this in detail elsewhere; cf. my "Tacit Knowing and the Pre-Reflexive Cogito," in *Intellect and Hope* (Durham, N.C.: Duke University Press, 1968), or my

review of Manser's *Sartre* in *Mind,* 78 (1969): 141-152. [Note, 1975: This material is included in essence in my *Sartre* (New York: Franklin Watts, 1973).]

10. Cf. Merleau-Ponty, *Les Aventures de la Dialectique*, p. 271.

11. Ibid.

12. Merleau-Ponty, *Le Visible et L'Invisible* (Paris: Gallimard, 1964), p. 290.

13. Merleau-Ponty, *La Structure du Comportement*, 5th ed. (Paris: Presses Universitaires de France, 1963), p. 190.

14. Merleau-Ponty, "Le doute de Cézanne," in *Sens et Non-Sens* (Paris: Nagel, 1948), pp. 15-44, 19-21.

15. *L'Oeil et l'Esprit*, pp. 29-30. Merleau-Ponty's account here comes close to Polanyi's theory of tacit knowing; my use of "from-to" in particular is borrowed from him. See, for example, Michael Polanyi, *The Tacit Dimension* (New York: Doubleday & Company, 1966), or *Knowing and Being* (London: Routledge & Kegan Paul, 1969) and my Introduction to the latter.

16. *L'Oeil et l'Esprit*, pp. 26-27.

17. Ibid., p. 31.

18. Ibid.

19. Ibid., pp. 67-68.

20. Ibid.

21. Ibid., pp. 68-69.

22. Ibid., p. 35.

23. *Situations II*, p. 61; quoted in Merleau-Ponty, "Le Langage indirect et les Voix du Silence," in *Signes* (Paris: Gallimard, 1960), p. 69.

24. *Signes*, p. 69.

25. Ibid.

26. Ibid., p. 70.

27. *L'Oeil et l'Esprit*, pp. 86-87.

28. Ibid., p. 87.

29. See A. Portmann, "Die Zeit im Leben des Organismus," reprinted from *Eranos Jahrbuch* in *Biologie und Geist* (Freiburg: Herder, 1963), pp. 123 ff.

30. *La Structure du Comportement*, p. 190.

31. *L'Oeil et l'Esprit*, p. 19.

32. Ibid., pp. 21-22.

33. *Sens et Non-Sens*, pp. 34-35.

34. *Signes*, p. 99.

35. Ibid., p. 87.

36. Ibid., p. 95.

37. Ibid., p. 71.

38. *Sens et Non-Sens*, p. 35.

39. Ibid., p. 44.

40. *L'Oeil et l'Esprit*, pp. 92-93.

41. Ibid.

42. Ibid.

43. In particular, for example, Polanyi, Portmann, Plessner, perhaps also David Bohm. See my *Knower and the Known* (Berkeley: University of California Press, 1975), and *The Understanding of Nature* (Dordrecht: Reidel, 1974).

X

The Career of Action and Passion in Sartre's Philosophical Work

1974

THE GREATNESS OF SARTRE AS PHILOSOPHER LIES NOT SO MUCH IN THE truths he has to tell as in two other philosophical merits: on the one hand, the rigor with which his conclusions follow from theses of the philosophers who have most influenced him—first, Descartes, then Husserl, perhaps Heidegger, then, via Marx and Marxism, Hegel and the force of dialectical thinking—on the other hand, the subtlety and richness with which he has woven his texts, especially *Being and Nothingness*, out of these basic themes. I have attempted elsewhere to describe the relation of his thought to that of his major predecessors, and to analyze critically the structure of his own philosophical works. One question, however, often though it has been asked and even answered, continues to plague any student of Sartre as philosopher: the question of agency. Is there, has there been, can there be, a Sartrean theory of action? We touch here on the central flaw in his philosophy, which must trouble every reader, much as, for all "resolutions" of the problem, the question of freedom is bound to vex all students of Spinoza. Indeed, in this, Sartre and Spinoza are as close to one another as they are diametrically opposite. As a recurrent reader, and teacher, of Sartre, I too have been plagued by this central question. Its formulation here, I should add, owes a great deal to my reading of Pierre Verstraeten's brilliant work, *Éthique et Violence*.[1]

I am asking, then, about the possibility of a Sartrean theory of action, and want to put this question in terms of three subquestions. First, what is the role of role playing for Sartrean man? Second, assuming that action is not wholly solitary, but entails the Other, what is Sartre's theory of communication, primarily of language? Third—and this is the most fundamental question—what is the relation, according to Sartre, between action and passion? Sartre has worked, according to his own account, in three successive stages of his philosophical development, with three basic concepts: the "for-itself" in *Being and Nothingness*, "praxis" in the *Critique of Dialectical Reason*, and "the lived" in *The Idiot of the Family* (as well as in *Question of Method*, which forms the prologue to the *Critique*, but could as well, or better, have formed its epilogue). I shall try to apply each of my questions in turn to each phase of Sartre's philosophizing.

I

First, role playing. What role does role playing play in each of Sartre's three periods? This is where Sartre himself, I believe, has most clearly seen the problem of action and his own dilemma in the face of it. The problem is certainly central in *Being and Nothingness*: the question of bad faith or its (im)possible contrary revolves around it. The waiter acting as waiter, playing his social role, has fled his freedom. The attractive girl, playing the innocent, while her would-be (and to-be) seducer holds her hand, is practicing a self-deception which her lover perfectly understands though she does not. One seems to have a choice between an honest agent playing no role—then what *can* he do?—or a role player who by accepting a role has already betrayed the total responsibility to himself of the free agent.

Let me put the question literally. What kind of agent is a professional role player, that is, an actor? Sartre has put this question on the stage in his dramatization of Dumas's *Kean*. Henri Peyre, in a review of several of Sartre's plays, finds nothing of philosophical import in *Kean*.[2] Yet, far from containing no philosophical message, *Kean* seems to me the best possible vehicle for Sartre's most fundamental problem. Man must make himself. He is born essenceless; he must make himself be what he is not and not be what he is. That is exactly the task to which, as Plato saw, the actor is professionally committed. Plato could reject such endless self-transformation, and therefore, in his view, self-betrayal; he could banish drama from his ideal city in the name of the Good it was to serve. For Sartre, on the contrary, the Good is worse than evil, for evil, like freedom, is negative, and therefore can be human, while Good is positive and so inhuman. Nowadays, what's worse, the Good is not only substance, like Plato's Ideal Good; it is bourgeois substance, the property of proprietors, who take refuge from the emptiness of freedom in the passive and meaningless solidity of their possessions. It is Podsnappery. So man is left as agent without anchor in the Good, that is, precisely, as Plato's actor. Sartre suggests, in the program notes for

Kean, that after a hundred years the play still appeals to actors as a vehicle, because this is the closest they can come to playing *themselves*.[3] The actor playing an actor is playing what he is: he is assuming, while not being that other, the being of an Other. Acting is like living in a hall of mirrors: images of images in a dizzying regression and multiplication of nonentity. But isn't that the condition of each of us, unless indeed we have given in irretrievably to the more sinister illusion of Decency or Sovereign Good? Even Sartre's hero Genet is not only "martyr" but "actor" (*comédien*). Of the tricks of his passive homosexuality Sartre writes:

> Is it a comedy? Yes and no. His obedience is *real* because it truly fulfills his mission, because he runs true risks to carry out the orders of his beloved; but on the other hand it is *imaginary* because he is submitting only to a creature of his mind.[4]

And of Genet himself:

> We have returned here to the paradox of which we had seen earlier that it was the original and profound structure of Genet's sensibility: it is that he cannot distinguish between what he feels and what he plays at feeling.[5]

Not only Genet's paradox, but humanity's. The for-itself makes itself, by its own act, either as nihilation of being, and so as translucent emptiness, the very quintessence of the actor, who as himself is nothing, or through the bad faith of submission to society, assuming a quasi solidity that is equivalent to self-loss: one has been made an object, as Genet had been at the outset of his long pilgrimage; one can only make a pretence of humanity. Playacting or hypocrisy, that is our choice.[6]

I have put my question in terms of the problem of the actor, but it is equivalent, for Sartre, at least in the period of *Being and Nothingness*, and a decade later in *Kean* or *Saint Genet*, to the problem of the agent. The failure of Hume's theory of experience, of the person as a congeries of psychological atoms, consisted, as he himself saw, in the fact that there was nobody there. The failure of the Sartrean free agent, strangely, is the same: the house is empty, unless full of fools and knaves.

Is there a change in the *Critique*? If there is to be history, praxis must be its foundation, and praxis is still the infinite choice of the totally free consciousness. (That it is the praxis of the "practical organism" makes no essential difference.)[7] True, the past—mine, my family's, my nation's, mankind's—has made me what I am. Facticity, the necessity of contingency, Sartre had always recognized. But I have still the total, indivisible responsibility of making of that made-me the I *I* choose to make of it. It is praxis as free action that Sartre claims to have inserted into the heart of a "Marxist" theory of history. Does this mean, then, that, in terms of the *Critique*, I could freely and honestly take on a social role? On the whole, I think not. Although there is, or was once, on July 14, the group in fusion where men acted freely together, that ephemeral configuration fails on at least three counts to validate the free assumption of social roles. First, Sartre's device for establishing a foundation for social action is far too contrived. This is the third man; in Sartre's example, *A*, from the window of his country inn, sees on one side *B* working on the road, on the other side, *C* working in the fields, and so brings these two otherwise unconnected praxes together by his observation. Second, moreover, the situation that allows such mediation to produce a group in fusion is still the total opposition of *Being and Nothingness*, which needed only the slightest touch to become classical Marxist *Klassenkampf*. The men of the Faubourg St. Antoine together hate, together combat, the *they* who threaten them with death by famine or gunfire. There is no society here, let alone roles in society, but a crisis, which brings together for a moment basically isolated agents. It is I who will starve or be shot. And, if you and you and you face the same lethal alternative, we are, transiently, united in the negative aim of fighting to the death the common enemy. There is so far no we-ourselves, hence no society; hence there are no social roles, except in the indirect fashion of a shared outbreak of violence against the Other we each singly and, by mediation, jointly hate. And third, the *praxis* of the group in fusion, passing, gives way to the practico-inert, to series, to institutions, where roles, again, are solidified as *in*human, even more clearly and irretrievably alienations of freedom than was the bad faith of Sartre's earlier period. The same holds, moreover, of the second oath, which is said to produce "organization" and to permit the initiation and acceptance of social functions. It would be here, if anywhere, that the free enactment of social roles might, one hopes, be realized. But even "organization," Sartre argues, produces *norms*, and these, he still insists, entail the gap between consciousness and object that constitutes alienation. Kantian autonomy, "respect for the law," is for him still unintelligible. Where there is law, it seems, there is so far always loss of freedom, always dishonesty and enslavement.[8]

Sartre's third fundamental concept, *le vécu*, the lived, finally, seems at first sight to remove him still further from discovering a synthesis of agency and action, of freedom and social role playing. He is asking, Can one person understand another? and seeking in the case of Sartre vis-à-vis Flaubert to find out. But if we try to assess the import of this task from the perspective of *Question of Method* or of *The Idiot*, we are faced with an even sharper dichotomy than before. On the one hand, the "lived" Sartre is looking for seems to be the very inwardness of consciousness experienced, a for-itself somehow experienced by another for-itself, not as the Other, but as for-itself. Society will be wholly external to this wholly inner lived consciousness, as external as were the efficient but unloving hands of Mme. Flaubert ministering (in Sartre's "fable") to the needs of the infant Gustave. Gustave, coming to consciousness, is prey to society: to his father's status, his elder brother's seniority—facts as dead as the cold corpses in the morgue downstairs. On the other hand, the adolescent Gustave does play a role, that of Le Garçon in the obscene farce he and his schoolfellows contrived. But that role, like the other roles Flaubert assigned himself in the juvenile writings Sartre quotes at length, is meant entirely to corrode; it is directed against society by its "idiotic" reject. The lived, an inner and impotent reality, and the role, an external, quasi-active illusion, are wholly opposed to one another, as were the nonentity of the actor and the part he plays or the praxis of the individual in history and the institutions that take him over and estrange him from himself. True, there is one role that is to rescue Flaubert, as there was one role that has saved Genet. Genet made himself a poet; Flaubert, one hoped, in volume four, was to make himself maker of Emma, who, by his own avowal, was himself. To this seemingly unique resolution of the conflict, the role of the poet or the novelist, I shall return in the context of my third question.

Before I proceed, however, let me refer to another treatment of roleplaying in human life, from which the incentive for the above reflections was at least in part derived. In a series of lectures delivered at Boston University in 1972-73, most of which I heard but which I have not read, Alasdair MacIntyre compared the sociological analysis of roles by Erving Goffman (in *The Presentation of the Self in Everyday Life*) with the Sartrean theory of free self-choice. Goffman describes roleplaying and equates it smugly and unreflectively with being human. For him, it's a nonproblem. Sartre wants to reject roleplaying as unfree or self-deceiving, yet, as I have argued, cannot escape its fascination. Goffman's unproblematic data pose, for him, an inescapable problem. MacIntyre, rightly enough, is satisfied with neither position, but wants to develop a "narrative" model of man which will both accredit the role of roles and tie them, when "authentic," if I may borrow that ill-used term, to a core that is the person, not just the *personnage*, nor even, as for Goffman, a collection of *personnages*. (It comes, in English, to the difference between "character" and "character.") Whether Sartre can develop such a hopeful issue of his dilemma remains to be seen; again, that is a point to which I shall return in conclusion.

II

My second question may appear irrelevant. "Action theory" and "philosophy of language," philosophical "specialists" may protest, are two different subjects. Yet "speech acts" are acts, and, conversely, all human action, however mute, is imbued with speech. For it takes its origin in a culture, which is made by and in a language. Even if preverbal or subverbal expressions, like smiling or frowning, are species-universal as well as species-specific, they are minimal expressions of humanization. It is as the child takes on the use of his mother tongue, as he becomes a language user, that he becomes a human agent. A philosopher's theory of language seems, therefore, a good touchstone for his theory of action. One might argue, too, that this should hold especially for Sartre, who is to the core "a man of words." When asked if he might continue his autobiography, he replied, "Why? I've shown how I came to be a writer. What else would be of interest?" And he has analyzed, for example, in "What is Literature?" or in an interview on "The Writer and His Language," the vocation of the writer, the poet, the dramatist, the philosopher. Besides, he was, when he wanted to be (which was by no means always), a superb master of prose style. So one might expect of him, if any philosopher, a developed theory of language. What do we find? Again, let us enquire, if we can, of each of the three stages on Sartre's way, what, according to him, language is, and how it relates to the possibility of action.

In the period of the for-itself, the word, like every cultural artifact, is a tool for the conquest of the in-itself, or for the transformation of a recalcitrant Other into the in-itself (or nearly so). Language is a form of seduction. It serves to nihilate the threat of the Other by reducing him (her?) to flesh. Indeed, in terms of the categories "Being" and "Nothingness," it could serve no other purpose. Except for the "we" of the class struggle, which is indirect and negative, the only possible relations between one for-itself and an Other are sadism or masochism. Sadism says, let me violate you; masochism says, Yes, I like to be hurt. A strange view for a master of language? But he *possesses* language; indeed, it was, in the adoptive home of his grandfather, the child Jean-Paul's only possession. He can do his will with it, use or abuse it, caress or torture it, as he likes. Besides, for a radical Cartesian, whose primary medium is consciousness, language comes a poor second to thought. It is ironic that Chomsky should have written a *Cartesian Linguistics*, for Descartes doesn't have a "linguistics." It is the properly ordered series of *ideas* that matters, not their verbalization. And in this, as Iris Murdoch pointed out some years ago, the Sartre of *Being and Nothingness* is still a rationalist. It is the for-itself making itself in its pure, inner freedom that he is after, not the words it ejects into the world to confess, if, *per impossible*, it can, its agonizing task. So language, uninteresting in its own character, is a tool, like any other tool, for conquering the world.

This is a wretched theory of language; I know few worse. And, as I have suggested, it shows up by its poverty the poverty of Sartre's view of action as well. There can be, Wittgenstein and Wittgensteinians have argued to good effect, no private language. Even inner thought, Plato insisted, is the dialogue of the soul with itself. In other words, language requires as its necessary condition not only *an* Other whom I seek to cast down toward thinghood, but the *world* of others, an intersubjective world within which I can come to myself as language user, and therefore as human agent. But it is just this "kingdom of ends," this world of agents among whom I act, whether with or against them, that Sartre radically rejects:

> Someone I once here pronounce the words "we doctors . . . ," I know that he's in bondage. That "we doctors" is his me, a parasitic creature that sucks his blood. . . . I don't like inhabited souls.[9]

Now of course I know, as every victim of American medicine knows, that in many, though not all cases, to belong to the A.M.A. is indeed to have enslaved one's soul, to fatten oneself on the sufferings of others. And of course I know, too, as any halfway honest appointee of any institution knows, that there are bureaucrats, legions of them, in every calling, people like "the man in the case," who take their very being from their profession or from their club membership or even still sometimes from their birth. I know, too, that I, as a "good citizen" of a public institution, as a committee member, an examiner, an officer of a professional organization, a professor-who-gets-on-well-with-the-dean, etc., etc.—that I, too, am "an inhabited soul," not like the souls of Plato's myth, stripped down to their fundamental uprightness or iniquity. But it is also true that it is the inhabitant, or better the habitation, that makes the person: what makes him is the content through which, or the shelter within which, he can become whatever human being he has, within limits, the power to become. I refuse to believe that whenever I say "our department" or "our college" or even "our university" I have necessarily thereby enslaved myself. No, when I use such phrases I am also expressing the fact that I am what I have, with luck as well as effort, become: a teacher of philosophy to the American young. Moreover, that is also, like writing, a verbal profession. Is it a form of seduction? Sometimes, indeed, it is. Every teacher has his bag of tricks, with which he amuses and ensnares his audience. But those are trimmings. Fundamentally, "we philosophy teachers'' are neither clowns nor slaves, but workers, whether with more or less success, at the task of conveying, and developing, the thoughts to which philosophical reflection has long given, and still gives, rise. However corrupt our government, however evil a civilization founded primarily on greed, the fact remains that teaching philosophy to our undergraduates, and even graduates, consists basically in the free communication, through language, of one mind, or one person, with others, and, reciprocally, of others with oneself. Despite the admitted dishonesty of all institutions, they can also furnish, as every cultural artifact does for its participants, a framework for the growth of freedom. And despite the inevitable hypocrisy of language, despite the fact that we often say what we do not mean, and that even wanting to speak truly we can never wholly say what we do mean: despite all that, a verbalizing profession like that of teaching *can* also furnish, as every form of verbal communication ought to do for its speakers and hearers, a framework for the growth of freedom—the growth of freedom, in this case, for teachers as well as learners. Language, and philosophical language in particular, whether in a teaching situation or in conversation with one's peers, far from being a form of seduction, or, alternatively, a pronouncement of bureaucratic solidarity, is the expression of a shared freedom; of a freedom limited, as all freedom is, by circumstance (as Merleau-Ponty put it, we never see our freedom face to face), but existent, lived and living, sometimes frustrated, sometimes growing, yet undeniably real. All this Sartre's early theory of language would deny, and must deny.

Yet there is still worse to come. Language for the for-itself was at least the for-itself's own instrument, just as the seducer's every gesture is something he *does*, not a brute fact. In the *Critique*, however, language has been exiled altogether to the in-itself. "The word is matter." Totally other than praxis, or the act of the "practical organism," it is in fact the contradiction that gets the dialectic going. Nonsense! Is *Nausea*, is *Being and Nothingness*, is *Words* "matter," a mess of marks on paper? True, such works are not thoughts either, or even *praxes*: they reside neither in consciousness nor in matter, but in the human world, which is neither and both at once. Indeed, it is language more than any human artifact which exhibits most clearly the embodiment of mind and the mentality, if one may call it so, of our bodily being. On this, it seems to me, Merleau-Ponty's chapter on language in *The Phenomenology of Perception* answered, or should have answered, Sartre (as well as Descartes) once and for all. For on the one hand (despite Sara and Washoe), language is still the plainest mark of man's uniqueness, and on the other hand, language exists only as speech or writing, that is, as sound or visible marks—but sound or visible marks imbued with meaning. Language re-presents meanings in the audible, visible, public world. True, the meaning doesn't "originally" inhabit some secret inner place; it is intentional as pointing to an objective. That is the lesson Sartre learned from Husserl, or so he says; but what he has done with it, as early as *The Transcendence of the Ego*, then, dialectically, in *Being and Nothingness*, and even more strikingly in the developed dialectic of the *Critique*, is to exile the *signifié* to the sphere of meaningless matter and to retain the *signifiant* as an empty, would-be act of sense-giving, a would-be act that necessarily fails because there is only the total other of the in-itself, of "matter," to set its intention to work. Just as the in-itself is the totally Other of the for-itself, so is matter the totally Other of *praxis*. How could such a radical contradiction somehow reconcile itself to produce one significant sentence, let alone human history? So far as the theory of language goes, and by the criterion I have adopted, therefore, the theory of action with it, the *Critique*, far from advancing Sartre's position beyond the impasse of *Being and Nothingness*, has taken it one step backward—or sideways—to show up, more plainly than ever, the endless volley of consciousness-matter, freedom-enslavement, activity-inertia, which is for him, or has been so far, the essenceless essence of humanity.

Does the *vécu* take us any further? Again, as in the third part of my first question, one would suppose not. Sartre's hope here is to penetrate by devious constructive methods to the very inwardness of another's lived experience, which would be prelinguistic, as it is pre-role playing. It would be the singular and secret medium in which both acting and the actor's lines have taken root, the soil from which they sprang. True, in the case of Flaubert, as for Sartre himself, it is language, the vocation of the writer, that constitutes the very fabric of his existence. And it is through writing, we were told, that Flaubert's experience was to be transmogrified from suffering to achievement. But with respect to the *theory* of language there is, so far as I can tell, no important innovation in the *Idiot*. The reflections of volume three on the status of the writer in nineteenth century France are standard Sartrean-Marxist arguments about the alienated intellectual in bourgeois society; but the peculiar nature of Sartre's Marxism, fortunately, is not my problem here.

III

My fundamental problem, as I said at the start, is the question whether there can be a Sartrean theory of action. And my two preliminary questions, about the role of roleplaying and about the theory of language (taken as touchstone for the theory of action), have been runners-up to the final question: How, in each stage of his development, does Sartre interpret the relation between action and passion, between the active and passive components of human life?

The position is clearest, and most paradoxical—which, for Sartre, comes to the same thing—in the first period, from the *Sketch for a Theory of the Emotions* and *The Transcendence of the Ego* to *Being and Nothingness*. The for-itself, for itself, is sheer activity, purely, transparently active through and through; the in-itself is pure passivity, pure opaqueness, it is what it is with the heavy unthinkingness of a stone or a clod of clay. Yet I, the for-itself, feel as well as act. I suffer as well as inflicting suffering on the world outside me. Doing is having, assimilating, digesting; but I am done to, had, assimilated, devoured as well, by the Other, by society, by all that stands opposed to me. What can Sartre make, at this stage, of this reverse, dark side of the lucidity of consciousness? What can he make of passion? On the one hand, in a phrase whose rhetoric he regrets, but which nevertheless follows compellingly from his initial premises, man is a useless passion. To be what one is not, to be project, never fulfillment, and to not be what one is, to be lack, absence not presence, emptiness not fullness, *is* to suffer. It is not, indeed, to suffer as Christ allegedly did, being God for man, being man for God; but to suffer uselessly, seeking the impossible coalescence of for-itself and in-itself which only *causa sui*, that inconceivable and unrealizable Spinozistic substance, could have actualized, had it existed. Alas, *we* exist instead, and are doomed forever to act out our impotence, to suffer our vain attempts at action.

Is it then passion that exists, not action? The only action we can find so far, as we have seen, is either the playacting of the sheer performer or the fall from action to self-deceit in the false substantiality of the man of good will. Yet Sartre at this stage, Cartesian to the core, cannot admit passivity to the human scene. Even the actor, after all, only pretends to give himself to the part of Romeo or Othello; the good citizen, certainly, only pretends to take on the imperatives which, heteronomous as they are, can claim, and confer on him, only a secondhand, a fraudulent "reality." Both are *acting* the roles to which they only seem to give themselves. There is no free action, so far as one can tell. Yet there is nothing else either except free action. The for-itself in its very impotence is all-powerful, infinitely free. Passion, Sartre insists in this period, *is* action, but by magic. Where we seem to give ourselves—to ambition, to curiosity, to a "good cause"—we are casting a spell, calling the grapes sour because we cannot reach them, sticking pins in the waxen image of the enemy we cannot defeat. There is, or would be if only there could be, the active activity of the liberated for-itself, choosing itself in anguish and alone. There is the passive passivity of the in-itself, which is full, meaningless, sated with its sheer state of

being no more than what it is, and being all there is. And, surrogate for
the first, there is the pseudo-activity, the magical activity of passion,
where I cry for what I cannot do or get, invoking in my irrationality and
impotence—which, if human, must yet in some sense be rationality and
power—what I cannot by technical, active means, achieve.

It is a bad lookout—and incidentally, an entirely male one. When,
many years ago, I reviewed Simone de Beauvoir's *Second Sex*, I
ventured to suggest that perhaps the apparent "relativity" of the
female, or the feminine (of course the distinction need not be biological), should be taken as an alleviation, not as an added burden to the
already burdensome human state. For to be feminine is to give rather
than exclusively to take; and giving is precisely what the for-itself can
neither live nor know. It acts; or when it cannot act, stamps its feet in an
enraged pretense of acting. It knows no surrender, no generosity, no
prayer, no openness to grace. It is not surprising that, for Sartre, "il
n'est jamais drôle d'être homme."[10] I don't know, perhaps it isn't, and
certainly being female is painful too, but at least we have a start at
giving: that is our calling. And without such giving, I submit, there is
only half humanity. Not that only female beings give; I intend no such
absurdity. The scientist gives himself to his problem, the artist to his
painting or his poem, the general or the chess player to his strategy. But
it is that aspect of free surrender, of a giving that is not betrayal but
fulfillment, that the Sartre of *Being and Nothingness* wholly ignores, in
both the French and English meanings of that word. From the triangular
contradiction of active activity (for-itself), passive passivity (in-itself),
and the *Ersatz* activity of passion, there is no sign of an escape. The
doors are shut.

Dialectical reason, one may hope, will open them a little, though the
hinges creak mightily with the cumbersome contrivances of Hegelian-
Marxist apparatus. It is still an all-or-nothing dialectic, but now it's the
whole human race or nothing: history is totalizing, or it is not history.
Why these sweeping abstractions should be thought by so many
ingenious minds to be more concrete than any less universal and less
dogmatic categorizations, again, fortunately need not concern me.
What does concern me is the way out from the turnstile action/"passion"/action through which for so many years and pages Sartre had
been driven by his own philosophical consistency to torment his readers
and himself. There are two moves in the *Critique* which, while they do
not effect a rescue, at least suggest the way toward one: first, in the
interpretation of the practico-inert and of its consequences, and secondly, in the account of the "second oath" and the social functions it
institutes. The concept of the practico-inert as the contrary of praxis,
takes, in effect, the place of the in-itself as the contrary of the for-itself.
On its own, the practico-inert is more inert than practical; the formation

of a dustbowl, for example, is a *physical* consequence of actions, of the act of cutting down trees, which those who made the dust bowl freely and greedily performed. This performance, however, produced more than physical consequences. It ensnared a future generation, who became its victims, victims like the characters of Steinbeck's *Grapes of Wrath*, driven from Oklahoma to an unwelcoming far West. Such consequences—Sartre's example is the deforestation of China, but we know our own vices better—exhibit the entrapment of most human agents in their environment. The activity of most of us, of all of us, qua alienated, is *passive* activity. This is, of course, humanity *de*human-ized, *in*human humanity; it ought not to exist. On the contrary, it must be the total choice of the for-itself, or praxis, which is its synonym, from which, ultimately, history will flow. But at least Sartre has seen—and this, perhaps, his "Marxism," as well as the experience of the war years, has taught him—that most people are a herd, driven by their own needs as well as by the iniquities of bosses past and present. Activity *in* society, not only in bourgeois society, but in feudal society, in every society history records or prehistory indicates, is *passive* activity.

But second, Sartre, being the dialectician that he is, can now glimpse, at least, another possibility. If there is passive activity, can there be active passivity? For the Sartre of *Being and Nothingness*, the answer was a ringing "No!" To give oneself is betrayal. Agency must be pure and unalloyed or it is no agency at all. But active passivity is precisely the category that was missing in the earlier Sartre: to give oneself to anything, to any cause, to any role, was to produce either the insubstantial kaleidoscope of playacting or bad faith. Only Genet, by the endless self-transformations of the victim into invert, traitor, saint, and poet, only Genet of all the inhabitants of this planet, it seems, could save himself and act freely out of his total unfreedom. Charles Scott has suggested ingeniously that Sartre too has perhaps once acted freely, in the composition of *Being and Nothingness* with its impossible outcome, or nonoutcome.[11] Be that as it may be—and it may be—these were grand and tragic exceptions to our otherwise universal human fate. The rest of us suffered uselessly indeed in the vain gesturing of activity that was no activity at all, but self-deceit. Now, however, there seems, theoretically at least, to be another alternative; perhaps there *can* be a giving of oneself that is yet free. What does the *Critique* offer in this respect? As I indicated earlier, only a hint. The concept "active passivity" is introduced in connection with the second oath, the stabilization of the group in fusion, which produces organization and social function, that is, one would suppose, freely accepted social roles. So far, however, the concept is introduced abstractly and fleetingly. For the "organization" or "social function" brought forth by the second oath soon relapses into serialization and institutionalization and we are once more enslaved. That this is so, Sartre argues, as I pointed out earlier, is plain from the fact that functions within an organization produce *norms*, and norms of course throw those who respect them out of themselves into the old condition of alienation and subservience. To act *according* to a norm is not wholly to fulfill it—to not be what one is and be what one is not—and there we are again. The doors snap shut once more. It seems as if Sartre had simply imposed the carapace of Marxist dogmatism on the unprotected but uncompromising Cartesianism of his earlier period: he is still seeking the unalloyed instant of pure freedom, which action in submission to standards—*any* standards—has already abandoned in temporizing flight.

It is a sad story. For Sartre himself in an early paper on Husserlian intentionality[12] had glimpsed active passivity at work, only to turn his back on it in favor of a more rigid—and false—interpretation of what "intentionality" means. Husserl had shown us, of course, that all consciousness is consciousness of—an object. Husserl had thrust the content of consciousness out into the world. So why can't anyone see, Sartre asks, that if I love a woman, that is not just my subjective state; I love her "because she is lovable." Of course. There is something, not me (and not the Other either, but what is lovable *in* her) to which I *owe* my affection. Admittedly, love as Sartre expounds it elsewhere is either wanting to make the loved object into flesh or seeking to become flesh oneself. But shorn of that Latin analysis, the statement "I love her *because she is lovable*" carries quite a different weight. She is worth giving myself to; conversely, her lovableness comes to me as a grace which I cannot but freely, passively yet freely, accept. Nor are only women "lovable," nor only men either. Knowledge is lovable, justice is lovable, beauty is lovable. Perhaps to search for knowledge is only to try to push back a little the barriers of ignorance, but knowledge *is* gained sometimes, and it is worth giving a life to its pursuit, as Kepler gave twenty years in search of his third law, or Darwin the same span to the theory of natural selection. Further, and much more emphatically, one may object, to search for justice is only to seek to lessen a little the omnipresence of injustice. Indeed, the nearer we come to 1976, the less we may feel, in present-day America, like boasting of equity or civil rights. Yet, if we did have Nixon and political burglary and if we still have the C.I.A. and police brutality, we do not have Auschwitz or the Gulag Archipelago, and there *is* a difference. And if we do have Greed as king and Corruption as his henchman, we have had, and still have, honest judges, and even now and then honest senators or congressmen: nor do I mean "honest" in Sartre's sense of *honnêtes gens*, that is to say, stuffed shirts, but honestly honest. True, Sacco and Vanzetti died, innocent or no; but Angela Davis was acquitted by the very system whose operation she, and of course Sartre, so totally condemn. Granted, there is no holy will—what a Kantian purist Sartre is after all!—but that does not mean that everyone and everything is totally evil. There *can* be the free giving of oneself to the standard of fair play even when one sees around one, and in one's own person, too, a failure to embody that standard in daily life. No pound weighs exactly a pound; no just act is wholly just; yet one can try to weigh fairly, whether as shopkeeper, statesman, or citizen. Moreover, beauty is lovable, not only as "lack seen across the ugliness of the world," let alone as the "horror" that is Genet. Natural beauty is lovable; this, one gathers from Simone de Beauvoir's memoirs, Sartre has just never noticed, any more than Socrates usually did. The beauty of works of art—though it may seem quaint nowadays to give it that unfashionable name—is lovable, that is, worthy of the discipline required to see or hear or read it, worthy of the infinitely greater discipline and self-sacrifice required to create it. In this dimension, as for the theory of language, Merleau-Ponty tried, again and again, to speak to Sartre, in *Signs*, in *Sense and Nonsense*, in *The Eye and the Mind*. In his lifetime, at least, he did not succeed; I shall certainly not attempt to better his instruction.

Nor, perhaps, need one make such an attempt. For there is *some* evidence, not much but a little, that, in the fourth volume of the *Idiot*, active passivity was to come into its own: within a limited sphere, as the making of a literary masterpiece, but also in a life, as the agency of its transformation. I have discussed this aspect of Sartre's Flaubert elsewhere,[13] but must touch on it again here, in conclusion. In particular, I want to make two points, one an assertion, the other a question.

First, the assertion: It is indeed active passivity, the autonomous self-submission to one's freely chosen standards, the resolution to play freely, out of oneself, one's social roles, that alone can transform the human condition from the tragic impasse Sartre—with all the weight of Descartes and Marx and the horrors of our century behind him—has made of it, and make it bearable, or even, as it occasionally is, joyous. In his first two volumes, Sartre presented the life of Gustave Flaubert as one of passive activity only, with a suggestion, late in volume two, that the transformation to active passivity would yet permit him to escape his infantile fate. Perhaps that was true of Gustave, unloved younger son, retarded at school, unwanted at home. I don't know. Not every human person, however, need go through quite such torments to find the destiny to which he can give himself in freedom. Nor need Sartre, had he not been Sartre, have taken so long and so tortured a route to the discovery (if he yet makes it) of the synthesis, in agency, of action and passion. It is a difficult synthesis in our philosophical situation, at the deadend of the Cartesian tradition in both its branches, or even at the close, as many insist, of philosophy itself. But it can be produced, and, indeed, has been produced, in a way by Merleau-Ponty in *The Phenomenology of Perception*, in another way by the Wittgenstein of the *Investigations*, in yet another by Michael Polanyi in *Personal Knowledge*, in another way again in the philosophical anthropology of Helmuth Plessner, also in some of the work of some Anglo-American philosophers, like Charles Taylor or Anthony Kenny or Alasdair MacIntyre. The freedom so discovered and articulated consists, however, not in the either-or of radical self-choice, but in the process of coming to oneself within the limits of one's situation and of the choices it permits one; it consists, not in pure activity, but in the free submission to standards that one accepts as universally valid, while recognizing one's own accountability, not only to them, but for them. Such is the thesis that needs to be, and in some quarters is being, elaborated.

Second, a concluding question: Why is it that in fact the only examples of active passivity Sartre has discovered are instances, not of social action, of doing in the real world, but of literary creation, and indeed of literary creation of a particularly self-corroding, self-denying kind? Roquentin decided to become someone through writing a novel, as the child Jean-Paul Sartre had decided to make himself remembered by posterity as teller of tales. There was something a little strained about that resolution. But Genet, we are told, truly saved himself by becoming a poet. Hegel had called the work of the artist "determinate consciousness." Genet, Sartre writes, evaded that determination:

> In determining himself *in his works* as the Thief, Genet escapes that determination, he opposes himself to it as free creative consciousness which would know how to define itself only in terms of indeterminate free activity; in creating himself in the Other (*chez l'autre*), he empties himself of himself and becomes the absolute void as unconditioned power of creation. In making himself the Thief for the Other, he makes himself creator for himself.[14]

True, "creation is passion"[15] 'the author suffers his characters' sufferings. Genet undergoes an asceticism "which is realized in the Word and whose fulfillment must dissolve language in silence.[16] Yet this, it seems, is a passion, not useless, but liberating. Something similar, one supposed, would turn out to have happened in the case of Flaubert. Making his hateful self-image in Emma Bovary, he would have given himself freely to the imaginative task that would break the chains of his neurotic passivity. By making himself, or better perhaps the inverse of himself, he would have achieved his long-sought and dearly purchased freedom. Now, both these cases of salvation are through imaginative making: through poetry or fiction. And imagination, for Sartre, is pure negation: it is the sheer appearance of what is not. In both cases, also, it is imagination turned *against* the imaginer that liberates him. Not for Sartre, or for his subjects, Genet or Flaubert, the arrogant self-assurance of *Le Temps Retrouvé*. It is the utter hatefulness of Genet's self-image, of his multiplied self-projections, or of Flaubert's single one, that mediates the transformation, in each case, from passive activity to active passivity, from helplessness to creative action. Is that the best that can be done? May one give oneself, truly and without self-deception, never to something greater than oneself, but only to oneself? May one give oneself, truly and without self-deception, never through respect or loyalty, but only through treachery or hatred? May one give oneself, truly and without self-deception, never to what is, or may be, or ought to be, but only to what seems?

Postscript, August 1975
   Sartre's statement in the *Novel Observateur* of 23 June, 30 June, and 7 July 1975 (translated in part in the *New York Review of Books* of 7 August 1975) shows clearly how he would answer not only my final question, but my whole argument. When, if ever, there is no material scarcity, there will be total openness of each to all, and, after all, it seems, the pure activity that Sartre himself, in his own best philosophizing, had shown to be impossible. The last message, like the first, is only "One is always right to rebel."

Notes

   1. Pierre Verstraeten, *Éthique et Violence* (Paris: Gallimard, 1973). For my own analysis of Sartre's major work and of his relation to his predecessors, see Marjorie Grene, *Sartre* (New York: Franklin Watts, 1973).
   2. Henri Peyre, "Jean-Paul Sartre: The Philosopher as Playwright," *New York Times Book Review*, 6 March 1960, p. 5.
   3. Jean-Paul Sartre, *Un Théatre de Situations* (Paris: Gallimard, 1973), pp. 282-291.
   4. Jean-Paul Sartre, *Saint Genet: Comédien et Martyre* (Paris: Gallimard, 1952), p. 155.
   5. Ibid., p. 156.
   6. Jean-Claude Lebensteyn, in a recent review of a production of *La Dispute* (*digraphe 2*, 1974, p. 119) has said, in effect, the same thing:

   (Mais, derechef, les acteurs de bonne foi sont des acteurs de mauvaise foi, des acteurs jouant sciemment à être des acteurs qui s'ignorent, devant des spectateurs qui sont des acteurs qui s'ignorent,

   ou qui, peut-être, jouent à leur tour sciemment à être des acteurs qui s'ignorent, les uns pour les autres, dans un entrecroisement sans fin.)

7. M. Grene, *Sartre*, chap. 7.

8. Cf. ibid., p. 213.

9. *Saint Genet*, p. 100.

10. *L'Idiot de la Famille* (Paris: Gallimard, 1971), 1:142n.

11. Informal communication.

12. Jean-Paul Sartre, *Situations I* (Paris: Gallimard, 1947), pp. 29-32, p. 32.

13. M. Grene, *Sartre*, chap. 8. (Unfortunately, Sartre's recent renunciation of writing means that the hints given in the *Idiot* are all we are to have.)

14. *Saint Genet*, p. 614.

15. Ibid., p. 618.

16. Ibid., p. 620.

XI

The True Teachers of Mankind

1973

THE FOLLOWING ESSAY WAS WRITTEN IN THE WINTER OF 1972-73 FOR delivery in May 1973. After it had been completed, my attention was called to a passage by Coleridge which says, in brief and metaphorically, what I had wanted to say, and, I believe, what Derrida is saying in much of his writing on "texts" and "writing." Since I had used Coleridge here only for the distinction between Imagination and Fancy, I could not easily incorporate it into my text. But perhaps what I am trying to do will be clearer if I call on Coleridge for an epigraph. In "The Principles of Genial Criticism," published in *Felix Farley's Bristol Journal* in 1814, he wrote:

> When I reflect on the manner in which smoothness, richness of sound, etc., enter into the formation of the beautiful, I am induced to suspect that they act negatively rather than positively. Something there must be to realize the form, something in and by which the *forma informans* reveals itself: and these, less than any that could be substituted, and in the least possible degree, distract the attention, in the least possible degree obscure the idea, of which they (composed into outline and surface) are the symbol. An illustrative hint may be taken from a pure crystal, as compared with an opaque, semi-opaque or clouded mass, on the one hand, and with a perfectly transparent body, such as the air, on the other. The crystal is lost in the light, which yet it contains, embodies, and gives a shape to; but which passes shapeless through the air, and, in the ruder body, is either quenched or dissipated.[1]

Poets, said Hume, are "liars by profession."[2] Poets themselves have said, in effect, the same—though not, one hopes, *to* the same effect. For in this quip as in so much else, Hume brings to a literal-minded logical consequence what was implicit in a long tradition: in this case, the controlling conception of art as mimesis. Imitation is a kind of foolery, *meant* to fool us, all right in its (minor) place. The serious business of life, on the contrary, whether in praxis or in the search for scientific knowledge, is to get through *from* our sign making to reality. Aristotle complained of Plato, for example, that the doctrine of participation is a mere metaphor and hence poetic; such talk should be banned from cognitive pursuits, reserved for what is now called the entertainment business.

This parceling of human activities into pigeonholes has had disastrous consequences for the interpretation of the sciences as well as of the arts, consequences which can be corrected, or at least alleviated, only in terms of a philosophical rethinking of the whole human condition which will display coherently the interrelations, likenesses *and* differences, in the class of human artifactions, arts, sciences, religions, moralities, social institutions and above, or beneath, all, languages. We make ourselves not simply in action, as some existentialists have tried to say, but through what we make, and have made, in and of the human world. To say this right, to remake our philosophical self-knowledge, is a task no one philosopher has yet succeeded in performing. Far be it from me to try to report in an hour on such attempts in general, let alone try to bring them to fruition. To describe the place of art in such a renewed philosophy of man, it may be that some version of Riegl's concept *Kunstwollen* will prove appropriate. That perspective, however, would be still too general for my more fragmentary aim today. Restricting my remarks to the arts of language, and in particular to the poetic use of language (whether in poetry or prose), I want to report (with some comments) what some philosophers have said, or intimated, about the relation of the art of poetic speech to cognitive or other verbal skills.

As I have already suggested, Hume speaks here for the mainstream, certainly of the British or "empiricist" tradition. There have been times, like the heyday of the Vienna Circle, when scientific language was our ideal (the time, mercifully gone, of *The Meaning of Meaning*, not to mention *Language, Truth and Logic*). Then of course this orthodoxy was replaced by so-called "ordinary language philosophy," a practice, one must admit, not necessarily as simpleminded as some of its critics *or* its practitioners have said, or shown, it to be. But even in late Wittgenstein, in the master himself, as distinct from the epigones, it is certainly the everyday rather than the "poetic" uses of language that are the chief object of reflection. Although the later works work largely metaphorically themselves—ice is slippery, beetles live in black boxes, engines idle, language goes on holiday, and so on—the language games they reflect on are usually "literal," not indeed any longer in the *Tractatus* sense of seeking to mirror the world, but in the sense that practical jobs of getting things done, building, winning at chess, teaching chemistry, rest chiefly on usages devoid of poetic resonance. Moreover, even the continental tradition, however much we associate it with the Romantic, obscurantist, and hence in some perverse sense "poetic," uses of speech, is in fact founded on the ideal of strict, "scientific" meaning, in this century especially through the work of Husserl with his conception of philosophy as *strenge Wissenschaft*. Recently, first, as we'll see, through the influence of Heidegger and then, especially in France, through interests in linguistics and in rhetoric, this is changing. But, again, in the main, the orthodox philosophical tradition in its view of the uses of language has given poetry a very secondary place, if any place at all.

What I want to argue—or, better, to use some statements of some philosophers to suggest—is that Hume and the tradition are wrong. Poets are not professional liars, inferior to good humdrum truth-tellers. But what I want to suggest is not strictly the contrary of this, that poetry has some cognitive import, nor even, in I. A. Richards' words, that "poetry is the supreme use of language, man's chief coordinating instrument, in the service of the most integral purposes of life."[3] What I want to put forward is a series of possible grounds for a defense of poetic language in the form of a transcendental argument. (I shall not construct such an argument, but try to prepare the way for one.)

Let me remind you what this piece of philosophical, specifically Kantian, jargon denotes. A transcendental argument starts from an agreed state of affairs, not just a particular state of affairs, like that referred to, for instance, in Moore's famous statement, "This is a hand," but a general feature of the human condition on which we all agree. Let me give an example from Kant himself. In one of the two branches of his central argument in the first *Critique*, the objective deduction of the categories, the starting point is the fact that we have experience of objects. That's where the argument begins. We then ask: What activities of the human mind must we presuppose as the necessary conditions for the existence of what we have originally taken as given? Thus in the objective deduction Kant argues that the experience of objects necessarily presupposes the basic rule-giving activities which he calls categories, the organization of experience in terms of the concepts of quantity, quality, substance, cause, and so on. And these in turn presuppose my ability to unite all my experience as mine, to bring it all together with the tag "I think" (not that I do do this, but that I could). The presuppositions so discovered, finally, are necessary and universal, not in themselves, but *for* the experience whose necessary presuppositions they are. The conclusion is not detachable from the premise, but tied to it. The argument is circular, though benignly so. It is important to notice, moreover, that the presuppositions *to* which we argue in a transcendental argument are activities of the human mind, not characters of things in themselves or even of phenomena passively given. In other words, they don't belong to nature (conceived either as reality or appearance), but to us. Some contemporary philosophers who use this type of argument have neglected this aspect of it. They look for necessary conditions in general, not just necessary conditions in the field of "mental" activities. One can hardly blame them, since Kant's conception of the mental is irredeemably, I would even say naïvely, tied to dualism. Kant simply takes it for granted that body is foreign to mind and hence to mental activity. As most of us nowadays see things, this won't do. But dualistic metaphysics is not a necessary adjunct to the Kantian form of argument. We can argue from an agreed proposition about human experience to its necessary condition in human activity without making that activity "mental" in some dualistic, let alone idealist, sense.

Well, then, what I'm looking for, and asking some philosophers past and present to help me discover the approach to, is a transcendental argument that would run as follows. We speak. There is human language, in its ordinary as well as its scientific uses. That is our given. What kinds of human activity, then, must we presuppose as the necessary conditions for the existence of language? One of these necessary conditions, I would like to argue, is uniquely exemplified in poetic language. In other words, there could be no discourse were it not for *some* human power that is expressed par excellence in the work of the poet. This sounds peculiar. Language is used prosaically and poetically. I seem to be saying, given A_1 and A_2, prose and poetry, that A_2 is necessarily presupposed, and so is valid, for both A_1 and A_2. A kind of skewed circular argument and perhaps a trivial one. But maybe it is not so obvious. What I am trying to say is that A_1 and A_2, prosaic and poetic ways of speaking, depend for their existence on an activity that we ordinarily take as characteristic only of the second of these. In other words, M. Jourdain could not have spoken prose, were it not for the poetic use of language which underlies both its more prosaic and more poetical uses. The paradigmatic use of language, the use that can lead us to the heart of language itself as a human power, is the poetic rather than the "ordinary" or even the "scientific."

In relation to the traditional view of language, we have agreed, this thesis is heretical. Yet there have been philosophers who support, or seem to support, it. I want now to look at a series of such statements, ranging from some that are very general to some that converge more exactly on poetic language itself. (I shall try to avoid reference to the theoretical statements of poets themselves or of critics, partly because I don't know them well enough, or know enough of them, partly because I find them too difficult. Literary criticism, like social science, is a form of discourse often peculiarly obscure to students of philosophy, at least to this one. It sounds theoretical, and then somehow it isn't. So if I repeat what some literary theorists have said, I hope—if they hear about it—they will forgive me. I have to come at my question out of *my* kind of literature, not theirs.)

The first proposal I want to report is Plato's, arch enemy of the poets if you will, but also in the *Symposium* their defender. There Diotima, the wise woman of Mantinea, is trying to explain to Socrates that what is usually called "eros" is but a part of a much more general activity. We give the name of the whole to what is really a part. Socrates is puzzled, so she gives him an analogous case. *Poiesis,* she suggests, is *any* kind of bringing into being what formerly was not. It is making in general. Yet we give the name "poetry" to one segment only of this general class of skills. One part, she points out, namely, the one that concerns music and metres, which has been separated off from *poiesis* as a whole, is called by the name of the whole, for only this is called *poiesis* (making) and those who have this part are called *tes poiesews poietai*—makers of making.[4] Now admittedly this passage could perhaps be read as a demotion of poetry from any special standing. Both strategies, for eros and for making, might be taken as leveling operations. Just as what is usually called eros, as Diotima explains, is one way among many of seeking immortality, so poetry is simply one sort of craft among others—carpentry, masonry, fishing, or what not. But this passage in the dialogue is after all the first approach to the ladder of love, the first warm-up before we come to the ladder itself. And in that culminating account, true loving will turn out to be, not just one way of seeking immortality, but the best way. Only he who has seen the beautiful itself can breed true virtue, Diotima will say, because only he is in contact not with illusion but with truth. So if we return to the parallel between eros and poetry we may take poetry too in the narrower sense, not as simply one member of the class of makings, but as the truest making, the making that sets the standard for all others. The trouble with this interpretation for our present purpose, however, is twofold. On the one hand, there is no special reference here to language, or to varied uses of language. And on the other hand, Plato's aim, I believe, in introducing "*poiesis*" into Diotima's discourse, is not so much to tell us anything about poetry itself as to bring *true* poetry into an equation with philosophy. In the central movement of the *Symposium*—indeed, as in Plato's other dialogue on love, the *Phaedrus*—love turns out to be philosophy, or a philosopher; and in our passage what is being suggested, I believe, is that at the pinnacle of human seekings for immortality not only love, but poetry, too, will be assimilated to the one effort of making discourse in the light of beauty and truth. The thrust of the analogy, therefore, is similar to that of the *Phaedrus*, where Plato tried to demonstrate, much more explicitly than he does here for poetry, that true rhetoric is identical with dialectic, that is, with philosophy. So this first suggestion, though it relates the poet's task to the highest human efforts, as Plato ranked them, is neither sufficiently specific nor appropriately oriented to help us much in the present context.

What Plato's pun with *poiesis* does suggest, however, is a very familiar thesis, one which again I shall have to dismiss regretfully as not of much use to us at this juncture. I mean of course the thesis that poetic making is paradigmatic of creative activity as such because it is in poetry that Imagination comes uniquely, or most conspicuously, into play. True, I have promised to leave poets and critics out of my account where possible, but *some* reference to Coleridge, I fear, can scarcely be avoided. I could indeed invoke Schelling instead as philosophic source for the concept of Primary Imagination, as well as of the view that art (if not specifically poetry) is the highest human expression of the Infinite Self-Consciousness in which ultimate reality is lodged. Better yet, I could invoke Fichte, from whom one way or another, all Romantic doctrines flow, as source for the view that "all true reality has both its ground and its evidence in the will."[5]

But it is not Romantic idealism I want to refer to here, whether Coleridge's version of it or any one else's. Its present heir will meet us later in Heidegger (vehemently though he would probably deny any such kinship). What I want to mention as my second possible ground for the transcendental argument I am in search of is not the infinite I-Am, but the distinction between Imagination and Fancy, which has after all had direct application, from Coleridge's own use onward, to the understanding of poetry and of the essential task of the poet. Couldn't we argue that Imagination's unifying principle, rather than the craft of bricklaying Fancy, is the necessary condition for our being able to speak at all? Some such hunch, I suppose, is back of one's impatience with the efforts of Chomskyan or post-Chomskyan linguists to uncover a machinery that will explicate linguistic competence. The machinery remains a mystery because the power to be explained is *not* mechanical. Not the programmed rearrangement of fixed units, but art's unpredictable shaping of disparate parts into a whole that defies total analysis—such, or something like it, is the precondition of linguistic competence. That is true, I believe. The work of Creative Imagination, as distinct from Fancy, *is* a necessary presupposition for the fact that we do speak. Nevertheless I do not think this argument will do the job for us here, since the concept of Creative Imagination, and even of its difference from Fancy, has by now been assimilated into the interpretation of too many activities, not only poetry, not only the arts, but science too. It is not so much a creed outworn as a creed too well worn in its passage through too many hands. Thomas Kuhn's distinction between revolutionary and routine science, for example, which has acquired immensely wide-ranging influence, is, it seems to me, the exact analogue of Coleridge's distinction. New "paradigms" are produced by the revolutionaries of science, those who forge ahead, under Imagination's guidance, to a new vision. The routine laborers, in contrast, do their journeyman's work, within the style set by one epoch-making achievement or another, well trained but within the range of Fancy only. So the conception of Creative Imagination no longer says anything uniquely about art, let alone poetic art. It applies in general to the originating activities of human beings in many fields. We must look elsewhere for philosophic insights or arguments with a special bearing on poetry.

The contemporary philosopher who most explicitly claims to invoke poetry in the service of philosophy, or philosophy in the service of poetry, is Heidegger. His one aim has been to ask the question of Being, *die Seinsfrage*. He sought to ask it, first, by means of what he called the "destruction of ontology," that is, by an attempt to move back through the successive wrong turnings of western thought to a reliving of its beginning in the unhiddenness of Being, as we may, with effort, yet glimpse it in the thought of the first great Greek thinkers, Heraclitus and Parmenides. In his later work, however, he relies recurrently on the poets, Hölderlin, Rilke, Trakl, George, to inspire his quest. That his changed emphasis represents a break in his thought—a *Kehre* or conversion—seems to me dubious; fortunately that question need not concern us. We need only notice that from the early thirties on he *has* reflected repeatedly on the philosophical import of poetry, and ask what we can derive for our present purpose from these reflections.

I should say, by the way, that I am by no means an enthusiast for late Heidegger. I have tried, honestly, to find what I could in it, and have found more than I expected, though, as we'll see, less than we need, and much less than his prestige in some quarters would presage. That prestige is such, however, that I must take account of him in some detail, even if most of what I have to report is negative.

What, then, let us ask, does Heidegger as philosopher have to say about the priority of poetic to ordinary or scientific discourse? My answer is in three parts. First, it is the poets, he tells us, who can bring us back to Being. Our destiny has been to "fall out of Being" (big B), to busy ourselves with beings (little b). We are caught in what he calls the "ontological difference," the gap between the many things, beings—gadgets, mostly—with which our lives are entangled, and Being, what it *means* to be. But man is the shepherd of Being; he needs to be recalled from his distraction by the silly toys of science and technology to his true destiny. In this task, Heidegger announces, it is the poets who can guide us. For poetry is "the primal language in which a people founds Being.'' What does this dictum mean? Here again—with respect to my question about the first answer (Heidegger recalls us to Being)—my answer is in three parts.

First, Heidegger's pronouncement is partly an outcry against the mechanization of mind that seems to characterize our technocracy-dominated world. Take one example (mine, not Heidegger's), the conception of validity in argument. For Descartes, in the seventeenth century, the desideratum for each step in the building of a system of knowledge was what he called ''intuition,'' the grasp of a clear and attentive mind so plain that no doubt remains about what is apprehended. *Now* it is not the mind's grasp of anything, but a set of mechanical relations ideally feedable into a computer that seems to be the logician's aim. A colleague once told me the definition he used in explaining the ''distribution'' of terms to a class in elementary logic—traditional logic, it's true, a subject much out of fashion, but still I think the example is apposite. For when I complained that the definition struck me as counterintuitive, he replied that that was its virtue. Since no one could claim to understand it, it was bound to work. The machinery of thinking is to be, if possible, detached from the minds that think. That kind of separation is impossible for poetry, or for language ''poetically'' used. Not that poetry is ''subjective,'' but it is, to use a phenomenological term, intentional. You cannot divide the signs it is made of from their possible meaning to some mind. Yet this recourse to poetry doesn't tell us very much. The recall to Being is an exclamation by a thinker impatient with science, impatient with anything ordinary, anything less rarefied than he believes his own thought to be. It is a reenactment, as I suggested earlier, of the Romantic reaction to the successful and the stuffy. Compared with Heidegger's lucubrations, however, Schumann's musical response to the philistines seems not only more euphonious, but also more profound.

What else does the Heideggerian dictum mean? ''Poetry is the primal language, through which a people founds Being.'' Put in a less prophetic tone, his statement might be saying what T. S. Eliot has told us in his essay on ''The Social Function of Poetry.'' The poet's first obligation is to his language, and his language—not his individual utterance, but his mother tongue—owes its persona, its untranslatable quintessence, to its poets. Even those who never read a line of poetry speak nevertheless a language enriched, or impoverished, by its poetic tradition. Heidegger, I must admit, is ingenious in choosing his poets and their poems to exemplify this theme, such as Trakl's ''Ein Winterabend,'' for instance, on which he elaborates in the first essay of *Unterwegs zur Sprache*. Yet this aspect of his appeal to poetry is not only restricted for my present use, as any such appeal must be, by the untranslatability of the examples. It is flawed also by the chauvinism that envelops much of what he writes. No native English speaker will assent, I trust, to the proposition implicit in much of Heidegger's speculation, that there is *only* German poetry, or only German thought. Of course a poem can't be universal like universal grammar. That is part of its superiority to such poor abstractions. But neither is there only one tongue that is the unique nurse of poetry. Besides, if language is shaped by poetry, we have still to ask *why* that is so. What is it about poetry that is so basic to the physiognomy of a language, indeed to its flesh and bone? I shall return to that question in a moment.

But I must ask finally what more there is to the primal language theme than the two motifs I have suggested: down with machinery and up with *Blut und Boden!* I'm afraid what it really amounts to, though devout Heideggerians would of course deny it, is a sellout of philosophy. Heidegger never could, so far, continue his magnum opus. When philosophic thought failed him, he turned to poetry. Hume, when philosophy proved too much for him, played backgammon; Heidegger read Hölderlin. Such flight can scarcely help us in our present search.

Over and above the call to Being, however, second, Heidegger does after all report to us *what* the poets say, and their message is often about language, or about their own vocation as speakers. This is true, for example, of all the five *Leitworte* (slogans?) he deals with in "Hölderlin und das Wesen der Dichtung," as it is of the George poem "Das Wort" in the essay of that name. So we might expect to learn something from these expositions about what the poetic use of language amounts to. Instead, however, we are chiefly told, again, through the poet's own assertions, of the special relation of speaking to Being: "Jedes wesentliche Sagen hört in dieses verhüllte Zueinandergehören von Sage und Sein, Wort und Ding zurück."[6] "Every essential saying harks back to this hidden togetherness [I can't render the *hören* in *gehören*] . . . to this hidden togetherness of saying and Being, word and thing." The poets bring us back to the insight that language is "the house of Being." In all these adjurations through poetry and citations of poetry, however, Heidegger seldom, so far as I can discover, really analyzes a poem. He usually talks around them, even though he may repeat, prophetically, successive lines or stanzas. In short, we shall have to look further for some other philosophical writers who take seriously the fine structure of poetry, the uses of language, whatever they are, that distinguish poetry from prose.

To these two negative points, finally, I must add one more, not quite so negative. Heidegger has always worked by the oracular method. His key sayings about language are, for example, "Die Sprache spricht," "Speech speaks," or, to parody Carnap's old parody of Heidegger, "Language langs." Or else, "Die Sprache ist . . . die Sprache,"

"Language is . . . language." Intonation and reputation may make such dicta *seem* to tell us something, but do they? Oddly enough, they might. And so might Heidegger's peculiar technique of pulling words up by their roots and replanting them in unaccustomed ways and places. But whatever the lesson to be learned from these techniques, and from those pronouncements, he doesn't himself state it as such, nor does he relate it explicitly to poetry or the poetic use of language. In the essay, "Der Weg zur Sprache," however, he quotes a statement by Wilhelm von Humboldt which puts more intelligibly what (I think) he means to say. Von Humboldt speaks of the discovery "dass die Sprache nicht bloss ein Austauschungsmittel zu gegenseitigem Verständnis, sondern eine wahre *Welt* ist, welche der *Geist* zwischen sich und die *Gegenstände* durch die innere Arbeit ihrer Kraft setzen muss,"[7] "that language is not merely a medium of exchange for mutual understanding, but is a true *world*, which the *mind* must set between itself and *objects* through the inner working of its force." Heidegger of course wants to go beyond this idealistic, basically still Leibnizian, expression to something more radical. But I still think von Humboldt is saying what Heidegger wants to say more clearly than he himself does, and is showing us, in particular, what poetry has to do with it. For it is the substantiality of language to which von Humboldt refers, its existence as a world *between* minds and things, that is uniquely evident in poetry, just because, as Auden says, "poetry makes nothing happen, it survives . . . a way of happening, a mouth." And if language without this quality would not *be* language, then the poetic use of speech is indeed a necessary condition for the existence of language as such. Heidegger never expressly says this, but he hints at it. "Language is . . . language." "*Language* speaks." But let's see where else we can find more detailed clues.

In what ways is poetic language prior to more prosaic usage? I mean this, of course, not historically, but in the manner of the transcendental argument I proposed at the start. My sources here are several, chiefly I suppose at this juncture, the writings of Jacques Derrida, but I shall not stop to specify my indebtedness at every point.

First, consider the contrast between the literal and metaphorical uses of language. A metaphor unifies two (at least two) meanings that are similar yet different. So there must be literal meanings before we can play this game. "An aged man is but a paltry thing,/A tattered coat upon a stick." If we didn't know coats, tatters, sticks when we saw them—routinely and literally—and aged men too for that matter, what could we make of the metaphor? Nothing. So there must be literal language first. Moreover, as I reminded you earlier, metaphor, in the view of Aristotle and the tradition, is an ornament of speech confined to the "so-called imitative arts." *Serious*, information-giving speech avoids it. But what if we break down the neat separation of the mimetic and the epistemic: speech for the fun of imitating and speech for the sake of stating the truth? This has happened in fact in the history of western thought in two directions. On the one hand, before Aristotle's tidying up of kinds of *logoi*, Plato found us all to *be* imitations, *eidola*; and so for him language, our efforts to voice the real we aspire to understand, was always metaphorical, never exact. Hence the metaphor of the sun and the cave, the myths of the soul's destiny, and so on. On the other hand, with the thinker who for Heidegger represents the end of metaphysics, that is, with Nietzsche, mimesis is abandoned altogether, and metaphor, for the contrary reason, is let loose and ranges everywhere. Language itself, Nietzsche says, is metaphorical, because after all what have sounds to do with things? To bring them together in language is to transfer—*metapherein*—one kind of thing into another. The sounds "aged man" have no more to do with aged men than aged men themselves have to do with tattered coats or sticks. This may be just Nietzschean perversity, but the pervasiveness of the metaphorical in language is not only a Nietzschean theme. The priority of metaphor over literal meaning seems to me, if I understand him, to be the theme also of Lévi-Strauss's chapter on the origin of language in *The Savage Mind*. The proper name is a limiting case of language, scarcely instantiated in reality. Language is classification, which brings together the nonidentical under some overarching concept. Derrida's essay, "La Mythologie Blanche," searches out in particular hidden metaphors in philosophic usage rather than in poetry; but the thrust of his argument is the same: it is not the literal use but the metaphorical, and hence, in Aristotle's view, the poetic, that is fundamental to all speech.[8] This is of course a paradoxical thesis. As I've admitted, metaphor depends on the bringing together in one word or phrase of a number of nonmetaphorical terms, concepts, or meanings. How can we *first* unite what we have not yet got? Metaphor is indeed caught, Derrida admits, between two deaths: death in the literal on the one hand, and on the other, in the confusion of total ambiguity. But just that pulling ourselves up by our own bootstraps *is* what language is. Language *is* a world between ourselves and things. It never mirrors them precisely; yet only through its images, its resonances, do we have the world at all. Hence Hölderlin's saying, "Darum ist der Güter Gefährlichstes, die Sprache dem Menschen gegeben . . . damit er zeuge, was er sei. . . ."[9] "Therefore the most perilous of possessions, language, is given to man . . . that he may bear witness, what he is. . . ."

Against, say, the effort of some philosophers to reduce language to proper names, or of others to eliminate proper names in favor of extensionally interpreted predicates, this is a move in the right direction. But metaphor of course is not by any means limited to poetry. For the new corpuscular philosophy of the seventeenth century the world was a machine. For some identity theorists of the twentieth century, minds are machines. Or take "field" theory or "wave" theory: metaphors are everywhere. What is it about *poems* as exemplifications of poetic language that shows this kind of usage to be constitutive for language as a world, in von Humboldt's sense?

This is, of course, much too large a question to answer here, and much too subtle a question for a literary layman to answer at all. But let me draw briefly and inadequately from several sources to try to suggest the direction for an answer.

Language in its ordinary or its scientific uses is transparent. We go through it to things, to get on with the business of living: greeting, promising, praying, reporting information, shouting for help, or what you will. Even if, as Benjamin insisted, the history of two peoples lingers in the words *Brot* or *pain* respectively, what we want usually when we ask for bread is food. The poetic in language, on the contrary, is its nontransparency. Jakobson has christened this character *poéticité* and describes its effect as follows: "How is poeticity manifested? In this: that the word is felt as word and not as simple substitute for the object named nor as explosion of emotion. In this, that the words and their syntax, their meaning (*signification*), their external and internal form, are not indifferent indices of reality, but possess their own weight and their own value."[10]

"Their own weight and their own value": Sartre made a similar point with his distinction between the language of the poet and the prose writer. The poet, he said, works on the hither side of language, he dwells in his words, while the prose writer (especially of course in Sartre's quasi-Marxist view of him) tries to get *through* language to accomplish something by his words, to tell others what to do. But what does it mean to dwell *in* words? What is the point of this "weightiness"? I'd like to appeal here to two further authoritative texts—one, however, untranslatable, and the other really much too long and complicated to invoke hastily at this stage of my reportage. But I can only try. The first is Walter Benjamin's essay, "Zwei Gedichte von Friedrich Hölderlin."[11] This early essay had not been published when Heidegger wrote his interpretations of Hölderlin; yet Benjamin seems to be saying, with greater depth and density, what Heidegger should have said. The other is Roman Ingarden's phenomenological treatise *Das literarische Kunstwerk*, from which I can adduce here only the most general outline.[12]

First, Benjamin. The poem, *das Gedicht,* he says, should be distinguished from what the poem says, *das Gedichtete*—we could perhaps say from its intent, if it is clear that "intent" is here an impersonal concept. It is the ideal target, what the poem (not the poet) is after.

Relative to the poem as a series of sounds, words, images, thoughts, *das Gedichtete* is a limiting concept, *ein Grenzbegriff*. But it is a *Grenzbegriff* also in another direction, over against the experience of mankind, the life that the poem is intended to illuminate. This, again, is not "life" in the individual, biographical sense. Yeats's own reaction to aging has nothing to do with the poetry of aging he has left us, any more than Hölderlin's own individual wrestling with the meaning of Greece or of the relation of the poet's vocation to his people has with the import of the poems Benjamin is analyzing. Life *im*personally understood, then, as the world of forms the poem aims to illuminate, not the poet's own world, let alone yours or mine—life so understood is the other reality to which, as limiting concept, *das Gedichtete*, the intent of the poem, stands related. And what makes a great poem, Benjamin tells us, is the *identity* (not the sameness!) of the actual, physically sounding poem with "the life of the forms embodied in the poetic cosmos." Benjamin's argument is enforced by his precise and delicate analysis of a particular poem. "Blödigkeit," compared with what is in effect an earlier version. One should really try to convey his meaning, if one could, by working in a similar way with a given *whole* poem in English. But let me return to the lines I quoted earlier and put them slightly into context, taking it that the whole of the poem is present to all of you.

An aged man is but a paltry thing,
A tattered coat upon a stick, unless
Soul clap its hands and sing, and louder sing
For every tatter in its mortal dress.

What is said—*das Gedicht*— is before you. Beyond pernes and gyres and golden singing birds, the experience of time's flow and of eternity as artifact escaping it is clear too. It is the bringing together of both, on the one hand the words in their metered and melodious sequence, with the metaphors they carry and the images they convey, and on the other the sharp edge of time and eternity, nature and artifact—it is this identi-fication that is the poem's intent. What Yeats made in "Sailing to Byzantium" was neither a concord of sweet sounds nor a statement of a truth about aging; yet it was also both. It was, indeed, as it turned out, itself an artifice of eternity, an irreal entity in which sound and sense become identical, not flatly or logically, but in unceasing reverberation with one another. Benjamin's essay, he tells us, elaborates Schiller's dictum that the real secret of the master, in art, consists in his destruc-tion—or consumption—of matter through form. But that's not quite right either; and indeed Benjamin expressly avoids the standard "form-matter" or "form-content" division in the body of the piece. It is true, of course, that in ordinary language form chicfly points to content, while in poetry, as in all works of art, content points to form—but not exclusively so. The vector is always in both directions. As Eliot has put it, neither sound nor sense alone would do. They must interact, in one, endlessly. Sound and sense (shorthand for sense and sense, the sensuous and its meaning, or its meanings) meet in identity only at the limiting point that is *das Gedichtete,* the intent toward which, as limit, the poem is aimed. I don't want to mimic the Heideggerian trick of quoting and requoting the same poem again and again; but I think it will do, all the same, to indicate the difference between the ordinary, transparent use of language and the nontransparency, not opacity, perhaps iridescence, of the language of poetry. (Or if you want your example a little more opaque, less crystalline, just take "Byzantium" instead—"that dolphin-torn, that gong-tormented sea.")

In any case, this is, I think, the point we're arguing *to.* We do speak. We couldn't do so if language were not partly nontransparent, resonant in itself between sound and sense, or "sense" and "sense," as poetry is. *How* this is so, what it is even in ordinary or scientific language that has, or presupposes, this kind of weight, remains to be asked. Meantime, however, I would like to refer in the briefest outline to the other source I mentioned as pertinent to my argument here, the phenomenological aesthetic of Roman Ingarden. Ingarden is talking about literature in general, but what he says applies also to poetry in particular. A literary work of art, he argues, is a many leveled entity. We must distinguish in it the strata of sounds, of units of meaning, of intentional complexes (that is, of what the reader or hearer grasps as intended), and of objective structures (the subject matter, for example, the story in a narrative work). It is the polyphonic interplay of all these that make the work. Meter and rhyme, for instance, not only contribute to the "frame" effect, as Richards calls it, they *are* part of the body of the poem. It would be rewarding, I think, to apply Ingarden's careful account to the analysis of poetry. I'm only suggesting it here as a more manageable counterpart on the one hand to Heidegger's Delphic utterances and on the other to Benjamin's condensed but provocative essay.

But why, I have yet to ask, should any good prose-minded, science-oriented, or man-in-the-street-addicted philosopher of language listen to all this? Isn't it Frege or Wittgenstein who can really tell us about language, not babblers of verse or metaphor or poeticity? Does the existence of language really depend, not so much on whatever it is that makes possible logical discourse on the one hand or games like "Slab!" or "Checkmate!" on the other, as on the possibility of the weasel-words of poetry? Let me indicate a direction in which we might look for an affirmative answer, in reliance first on the reflections of Jacques Derrida about speech and writing, and, finally, on some examples from poetry itself which might lend themselves to interpretation along the lines that Derrida, or Ingarden, suggest.

The aim of language as traditionally understood, Derrida holds, has been to bring the mind, through speech, into the presence of the real. Living speech—what Merleau-Ponty called *la parole parlante*—uses sounds (*signifiants*) to point to thoughts (*signifiés*) which *should* in turn, ideally, express the Being present to the mind that thinks, and voices its thought in speech. But does that moment ever happen? Can it ever happen? Can Heidegger's ontological difference ever be truly overcome? Words themselves are beings through which, forever, we seek Being; we never find it. We speak, we exist, as encultured animals, always in the *difference* between utterance and expectation, between expectation and fulfillment. This trailing of meaning *after* speaking, this lack of closure, this missing of presence, however, Derrida argues, is best exemplified in writing. Indeed, he insists, in its "difference," its postponement of realization, its tension between meaning and what is meant, speech is always already writing—*archi-écriture,* a text to be read. But surely the text par excellence is the poetic text, with its clear enframing against the background of the ordinary muddle of experience, its artificial timing as against the unstructured, or less structured, flow of daily living, its images sharpened against the duller sensing of the inattentive eye and ear, its inter-reverberant, never completed meanings as against the indifferent sayings of everyday discourse. All these "differences" held together in the identity that is the poem, this single entity stretched once for all between its hetero-geneous elements—sound, rhythm, meter, rhyme, imagery, metaphor, hopes, fears, memories, "lion and woman and the Lord knows what"—that is the best paradigm for the world of speech, the world of mind we have set between ourselves and things. Wittgenstein exempli-fies language with a single-word game, "Slab!" Frege elucidated "true" and "false" as the designata of assertions by assuring us that the proposition "Odysseus was cast up naked on the shores of Ithaca" designates the false, since Odysseus never existed. Wittgenstein and Frege were both great philosophers; we can learn much, *even* about language, by studying them. But, I submit, we can learn something they both missed, something essential to the possibility of language, from the study of poetic discourse as the quintessential written word and from reflection on *its* nature.

Let me give you in conclusion a couple of small examples, not osten-sibly of the whole complex and many layered texture of poetry as text—though that too is implicit in them—but of the particular power conferred on language by what Milton called the "troublesome and modern bondage of riming," a blessed bondage sometimes, despite his exhortation, since it can heighten the artificiality yet reality of verse, its power to intensify meaning by its containment *in* an artifact, so that saying and said echo one another and language shows us, paradigmatically, what it can do, what, in a lesser way, it always does.

> Dust inbreathed was a house—
> The wall, the wainscot and the mouse.

Again, forgive me for quoting a single couplet out of context, but I hope if you think about these lines you will see what my argument means, or is meant to mean. There isn't much metaphor here, nor, so far as I know, hidden symbolism, but consider what the rhyme helps these lines say, and how it helps them say it. The whole polyphonic structure of the verbal art work, as Ingarden calls it, is present to us here. Consider, for example, what the *w*'s accomplish—wall, wainscot—and *the* mouse, not *a* mouse. Every old house has its particular mouse. All this, and of course much more, is bound, intensified, by the abrupt but rounded endings, "house," "mouse." Or take one more example:

> I have done one braver thing
>   Than all the worthies did,
> And yet a braver thence doth spring,
>   Which is, to keep that hid.

And in the final stanza:

> Then you have done a braver thing
>   Than all the worthies did;
> And a braver thence will spring,
>   Which is, to keep that hid.

"Hid," "did" is no extraordinary rhyme, any more than "house," "mouse." But the frame heightens the text, showing the text itself to be a kind of frame—a frame in which we find ourselves enframed—or better, perhaps, a film, translucent not transparent, which we have put between ourselves and things and through which things reflect themselves back to us. *Das Gedicht, das Leben, das Gedichtete* as the ideal identity of both: it is the possibility of such a language-borne existence that *is* the possibility of language itself. Kant's leading principle in the concluding section of the "Transcendental Analytic," the "Analytic of Principles," runs: "The conditions of the possibility of experience in general are likewise the conditions of the possibility of the object of experience." Let our leading transcendental principle run: The conditions of the possibility of poetic language are likewise the conditions of the possibility of language in general.

Notes

1. Reprinted in Samuel Taylor Coleridge, *Biographia Literaria*, ed. J. Shawcross (London: Oxford University Press, 1907), 2:238.

2. David Hume, *Treatise of Human Nature*, bk. 1, pt. 3, sec. 10.

3. I. A. Richards, *Coleridge on Imagination* (Bloomington: Indiana University Press, 1960), p. 220.

4. Plato, *Symposium* 205C.

5. Samuel Taylor Coleridge, *The Friend*, sec. 2, essay 11, quoted in Richards, p. 179.

6. Martin Heidegger, *Unterwegs zur Sprache* (Pfullingen: Neske, 1959), p. 238.

7. Quoted in ibid., p. 248.

8. Jacques Derrida, *Marges de la Philosophie* (Paris: Éditions de Minuit, 1972), pp. 247-324.

9. Friedrich Hölderlin, *Sämtliche Werke* (Munich and Leipzig: Georg Müller, 1916), 4:246.

10. Roman Jakobson, "Qu'est-ce que la poésie?" *Poétique*, 2 (1971): 307, trans. from the Czech by Marguerite Derrida.

11. Walter Benjamin, *Illuminationen* (Frankfurt am Main: Suhrkamp, 1961), pp. 22-46.

12. Roman Ingarden, *Das literarische Kuntswek*, 4th ed. (Tübingen: Niemeyer, 1972).

XII

Life, Death, and Language: Some Thoughts on Wittgenstein and Derrida

1973

HOWEVER DIVERSE HAVE BEEN THE STYLES OF PHILOSOPHIZING OF THE past half century, their practitioners have agreed on one thing: we need a new beginning. Even if, like Heidegger, they tell us to try to relive the *first* beginning of Western thought, that very repetition would be a renewal, and so new. In a number of these adjurations to a fresh start, moreover, reflection on the traditional interpretation of language has had a central place. I want here to compare two such language-focused enterprises, which look—and are—very different, yet feel—and are— somehow related, if only in the glaring diversity of their ways of dealing with *one* problem. What I am trying to do, I suppose, is take Wittgenstein (*Investigations* period) as more familiar to most of my readers (though he has long been, I must confess, very puzzling to me), consider some characteristics of his method for letting the fly out of the fly bottle, and compare these with Derrida's techniques for showing that, in fact, the fly can never get in. (Parenthetically, I should say that it might seem more appropriate, if one wants to interpret Derrida by reference to some one in the British tradition, to take Austin rather than Wittgenstein, since Derrida has written an essay on Austin; but the parallels with Wittgenstein, I find, are irresistible, and certainly sufficient unto the day; so, except for the briefest allusion, a comparison with other approaches to language will have to await another occasion.)[1]

Well, then, what of Wittgenstein and Derrida on language? They agree on their starting point: the traditional conception of language, both insist, immobilizes thought. Somehow this rigidity, this one-track thinking, must be overcome. But they differ both in their diagnosis of the pathology and in their prescription for treatment. (Neither, I should say at once, expects a quick cure!)

First, the diagnosis. Let's start from the Augustinian account with which the *Investigations* opens. Strangely for the author of the *De Magistro* (where it is Christ the teacher who teaches within), this is an almost physicalist description of language learning. There are things and there are sounds emitted by grown-ups, and the child learns to imitate the sounds and to correlate them in the same way with the things. What we begin with, in other words, is a good *Tractatus*-like mirroring of words and items in the world. But what the child learns, St. Augustine tells us, is ultimately to use the sounds, not *just* in order to refer, but to implement "his own desires." So there is something *in* him, something "inner" or "mental," that is served by those convenient correlations. The traditional conception of language includes all three: signs, things, and the inner life; the soul, the subject, whatever it is that *wants* something from speaking, wants to "express itself" in speech. So Wittgenstein remarks in *Zettel* that philosophy always seeks either a symbol system or a secret inner process. Philosophy wants language to be either monolithically objective, or subjective—or perhaps, as in Baby Augustine's case, one for the sake of the other: name-giving for the sake of my desires.

The same three ingredients—words, things, and mental life, or signs, substances, and souls if one wants an alliterative, and Aristotelian, tag—are universal in the traditional view of language. But in Derrida's version they come in a rather different mix. His paradigms in *De la Grammatologie* are Plato, Rousseau, and Saussure, but also Husserl (the last especially in *La Voix et le Phénomène,* a critique of one chapter of the *Logical Investigations*). What have all these, and, for Derrida, the whole tradition, in common? They all share an ideal of what the living voice can accomplish. The sound (the *signifiant,* those sounds the grown-ups make and the child learns to make too), designates, points to, a concept, or thought—or thinking—in the mind (that thought, or thinking, is the *signifié*). But that thought in turn reflects or expresses a reality, an object *of* thinking, which is luminously and evidently present to the mind *in* its thinking and as (so to speak) it speaks. The correlation of *signifiant* and *signifié* is of course conventional, as is the correlation of words and things in the Augustinian story. But what is conventionally correlated in this account is sounds and "inner" processes, and the relation to reality—to "things"—makes its appearance (or is said to do so) only in that presence of Being to the mind which is expressed (or is said to be expressed) by the speaker in living speech. I shall have more to say later about the relative places of nature and convention in

Derrida's, as compared with Wittgenstein's, interpretation of language; but for now let us just settle this much: traditional philosophers, Wittgenstein and Derrida agree, insist on the interaction of three ingredients, signs, thoughts, and reality (or realities) of some kind, in their account of language. For Wittgenstein, signs have been too single-mindedly, and simplemindedly, correlated with things, and/or the process has been stubbornly misdirected to some "inner" goings-on that somehow philosophers have thought it must be *for*. In Derrida's view, the single-×-simplemindedness of the tradition has resided in its belief that the outer (sound) refers univocally to an inner (thought), which in its turn is intuitively united with the Being present to it in that thought. True speech has been conceived as the speech of the lover who has climbed the ladder, of the philosopher who has escaped the cave to live in the light of the sun.

Now given these two very different diagnoses of the same disease, we shall not be surprised to find both the problems raised and the methods used to deal with them very different too. Wittgenstein has a seemingly workable model to start from, but one that turns out to be partly too simple and partly rather silly. On the one hand, philosophy seeks symbol systems, correlations of words and things, but they don't come out just right (this against himself in the *Tractatus*). And on the other hand, philosophy seeks to go from this outer, working—or not quite working—word-thing relation to some inner life—the desires of the child Augustine—on which the process somehow hangs. Here Wittgenstein is opposing not so much his own early view as almost everyone else; for this kind of inner something that philosophers are always chasing never gets caught at all. Given this simple, partly operative but limited, model, then, he asks: Why tie ourselves to this one very simple pattern of linguistic activity with its will-o'-the-wisp accompaniment? Doesn't language work in all sorts of other ways? Is language *always* like that? Derrida, in contrast, is looking not at a working machine too simply understood, but at a dream of language, an alleged machine that has never existed and never worked at all. True, it is a dream we cannot escape. The hope of presence is incurable. But it is "incurable" precisely because it is a dream, not reality: Being never *is* present as the myth of presence claims it is. And yet the dream also has a reality insofar as dream itself is an aspect of our reality, of the kind of beings we are. Now Wittgenstein, too, admittedly, takes account of what is *un*real or *mis*guided in the traditional view of language—not only of what is too limited or abstract. The thrust to an "inner" life, the beetle-in-the-box syndrome, represents, perhaps, half of the ideal of presence. But, in his version, the routine working of language, in the ordinary world of human interests and activities, overmasters the persistent dream. The ghost of inwardness can be shoved into the lumber room of superstitions where all ghosts belong. For Derrida, in contrast, it's a very live haunt indeed. He has to ask, not how we are to supplement a one-sided and partly foolish view of language, but how we are to dismantle a deeply mistaken yet inevitable conception. He has to ask, head on: Is language *ever* like that? To find what's happening when we speak, we must take the ghost apart—a tricky job, for ghosts are notoriously hard to catch, let alone to disarticulate.

Where have we got to? Both Derrida and Wittgenstein find philosophical thinking about language perversely inflexible, both seek to shake up somehow our thinking about it; but since they conceive the traditional triad so differently, the questions they ask of language are correspondingly different. Yet here too there is something shared in their two enterprises. Neither seeks to substitute for a wonted rigidity some new philosophical system that will replace it. On the contrary, they both cultivate techniques for questioning language, for catching it at work, techniques to free it from the illusions of philosophy, not to enslave it afresh. Let me try to characterize very briefly these two techniques, and then enumerate, somewhat randomly, some contrasts between them.

Wittgenstein's technique—forgive me for saying it once more—is to *re*construct language at work. Derrida's, in contrast, is to *de*construct its alleged working. Wittgenstein complexifies the traditional account by setting the real machinery to work in a whole range of ways, over and over, till philosophical simplemindedness withers away (or seems to) and the silly ghost of inwardness flutters harmlessly off (or so one hopes). His method, though deep and difficult, goodness knows, is *meant* to make things easy, as too many of his presumed disciples have too readily supposed. He wants to oil the machinery and declare our philosophical holiday over. Derrida, on the other hand, decidedly wants to make things difficult. He too complexifies the traditional account, but so that we feel both its power over us and its impotence to find its own, and our, fulfillment. Wittgenstein adjures us: treat the philosophic illness with constant exercise; make language games work! The ice of logic is slippery: back to the rough ground! Derrida plays *with* language. He takes it apart (''deconstruction'' is his own name for his own enterprise), and finds it, not working better, more wholesomely, than philosophy dreamed, but much less well. We are ensnared in language, trapped at once by the philosophic vision and its impossibility of fulfillment. Speaking is not playing games in the world, as Wittgenstein wants us to discover; it is the game *of* the world (*le jeu du monde*), it plays with us. As flies are to wanton boys, we could almost say, are we to our words——. Yet Derrida's path, too, I think, is meant in a way to be one of liberation. Spinozistically, perhaps, we should learn to see our destiny for what it is, to turn the game words play with us into an inwrought, reflexive, never ending and ever paradoxical game we play with them. I hope what follows may clarify somewhat these enigmatic pronouncements. For a start, I am contrasting, as I've said, the reconstruction of a reality with the deconstruction of a dream, games in the world with the game of the world.

But I must stop to insert a warning note here. Contrasting Wittgenstein's language games with Derrida's "game"—or "play"—of the world, I am doubtless contrasting also the divergent resonances of *Spiel* and *jeu*, complicated further, indeed, by *our* thinking of *Sprachspiele* as language *games*. How Wittgenstein himself thought of them, as between the German and English *Spiel* and "game" (which are by no means equivalent), who can possibly say? Maybe there is a Derridaan lesson here. If one of the most profoundly influential philosophers in the English-speaking world thought, and wrote, in a foreign tongue, what can we really know of his thought, or he of ours? Indeed, John Findlay has argued surprisingly, but convincingly, I think, that Wittgenstein was at bottom a solipsist, that all those games were licensed to go on in the hearty, public world while *he* struggled with an inner striving that *wouldn't* come out.[2] Be that as it may; what I am trying to elucidate is the *texts* of Wittgenstein and Derrida (another Derridaan admission, as we shall shortly see), and not their secret souls. Wittgensteinians will cry: But there are no secret souls! Yet Wittgenstein's lesson *could* be: If there are—or if there is one, mine—you'll never know because no one can every say. Certainly though he *tells* us he wants to make things easy, he writes (on the left-hand page) like one in agony.

But enough of this ornamentation: back to my theme. Reconstruction-deconstruction: how to elaborate this contrast? Let us have a look at a series of further contrasts that grow out of, or have bearing on, it.

Take first, or next, the contrast of inner and outer. Wittgenstein says, forget it! (Even if Findlay is right, that's what he *says*.) Forget the rigid reference of the Augustinian model, forget the foolish flickering of the "inner" happening. *When* does the "inner" happening of knowing how to play chess take place? What a silly question! I *play* chess. *When* do I know English? I speak it. The contrast of inner event and outer doing is simply an impediment to understanding what in fact goes on. From this position Derrida is just as different as possible. For him, indeed, *différance* is what it's all about, *différance* with an *a*, mind you, to show that the difference between inner and outer—or rather, the whole nest of differences inherent in speech—is not an ordinary difference. It is the *conflict* of meaning with what it is meant to mean (difference is what we fight about), the *gap* between meaning and what it is meant to mean, the spatialization, the spreading out into *re*presentation of what should have been a pure presentation of intuitive clarity; and by the same token, the deferring (one word in French: *différer,* to differ; *différer,* to defer), the deferring of the moment of truth, the temporalizing of experience, which is also always temporizing: we never make it home. It is not the inner that is strange, *seltsam,* as Wittgenstein keeps calling it. The inner, if we could really reach it, would be presence, the vision of the Forms, the mind at home. But we never do. We are caught in externality, not happily, but as our inalienable alienation from what we have always sought. Thus in *La Voix et le Phénomène* Derrida shows how Husserl tries vainly to reduce language to the purely expressive, to the expression of what is *evident,* but without ever being able to eliminate its *indicative* role. In *Grammatologie* he quotes Peirce's dictum, "We think only in signs," a self-externalization that never comes to rest in easy union with what the signs are *of.* For Wittgenstein the *working* of language permits us—or *should* permit us—to abandon the vain search for univocal correlation, whether of signs and things or of signs and mental events. Neither the inner nor the outer aim of language matters: they are fused, or canceled; there is no problem left. For Derrida, however, there is no such cancellation, or fusion, ever. Presence haunts us, inevitably, but there *is* no presence, only absence. Austin's performatives, he argues, can only be said to succeed because they can also fail. And indeed, he insists, in a sense they always do. For language, which is said to lead to presentation, always falls into *re*presentation. *Every* form of speech is quotable; and quotability entails absence. It is the very gap between inner and outer, which is also a gap between now and then, or then and now, that makes language what it is. Could we close it, we would be silent, with the silence of beasts or gods perhaps, but not of men.

The contrast of inner and outer, as Derrida elaborates it, is identified, further, with the contrast between speech and writing. This contrast, everywhere reiterated, constitutes in fact his chief innovative theme. His major work is entitled "On Grammatology." *Différance,* neither a word nor a concept, he insists—so I don't know what to call it—is developed out of reflection on *écriture.* What does Wittgenstein make of this contrast? He ignores it totally. If you look at the language games of the *Investigations,* some are written, some spoken; it doesn't seem to matter a bit. For Derrida, in contrast, nothing matters more. Nothing else even matters at all. There was the philosophers' ideal of the perfect moment of speech: for Plato the living soul could learn through recollection to *see* the Forms; Rousseau recounted the mythical occasion when living souls met one another in the perfect moment of the first words spoken at some rustic spring. But there never was such a moment. Language is always the trace of a trace. Even spoken words must linger in the air, a kind of skywriting. Sounds become words only when repeatable. The unique, perfect expression of perfect presence has never been, could never be. Language is already *text*, never present, always the *différance*: spatialization, conflict, temporalization, temporizing; gaps, gaps, gaps.

Wittgenstein argued: no private language, because only language in public works. Language must be public because that is where it succeeds. Derrida argues, on the contrary, yes, language must indeed be public—texts to be repeated, texts to be read, and misread—language must be public, because it always fails. Language is our *hamartia*, our missing of the mark. The moment we speak we introduce not a well-oiled machinery, but a species-specific neurosis. We invoke, like Oedipus, a self-referential curse. Our very riddle-solving ingenuity triggers—*has* triggered, when the show begins—the coming of the plague, which only our self-blinding can remove.

More frills, you'll say. Is this philosophy? Yes and no. After all, both Derrida and Wittgenstein want to show us what philosophy *cannot* do. But let me try another contrast, the contrast of explicit and implicit.

Wittgenstein recurrently attacks the notion that language needs to go by exact rules, not, however, as Merleau-Ponty does, for example, because of some trailing meaning that lags behind them. (Do we, he asks in *Zettel,* hear the music, and *then* the expression?) We don't need exact rules, not because of some underlying depths that escape them, but because the context decides. Operations operate where it fits them to do so. The very contrast, and so the conception of the "explicit" or "exact," is unnecessary to the way language games in fact go on. For Derrida, however, the Platonic or Saussurian or especially Husserlian ideal of truly precise meaning, the coalescence of thought with presence, still appears as the *telos* of language, and what we have in its failure is the failure of the totally explicit, of language as pure expression. But in this situation the explicit, which should have been the inner, turns round and assumes the place of the outer, the writing, which remains always at some remove from the inner, which should have been explicit, but never is. The play between the trace, the writing, absent from meaning, and the implicit, the thought that is meant, but never unequivocally achieved: this to-and-from between *signifiant* and *signifié*, in one direction or another, in every direction, never comes finally to a halt. We are always saying never quite what we mean; we always mean never quite what we say. It is, I should think, the coalescence of rule and operation as Wittgenstein adjures us to practice it that is, for Derrida, a philosophical will-o'-the-wisp. All we *have,* in the end, is traces of traces, inscriptions separable and indeed separated from their import. Even spoken language is a kind of primordial script, an *archi-écriture*. Moreover, though language does indeed work only in context, contexts themselves are never self-contained. Relative to the expression intended, they are fragments only, the place of adumbrations, echoes of what one meant to say.

This is odd, come to think of it. Wittgenstein wrote in fragments, *Zettel* are his style, while Derrida fashions essays of polished, Mallarméan elegance. But Wittgenstein's fragments *direct* us to language in its whole, and wholesome, operations in the world, while Derrida's beautifully turned phrases lure us into an unending maze of subtleties from which there seems no rescue into ordinary talk.

Let us leave that oddity and look at yet another contrast in the treatment of language, that between literal and metaphorical use. Wittgenstein uses metaphors liberally in his own writing: engines idle, language goes on holiday, the ice of logic is slippery, flies buzz in fly bottles, cities have suburbs, and so on. Indeed, both the "picture" and "game" theories themselves are metaphors, as is the "family" concept. But so far as I can recall he doesn't deal with the question of metaphor as such. The language he is concerned to free from philosophic cramp is chiefly everyday talk about toothaches, pieces of cheese, and such. Derrida, on the other hand, not only cares little for the speech of the man in the street and prefers to delve straight into philosophic, or literary, theories of language, but when he does talk about "ordinary" words or "ordinary" usage, his aim is to show, as I mentioned about his discussion of Austin, that even here things are not as simple as they appear; and in particular, that even in what looks like literal language, metaphor lingers. Univocal meaning, like the moment of pure, living speech, is a conceptual ideal rather than the reality we live with—or in. Not that this is just another theory of "open texture" or of vagueness in language. It is a question of the interplay of meanings which may in themselves be more or less literal, as well as more or less "metaphorical": the former, for instance, in Derrida's own use of the several meanings of *différer,* the latter, for example, in the "metaphorical" carry-over of one meaning into another in such traditional philosophical concepts as "theory" or in the phrase "natural light." In the rhetorical tradition it was held, following Aristotle, that metaphor should be restricted to the sphere of the mimetic; outside the arts, where one wants to state propositional truth, metaphorical use is taboo. But, Derrida insists, there is never *the* last, and therefore *the* literal, word for anything, not even, as Heidegger seems to hope, for "Being." Language is always loose enough to retain some transfer—some *metapherein*—between senses, some poetical resonance. We are caught up, whether we will or no, in the play of words which is the play of the world.

I have been talking so far about distinctions between kinds of, or aspects of, linguistic activity: outer versus inner processes, language spoken or written, explicit versus implicit sense or meaning, literal language as against metaphor. I come now to a contrast between language itself and something other than speech but related to it: to the contrast between speech and gesture. In the passage in *Confessions* from which we started, you will remember, Augustine remarks that the grown-ups show their intentions by their bodily movements, "as it were," he remarks parenthetically, "the natural words of all peoples," *tamquam verbis naturalibus omnium gentium.*[3] Wittgenstein makes little of this parenthesis at the outset, yet it plays an important role in his whole enterprise (some of the notes in *Zettel* bring this out especially clearly). Gesture is natural language, as it were. Language is then a sort of artificial gesture. If we put it back into the context of movement from which it sprang, we may free it from the immobilizing influence of philosophy and get it going again in its right and proper way. "Proper": there might be a whole Derridaan excursus here; but let me stay for now with Wittgenstein: let language come unstuck, let it work naturally once more. Hence the "form of life" formula: natural ways of movement, forms of going on, are the controlling medium, the limits, of the artifacts of culture, including words. Nature controls culture, or ought to control it.

Derrida's move, again, is just the opposite of this. Husserl, he points out, considered gesture external to language because it is not *said*, only done. But the universality of the indicative as against the expressive role of language shows that the moment of pure presence is unreachable; there is always a sort of trailing of the indicative, of the pointing aspect of speech, behind what is truly to be expressed. If presence were attainable, that would indeed be "natural language," like Rousseau's imagined first moment of speaking at the spring. Far from showing us, therefore, that language is a natural activity, the omnipresence of the indicative, of gesture—the omnipresence of absence, if you will—betrays the fact that language is wholly artificial, a product of culture through and through. We gesticulate through words, in their referring as against their expressive function; as Novalis put it, language is language of mouth and fingers, *Mund und Fingersprache.*[4] We mime at one another in the antics of social role playing, including the social roles of language, Wittgenstein's *Sprachspiele,* because the pure expression of our thought, the natural aim of language, always eludes us. Wittgenstein is content, at least on the surface (I can't dismiss entirely Findlay's interpretation), to put the conventions of ordinary usage "normally" and "naturally" to work. He seems to be satisfied, with Hume, that custom is second nature. Grease the machinery and let it rip; men have always taken naturally to their machines, become part of them—bows and arrows, boats, cars, planes, languages. So they have, Derrida would answer; but isn't that so precisely because we have no nature, because everything human is something made? Custom may indeed be second nature, but we can ask with Montaigne, What if nature were but first custom?

Of course we can turn this reversal round again. If, as it does, our very nature needs culture, then culture is nature, our nature. Even what is natural to us can only become what it is through cultural artifacts, which thus turn out, like *Sprachspiele,* to be natural after all. One can take it either way. Yet the difference in emphasis is glaring. Where Wittgenstein wants to restore the artifacts of language to their natural, unreflective roles, or family of roles, Derrida wants to show us that hope for a natural human life is vain: the artificial dominates the natural and holds it in abeyance with every step we take, certainly with every word we utter.

Nature is life. The roles Wittgenstein and Derrida assign to life and death may furnish us with one more, and, it seems to me, culminating, contrast between their views of language. What does the word "life" (strictly, *Leben* and *vie,* respectively) mean to each of them, what does this key word do in their respective prescriptions for treating our philosophic ills?

Physicians in general are supposed to want to save life, to fight the enemy death. So it seems to be with Wittgensteinian therapy. Language games of every style, from mathematics to religion, must be freed from the self-consciousness that philosophical reflection chronically produces and be let to live again, each in its own way. Philosophy is a kind of stage fright. That is death, or at least the image of death. We should learn to master it. We should learn to be able to abandon reflection when we like and get on with the job. Philosophy, compared to ordinary goings-on, is deathlike; it tries to stop the game in the midst of play. Forget it, or try to forget it. Let life go on.

Yet of course Wittgenstein recognizes the existence of another notion of life, that alleged secret "inner process," whatever life it is that belongs to the beetle in the box. In *Zettel* he writes:

Man könnte sagen: in allen Fällen meint man mit "Gedanke" das *Lebende* am Satz. Das, ohne welches er tot, eine blosse Lautfolge oder Folge geschriebener Figuren ist.

One might say: in all cases one means by "thought" what is *living* in the sentence. That without which it is dead, a mere sound sequence or sequence of written shapes.[5]

Then he gives his chess example, and continues:

Oder wenn wir von einem Etwas sprächen, welches das Papiergeld von blossen bedruckten Zetteln unterscheidet und ihm seine Bedeutung, sein Leben gibt!

Or what if we spoke of a Something that distinguishes paper money from mere printed slips of paper and gives it its meaning, its life![6]

But that is very like what, in Derrida's account, Husserl meant by *life*. It is in that sense, or one allied to it, that phenomenology appears as a "philosophy of life." That is also the meaning, I should say, of Sartre's *le vécu*, for if there is life, as against machinery, in the Cartesian tradition (and both Husserl and Sartre are diehard Cartesians), it can only be the secret life of the soul, the pure lucid moment of the *cogitatio* in the very presence of the Being it knows. Now admittedly, both Wittgenstein and Derrida are counter-Cartesians, but, as we have seen, their accounts of the "secret inner life" and their ways of dealing with it are as far apart as they could be in their direction and their style.

Wittgenstein wants to displace "life" from inner, not to outer, but to ordinary—which is neither "in" nor "out," neither hidden "subject" nor lifeless "object," but just the way things naturally do work. Thus the alleged inner "life," held fast to, is a kind of death; to come to life is to ignore it, to ignore beetles in boxes and their like, and go on talking, in the appropriate way for appropriate contexts, as real live human beings indeed do.

Derrida, however, is taking that ideal, never existent, inner life as an inescapable if unfulfillable *telos* of language, and of our "lives" as language users. If we could realize that goal, he admits, this would be both absolute life and total death. Yet, in contrast to Wittgenstein's "forms of life" message, I think it is fair to say that what Derrida chiefly wants to show us is, as against the life we seek but never find, the hand of death in speech. He wants to protect us from the ideal of life which in fulfillment would be death by showing us the role of death in the only life we have. Thus the thesis constant, in his view, from the *Phaedrus* to Saussure, of the unique superiority of *living* speech, can only be corrected by the counterthesis: the possibility of language depends upon the possibility of death. Hence his insistence on writing, on the *grammatic* as essential to speech itself. He does *not* mean, of course, that people wrote before they spoke. His is not a historical thesis in that sense—though it is a thesis about the *possibility* of history, of *Geschichtlichkeit*, to borrow Heidegger's term. We do learn from the dead, after all. True, a wild child, if there ever was one, on its own would never learn to speak and hence would never become human. We need the mediation of living language-users to initiate us into the language-borne, as well as language-born, historical, human, social world. But *what* do our elders teach us? What did little Augustine learn from the grown-ups? His mother tongue, an invisible, indeed inaudible, machine transmitted at a countless sequence of maternal knees, long turned to clay. Speech (*parole*) is of the living, but language (*langue*), which precedes speech, operates through death. It not only transcends death, it needs death to work as it does, to be what it is. Each living moment is unique; but the very quintessence of words is repeatability, nonuniqueness, and that is the nature of writing, of the text, which is not lived, which in itself indeed is dead, yet survives the moment of writing, can even survive the writer. Even Shakespeare's death didn't kill the English tongue—though, admittedly, life with the mass media may. That is by the way, or maybe it isn't. For the point is, what matters most in language is not speaking speech (as Merleau-Ponty called it), but the texts we leave, that is, the *habits* of speech, whether strictly "written down" or not, that will have become established ways of talking for those, not yet living, who will—God help them—have learned from us. And habits, *hexeis,* remember, are second actualities, worked up possibilities of acting, but still possibilities, not acts themselves. Language is texts to be read, not the very act of reading, let alone of speaking purely out of one's heart. If language were really *verbum cordis,* there would be none at all; silent prayer perhaps, but no talk. Plato called writing poison to the soul, but, Derrida argues, he *had* to find it also a drug (*pharmacon*) in the benign as well as the injurious sense. Why else, one may ask, did he keep on writing when he hated it so? Saussure called writing "language in drag": "L'ecriture voile la vue de la langue: elle n'est pas un vêtement mais un travestissement.[7] But his compulsive search for anagrams, for a secret writing behind the writing, suggests that he took it very seriously indeed. And it demands to be taken seriously precisely because the life of speech begins only with that death of the word which writing represents. *Re*-presents, since writing like any linguistic phenomenon is never *pre*sented purely. Maybe the only pure poem is the "Fisches Nachtgesang" of Morgenstern, and even it, though one can't quote it orally, is repeatable in print. Biologically, or genetically, considered, life can go on forever; but human life, the life of tradition and of language, is mediated by death.

We have been looking, spottily, at two divergent ways of facing a single quandary: the immobilizing of our minds by the action on them of our inherited philosophy of language. If in conclusion I ask why the methods of these two writers, faced with the same problem, are so contrary, I can only suggest a very obvious, indeed a platitudinous, answer. Both Wittgenstein and Derrida, we've noticed, are counter-Cartesians. They both emphatically *dis*believe, at least at the linguistic level: I still want to leave open the possibility that Findlay may be right, that Wittgenstein may have been a secret, and so silent, mystic, or secret, and so silent, solipsist—but at the linguistic level they both disbelieve in the Cartesian moment of truth, the inwardly self-warranting clear and distinct idea. Wittgenstein, however, came to these problems through Russell and Moore, the heirs of Hume, the last empiricists, whose search for pure atomic impressions motivated their philosophiz-

ing, even in occasional (though of course gentlemanly) rebellion against
that aim of thought. This is the, originally would-be objective, but
ultimately phenomenalist, issue of Cartesianism. Derrida, on the
contrary, comes through Husserl out of the idealist branch of the
Cartesian family, even if, with the help of Nietzsche (let alone Freud
and Marx), he rebels violently, or at least with the rhetoric of violence,
against that demitradition. The two branches have, of course, like all
cousins, something in common. Empiricism becomes idealist despite
itself. Hume is Berkeley without God. In that case, perhaps, as many
philosophers now like to argue, phenomenalism is but phenomenology
in everyday (that is, of course, English) dress, while phenomenology is
phenomenalism in the ceremonial robes of continental ex cathedra
utterance. But if one is caught in the trap of looking for passive bits of
experience—pains, inner happenings, momentary knowings how or
that—one has to try to get out and act. That is the right kind of therapy
for that kind of cramp. And if on the other hand one is fascinated by the
serpent idealism, by the Transcendental Ego, one has, as therapy, to
look elsewhere, to seek one's antidote not in escape, which is impossible, but in a kind of stretching here and there, a snake-charmer's
dance, as it were, a recognition of one's trancelike state through making
of it a kind of game with language, in language: a game, or a battle, of
inner with outer, implicit with explicit, expression with gesture, life
with death.

Yet opposite though these prescriptions feel when we read of them,
or try to practice them, they have, finally, one more character in common. They are both Wonderland philosophies. They both exhort us to
work terribly hard, to run terribly fast, in order to stay where we are.
Maybe that is the only new beginning we can manage. The ice *is* slippery, after all.

Notes

1. Cf. Jacques Derrida, *Marges de la Philosophie* (Paris: Les Éditions de Minuit, 1972), pp. 382 ff.
2. John N. Findlay, "My Encounters with Wittgenstein," *Philosophical Forum* 4 (1972-73): 167-185.
3. St. Augustine, *Confessiones* 1. 8.
4. Novalis, *Schriften II* (Stuttgart: Kohlhammer, 1960), p. 588.
5. Ludwig Wittgenstein, *Zettel*, ed. G. E. M. Anscombe and G. H. von Wright (Berkeley: University of California Press, 1967), sec. 143.
6. Ibid.
7. Quoted in Jacques Derrida, *De la Grammatologie* (Paris: Les Éditions de Minuit, 1967), p. 52; from Saussure, *Cours,* p. 51.

XIII

Appendix: Hobbes and the Modern Mind

1969

———————

I

IN HIS LECTURES, *Of Molecules and Men,* FRANCIS CRICK CELEBRATES the approaching end of what he calls "vitalism" and the triumph of a scientific mentality which will envisage all of nature, human and animate as well as nonorganic, in terms of the laws governing the behavior of its least parts. He writes:

> Once one has become adjusted to the idea that we are here because we have evolved from simple chemical compounds by a process of natural selection, it is remarkable how many of the problems of the modern world take on a completely new light. It is for this reason that it is important that science in general, and natural selection in particular, should become the basis on which we are to build the new culture. C. P. Snow was quite right when he said there were two cultures. . . . The mistake he made, in my view, was to underestimate the difference between them. The old, or literary culture, which was based originally on Christian values, is clearly dying, whereas the new culture, the scientific one, based on scientific values, is still in an early stage of development, although it is growing with great rapidity. It is not possible to see one's way clearly in the modern world unless one grasps this division between these two cultures and the fact that one is slowly dying and the other, although primitive, is bursting into life.[1]

The physicist W. Heitler, on the other hand, interprets the same vision, not as triumph, but as tragedy.

> Belief in a mechanistic universe is a modern superstition. As probably happens in most cases of superstition, the belief is based on a more or less

extensive series of correct facts, facts which are subsequently generalized
without warrant, and finally so distorted that they become grotesque. . . .
A mechanistic living creature presents the grotesque picture of a robot such
as is frequently portrayed in comic papers nowadays. The witch superstition has cost innumerable innocent women their lives, in the cruellest
fashion. The mechanistic superstition is more dangerous. It leads to a
general spiritual and moral drying-up which can easily lead to physical
destruction. When once we have got to the stage of seeing in man merely
a complex machine, what does it matter if we destroy him?[2]

Both these statements occur, it is true, in "popular" writings by men of
science, but they represent the implicit, and often indeed the explicit,
principles of many, both in and out of science. It is this confrontation,
and this conflict, with which I am here concerned.

A dogmatic and oversimple materialism like that of Crick can appear
as triumph only to those who close their eyes to the simple but
irrefutable argument stated as long ago as in Plato's *Theaetetus*: the
reduction of knowledge to an enumeration of least particulars denies the
possibility of knowledge itself, including this very knowledge. Yet this
vision, self-contradictory though it is, has held sway over Western
minds recurrently for more than two millennia and increasingly for the
past three centuries. It is by now as powerful as it is destructive; and it
can be overcome, therefore, only by the fundamental rethinking of our
philosophical premises. Such fundamental rethinking is slow and difficult. I want here to put the problem more concretely by taking as a
model for the contemporary dilemma a single seventeenth-century
thinker, Thomas Hobbes. To be sure, Hobbes was by no means
directly, or even indirectly, the most influential thinker of his day; but
he was the most revolutionary, and therefore the most prophetic, the
most paradigmatic for the dilemma we now confront.

II

It is primarily Hobbes's philosophy of nature with which I am concerned. Hobbes's politics, I agree with critics like Tönnies, Brandt,
Polin, or Watkins in believing, follows rigorously from his conception
of nature.[3] The concept of "endeavor," and the distinction between the
natural and artificial on which it rests, are direct consequences of his
rigorous materialism and determinism. In this view, to be sure, I
disagree with another authoritative group of Hobbesian scholars. But
this is not the place to argue this question; it has been exhaustively
examined by numerous experts and has, in my view, been settled defin-
itely in Mr. Watkins's recent book, *Hobbes's System of Ideas*.[4] In any
case, my exposition, in contrast to these specialized debates, can rest on

one of two grounds. The reader may take "my" Hobbes—or, if he prefers, the Hobbes of any of the aforesaid scholars—as a quasi-historical model, rather as Hobbes himself, like other natural-law theorists, took his "state of nature," not as historical fact, but as an idealized model of what *would* be, were men's passions given free rein outside civil society. Or he may take this Hobbes—as I join Tönnies, Watkins, and others in taking him—as in fact the historical Hobbes. In neither case, I must again emphasize, am I suggesting that the thought of this one man, or of any one man, *caused* our crisis. As I have already said, he was indeed less influential than other, more easily compromising figures. But if the Tönnies-Watkins axis of Hobbesian scholarship is correct, Hobbes alone among seventeenth-century thinkers saw through to where we stand today, and the problems we face are the problems that arise from our intellectual condition as minds dominated by Hobbism, or as the heirs of Hobbism. I may therefore take their Hobbes—or, if, as I believe, they are correct, Hobbes himself—as paradigmatic for our problem.

III

As I have opposed, at the start, two interpretations of the modern situation, so I may begin now by confronting Hobbism and its contrary in Hobbes's own time. Cudworth, in his *True Intellectual System,* was attacking, in his rambling way, "atheists" as such and, in some places, Hobbes in particular. Hobbes appears to him, and rightly, as the metaphysical leveler par excellence. Writing of "atheists" in general, but clearly attacking Hobbesian nominalism in particular, he writes:

> Wherefore they conclude, that there is no such scale or ladder in nature, no such climbing stairs of entity and perfection, one above another, but that the whole universe is one flat and level, it being indeed all nothing but the same uniform matter, under several forms, dresses and disguises; or variegated by diversity of accidental modifications; one of which is that of such beings as have fancy in them, commonly called animals; which are but some of sportful or wanton natures, more trimly artificial and finer *gamaieus,* or pretty toys; but by reason of this fancy they have no higher degree of entity and perfection in them, than is in senseless matter: as they will also be all of them quickly transformed again into other seemingly dull, unthinking and inanimate shapes.[5]

This thesis, the denial of hierarchy in nature and the assertion of a one-leveled ontology, is, indeed, the fundament of Hobbism, from which all else follows. Not that we could now—or would wish to, if we could—revert to Cudworth's orthodoxly theocentric world. But if we are to find ourselves again at home in a significant universe, we must somehow find, dialectically, a synthesis of what Cudworth asserted and Hobbes denied. If man is to find anew his place in nature, it will not be man as Cudworth knew him, yet somehow man as man, not as a congeries of macromolecules. And even more plainly, Cudworth's God has gone past recall—one can scarcely regret it; yet here, too, as Iris Murdoch argues in "The Sovereignty of Good," it is some analogue of the traditional deity we have to seek, and find, if the fundamental meaninglessness of the Hobbesian world, *our* Hobbesian world, is to be overcome.

What, then, is the character of the one-leveled universe so radically opposed to Cudworth's structured cosmos? First, be it noted, it is a universe constructed on the foundation of the contrast between the *natural* and the *artificial*. There can be here no "higher" and "lower" in nature. Yet in human life, in what we call culture, in language, custom, institutions, we find nature transformed by man. Whatever else we have done, we have changed the face of the earth, have destroyed much of it, indeed, but have also covered it with novel sounds and sights. To many, these products of human activity, laws, theories, works of art, have seemed higher realities, or the expressions of higher realities, to which we owe allegiance. In a one-leveled world, they can be interpreted only, in contrast to what "really" is, as artifacts, as what we have *made* in contrast to what naturally exists.

The contrast between "nature" and "convention," as Hobbes, of course, well knew, goes back to ancient Sophism. Indeed, the *Leviathan* may be seen as the *Republic* minus the Good, with Thrasymachus putting his position rigorously instead of shifting his ground, and with the elaboration by Glaucon and Adeimantus, and the construction of an *artificial* society based on natural need, standing as the final word on justice. Confronted with this contrast, Plato found it necessary, through the difficult indirections of the central books of the *Republic*, to establish a higher, and transcendent, Nature: the Good itself, as criterion for the problems of practice and of knowledge. In relation to this higher and really real nature, the restless, need-driven nature of the phenomenal world is judged, and takes its due, inferior place. Without it, need alone, and in the last analysis, the only "natural" need, self-assertion, dominates. Our "standards," rooted in no higher truth, become conventions only.

The heir of this sophistic view in modern times is the evolutionists' contrast of nature and culture. Thus evolution is either "natural," the play in endless statistical diversity of survival-for-survival-for-survival, the self-perpetuation of genetic combinations in a war of all against all at the level of gene-environment relations; or "cultural," the self-perpetuation of manmade artifacts, whose natural end, however powerful their apparent authority within a given society, is again survival alone. Not the good life, but life, is the goal of living.

Now this is precisely the contrast on which Hobbism essentially relies. Both Hobbes's theory of language (and of knowledge) and his theory of society rest explicitly on this foundation. "What," Hobbes wrote to Descartes in protest against the innatism of the third Meditation, "if reason be nothing but the stringing of names together?"[6] In a one-level universe, our discovery of the rational order inherent in speech appears, not as the mediator of a cosmic Logos, but as a pure *invention*. The conventional element in language takes over altogether and speech becomes an aggregate of insignificant noises or meaningless marks, used in order to tie together bundles of happenings—and in themselves a trivial series of happenings, too. Hempel has described mathematics as a giant juice-extractor: it conveys no information about the world, but serves to press out of the raw material we put in the juice we want to get out.[7] Hobbes, enamored from middle age of Euclid, saw all language as having this mathematical character. Word-borne thought, for him, is *calculation*; and deductive systems, the machines (computers, we would say) that we use to help us calculate. "For words are wise men's counters, . . . they do but reckon by them. . . ."[8]

It may be instructive to contrast here, very briefly, the reliance by Hobbes and Descartes on mathematics as the paradigm of scientific knowledge. Hobbes, as we all know, was a poor mathematician and Descartes a great one. Yet Hobbes's conception of mathematics and its uses comes closer to the conceptions now current than does Descartes's. For Hobbes had seen through to the positive outcome of the scientific revolution. It is not so much that, in Galilean phrase, nature is written in the mathematical language, as it is that mathematics, in itself blind and empty, is the only instrument through which we can suitably manipulate the happenings of nature as our senses record them. Descartes, on the other hand, was still sufficiently confident of the *real* power of mind to affirm the direct ontological import of geometrical thought within the bounds of clarity and distinctness. To be sure, this ontological claim had to be supported by God's unwillingness to deceive and by the vestige of hierarchy needed to enclose on the one hand such a nondeceiving God and on the other such well-coordinated finite natures as thinking minds and extended bodies. But within these boundaries Descartes's emphasis is on the active power of the mind to *know*, and, in knowing, to submit itself to the being whose luminousness is its judge. Hobbes, on the other hand, transforms this action into making, and this power into the sheer unrestricted doing of the artificer. Descartes, so far as I know, shows no interest anywhere in the problem of universals; but his theory of innate ideas marks him as, implicitly, a believer in a realist theory. For the mind has innately the power, not of inventing juice-extractors, but of acquiring from within itself insight into truth. In contrast, Hobbes is the archnominalist. Hobbesian systems have to have truth fed into them by means of sensory input; in themselves they are merely machines for the efficient storage and translation of such information. For Descartes, theory is still vision; for Hobbes, construction.

Tillich, in *The Courage to Be,* calls nominalism a forerunner of existentialism, in that it paves the way for that mood of anxiety, the anxiety of meaninglessness, which characterizes the thinking of our time.[9] This relation clearly obtains for Hobbesian nominalism: words are wholly deprived of meaning and so, as we shall see, is the nature through which, by their aid, we thread our way. Alienation is already complete and dread lies in wait.

One qualification should perhaps be made of this sweeping statement of Hobbes's conventionalism with respect to language. Frithiof Brandt, in his illuminating book on Hobbes's mechanical system, suggests that Hobbes, after his rash remark to Descartes about reasoning, came to realize that reason is not only "stringing of names together," that *concepts* must be correlated to words if the latter are effectively to serve our purposes.[10] Concepts, however, for Hobbes, are *images*, "phantasms" of sense. They are themselves both particular and meaningless. They add neither generality nor significance to the empty calculations of discourse. Indeed, as we shall see shortly, it is precisely the supplementation of verbal calculation by reference to sensation that gives Hobbes, three centuries in advance of Schlick or Carnap, the model in which the chief contemporary conception of science has come to rest.

I need not stop here to elaborate the way in which Hobbes's politics also rests on the opposition of nature and art. Warrender's subtleties notwithstanding, I need only point to the justification of the title, *Leviathan*: "Nature . . . is by the art of man, as in many other things, so in this also imitated that it can make an artificial animal."[11] This is, again, the *Republic* without the Good. The state has been devised to satisfy natural need, i.e., survival, by evading natural peril, i.e., the sudden death which threatens each from each other's fear, vanity, and greed. One-leveled nature controlled through artifice: this is still the one opposition which Hobbesian, like positivist, thought permits.

In such a one-leveled universe, what is knowledge? There are two possibilities, which Hobbes unites in a theory exactly equivalent to the conception of scientific explanation that was until very recently almost universally accepted. The single source of information about the world is sense; everything we know is fed in by the senses and retained, as they "decay," in memory. This is what Hobbes called "absolute knowledge." Science, however, is hypothetical: it imposes axiom systems, themselves empty, upon the sensory base. Thus we have what has come to be known as the hypothetico-deductive model of explanation. Theoretical constructs, like the atomic theory, for instance, are superimposed upon the sensory data expressed in protocol reports. In themselves, theories make no claim to truth; they are vehicles for calculation, for retroductive summary and storage of sensory input and predictive claims to future sensible results. The *explanans* is a statement with empirical content from which the *explanandum,* and its observable derivatives, can be deduced. True, Hempel and Oppenheim, in their classic paper on explanation, timidly (and in their own terms, unintelligibly) assert, "the *explanans* must be true."[12] But this is clearly an embarrassment, as Hempel testifies in "The Theoretician's Dilemma."[13] What hypotheses *should* be, really, on this view, are not claims to truth, since claims are personal and there are no persons in this universe, but paper-and-ink computers, machines for turning sensory input into sensory output.

There has seemed, however, to be a difficulty in this theory, a difficulty similar to that which haunts Hempel's "dilemma." Scientists construct, not arbitrary hypotheses, but hypotheses of one particular variety. Epicurus, holding a similar methodology, had insisted on multiple causality; an indefinite number of explanations, he argued, might be the premises from which a given phenomenon could be shown to follow and hence, in his sense, its causes. And until one hypothesis rather than another produces observable consequences, whether in confirmation or disconfirmation, this equivocity may indeed obtain. Yet scientific explanation does follow certain conceptual lines and not others. Why? Or why not? In particular, Hobbes, and his twentieth century positivist heirs, construct systems, the basic terms of which refer in one guise or another to *matter in motion.* For Hobbes, the proper vocabulary was still the traditional one of "substance," but substances for him were simply bodies, and motions and countermotions the accidents of bodies. For twentieth century physicalists, the proper concepts boil down to events, not substances, space-time coordinates, and ultimately the particles (or waves) specified in terms of such coordinates. Why only this materialist kind of system and no other? Hobbes's answer is essentially the Epicurean one: no other construct, no other verbal machinery, would fail to contradict the data of sense.

Admittedly, Hobbes does not state this principle explicitly in his mature work on nature, *De Corpore.* Here he simply constructs his hypothetical corporeal language, then applies it in what he calls "Physics," to the phenomena of sense. Nonmaterialist language, of spirits or ghosts or what not, he dismisses as self-contradictory. In the earlier *Elements of Law,* however, he makes this reason for his materialism somewhat more explicit.[14] Materialism is the only successful system because it is the only system not contradicted by sense. Despite, or even because of, the purely conventional character of science, its theories are restricted to the terms of matter in motion.

To support this restriction, of course, sense itself, which provides the content of our otherwise empty system, must be shown to be reducible to motion. So, Hobbes points out, if you strike your eyeball sharply, you see light. Seeing is the consequence of, indeed, *is*, a motion. And similarly for the other senses. This link given, he can construct a detailed theory of the causes of sensory phantasms in the rigorous terms of matter in motion. And, again, the translation of his now antique language, whether into terms of the electronics of brain action or the chemistry of enzyme specificity, has made no single jot of difference in the underlying philosophic view. All explanation is hypothetico-deductive, and the only meaningful hypotheses are such as reduce all phenomena to material or, in modern language, to physico-chemical terms.

Such reduction, moreover, means reduction of wholes to parts. Explanation is hypothetico-deductive, materialistic, and *particulate*. True, Hobbes is not in the Democritean sense an atomist. Hobbesian bodies are not atoms and the space that he postulates at the beginning of his system is an imaginary, not a real, void. His interest is different and the turn of his atomism differs accordingly. In sympathy with Descartes and Galileo, he is trying to formulate rules for a mechanical nature in which the new discoveries about motion will prevail. He is willing to take "substance" simply as equivalent to "body," and body as "filling some part of space." But the *motions* of bodies—and that is what all alterations in nature come down to—are analyzed in terms of their least unit, *conatus* or endeavor. All mutation is motion and motion is particulate: the continuity of motion is understood as a summation of minute motions. Nor, since all change is motion, can there be wholes not reducible to such least parts. There are only bodies moving, and the analysis of their motion resolves these into parts. Hobbes is an atomist, not a Democritean, but an atomist of motion.

Where we find wholes, therefore, they are either apparent or artificial. In nature the real accidents of bodies are their motions, which are, as we have just seen, analyzable into their least parts. The colors and sounds that seem to belong to bodies, however, are phantasms in the subject, and explicable in terms of the corporeal motions that cause them. Although he does not state it as such, Hobbes embraces wholeheartedly the Galilean-Democritean distinction between the mechanical qualities of bodies and those appearances which, in Galileo's terms, "would be mere names if the living creature were removed."[15]

Apart from these "phantasms," which are mere seemings, moreover, such wholes as we have to deal with in our experience are merely *made* wholes. They are language systems, which constitute sciences when applied to sense, or legal systems invented to assuage our fears and satisfy our needs—needs and fears which, in turn, reduce to a sum of "endeavors" or least motions of our bodies to and from other bodies which have in turn caused such minute internal movements.

All motion, moreover, is determinate. There are no tendencies, no aims. In this again Hobbes shares the Galilean and Cartesian resolve to eliminate final causes from nature, and equally the Spinozistic resolve to eliminate ends from the explanation of human nature. There are in nature only causes, no reasons. Appetites and aversions, which appear to be directed to and from objects, are summations of endeavors outward in reaction to endeavors inward from the thing. There are simply local motions, and, when these conflict, the resolution of the conflict has to be devised by artifice through the contractual institution of civil society, which our drives have driven us to contrive for the avoidance of our own destruction. Modern explanation, Stocks has remarked, neglects Aristotelian formal and final causes in favor of material and efficient causes alone, agencies that in Aristotelian terms would be intelligible only as correlates of their respective partners, form and end.[16] This program is rigorously carried through in Hobbesian mechanism: as wholes are explained through reduction to their parts, so ends through their reduction to a series of undirected motions. All "choices" are in effect Hobson's choices, "the choice of the junior at meat."

It is scarcely necessary to add that such determination also abolishes "oughts" and, like Hume's argument a century later, subordinates reason to passion. Where there are no reasons, but only causes, there can be, except by the devices of civil society—themselves motivated by the causes of fear, greed, and honor—no obligations. The laws of nature for Hobbes, as Watkins convincingly argues, are not "laws" in a normative or ethical sense; rather they are of the nature of a physician's prescription.[17] The doctor assumes we want to get well and prescribes means. First comes fear of pain or death and/or desire of health, then consultation, prescription, submission to a medical regimen, and, then, it is to be hoped, recovery. Similarly, self-interest, using the calculation that is "reason," reckons the need to keep the peace and submits.

One final, and fundamental, point. All this, for Hobbes as for modern empiricist philosophies, is meant to be no metaphysic but a nonspeculative system, arbitrary in itself, but tied down through control by sense. Yet Hobbes's materialism is only apparently nonmetaphysical or nondogmatic. As we have seen, the link between hypothetical system and observation depends on the thesis that all sense is motion. This is the single and indispensable link that ties theoretical calculation to sensory in- and output. But the thesis that all sense is motion is only fleetingly argued for in the *Elements,* in *De Corpore* not at all. Nor is it, either logically or empirically, self-evident. Logically, it would be in Hobbesian terms a mere matter of convention so to decree. Empirically, it must be admitted there is no phenomenal uniqueness about motion, let alone about "matter" in motion. As Berkeley has conclusively shown, primary and secondary qualities are, as phenomena, exactly on a par. There is no unique access here to motion, nor to some underlying bodies whose real accident it is to move. What remains, then, as the ground for Hobbes's essential thesis is pure metaphysical faith. Only the unquestioned belief that all alteration *must* be motion makes him so sure that in fact it is so, and that therefore his free-floating system of "reason" can, alone of all hypothetical systems, be tied down to it roots in sense. This is, in other words, like modern empiricisms, a singularly narrow metaphysic disguised as antimetaphysical. It is indeed the same metaphysic concealed under the same methodological disguise that we meet again, not only in logical positivism or in Russell's logical atomism, but in the central state materialism of Smart or Armstrong, or in the computer-ridden speculations of writers like Putnam or Scriven.[18] And it is the pervasive influence of this particulate, materialist, one-leveled ontology that generates in one way or another the barbarisms paraded, with all the armory of mathematical logic to protect them, by the heralds of the present philosophical Establishment.

Notes

1. Francis Crick, *Of Molecules and Men* (Seattle: University of Washington Press, 1966), p. 93.

2. Walter Heitler, *Man and Science* (New York: Basic Books, 1963), p. 97.

3. Frithiof Brandt, *Thomas Hobbes' Mechanical Conception of Nature* (Copenhagen: Levin & Munksgaard, 1928); Raymond Polin, *Politique et Philosophie chez Thomas Hobbes* (Paris: Presses Universitaires de France, 1953); Ferdinand Tönnies, *Thomas Hobbes Leben und Lehre* (Stuttgart: H. Krutz, 1925); J. W. N. Watkins, *Hobbes's System of Ideas* (London: Hutchinson, 1965).

4. See n. 3.

5. Ralph Cudworth, *The True Intellectual System of the Universe* (London, 1920), 4:126-127.

6. Thomas Hobbes, Objections, 3.

7. Carl G. Hempel, "On Mathematical Truth," in Herbert Feigl and May Brodbeck, *Readings in Philosophy of Science* (New York: Appleton-Century-Crofts, 1953), p. 160.

8. Thomas Hobbes, *Leviathan,* pt. 1, chap. 4.

9. Paul Tillich, *The Courage to Be* (New Haven: Yale University Press, 1952), pp. 129-130.

10. Brandt, p. 230.

11. *Leviathan*, Introduction.

12. Carl G. Hempel and Paul Oppenheim, "The Logic of Explanation," *Philosophy of Science*, 15 (1948): 136.

13. Carl G. Hempel, "The Theoretician's Dilemma: A Study in the Logic of Theory Construction," *Minnesota Studies in the Philosophy of Science*, 2 (Minneapolis: University of Minnesota Press, 1938), pp. 37-98.

14. Thomas Hobbes, *Elements of Law*, pt. 1, chap. 2; cf., for example, chap. 6 and passim.

15. Galileo Galilei, *Discoveries and Opinions of Galileo*, trans. and ed. Stillman Drake (Garden City, New York: Doubleday, 1957), p. 274; Galileo Galilei, *Il Saggiattore* (*Opere, Ed. Naz. 6*, 1965), pp. 347-348.

16. John L. Stocks, *Reason and Intuition and Other Essays* (London: Oxford University Press, 1939), pp. 62-63.

17. Watkins, p. 79.

18. [Note, August 1975: This reference was to Putnam's earlier work; he seems recently to have been changing his position.]

Index